THE POETICAL AND DRAMATIC
WORKS OF SIR CHARLES SEDLEY

Portrait of a Gentleman, said to be

Sir Charles Sedley

THE POETICAL AND DRAMATIC WORKS OF SIR CHARLES SEDLEY

Collected and Edited from the Old Editions

WITH A PREFACE ON THE TEXT, EXPLANATORY AND TEXTUAL NOTES, AN APPENDIX CONTAINING WORKS OF DOUBTFUL AUTHENTICITY, AND A BIBLIOGRAPHY

By

V. DE SOLA PINTO

VOL. I

AMS PRESS
NEW YORK

Reprinted with the permission of V. De Sola Pinto
From the edition of 1928, London
First AMS EDITION published 1969
Manufactured in the United States of America

Library of Congress Catalogue Card Number: 70-85905

AMS PRESS, INC.
New York, N.Y. 10003

PREFACE

THE works of Sir Charles Sedley have been read hitherto chiefly in editions published during the eighteenth century, and almost all the critical judgments which have been passed upon them are based on the texts of these editions. To cite only a few examples, the authors of the articles in " Cibber's Lives of the Poets " (London, 1753), and " Biographia Britannica " (London, 1747–1766), Sir A. W. Ward in the " Dictionary of National Biography " and his " History of English Dramatic Literature," and Edmund Plückhahn in his dissertation on the " Foreign Influences on English Comedy at the end of the Seventeenth Century, Illustrated from Sir Charles Sedley's ' The Mulberry Garden ' and ' Bellamira,' " [1] all appear to have used the edition of 1722. Karl Lissner in " Sir Charles Sedley's Life and Works " [2] admittedly used that of 1776, and the bibliography appended to Mr. C. H. Whibley's article on the " Court Poets of the Restoration " in the Cambridge History of English Literature names the editions of 1707 and 1778 together with the first editions of the plays published during the poet's lifetime, and of the long poem called " The Happy Pair," which appeared in the year after his death. Critics and biographers seem to have accepted the texts of these eighteenth-century editions without any inquiry into their origin, or any attempt to compare them with other versions which appeared during the poet's lifetime. Such an inquiry and such a comparison with the necessary accompaniment of a complete bibliography must provide the essential foundation of a modern critical edition.

No collected edition of Sedley's works appeared during his lifetime. Three plays, however, " The Mulberry Garden," " Antony and Cleopatra " and " Bellamira," were published in the quarto editions recorded in my Bibliography (see Vol. II, pp. 236, 242, 246). As they all have the author's name on the title-page and are the productions of trustworthy publishers, there is no doubt as to their authenticity. Besides these plays, one act of " Pompey the Great " (4to, 1664) can be assigned to him on good authority.[3] Various lyrics, translations and prologues

---

[1] " Die Bearbeitung ausländischer Stoffe in englischen Drama am Ende des 17 Jahrhunderts, dargelegt an Sir Charles Sedley's the Mulberry Garden und Bellamira or the Mistress." Hamburg, 1904, 8vo.

[2] " Sir Charles Sedley's Leben und Werke." Haller, 1905, 8vo.

[3] See " Sir Charles Sedley, a Study in the Life and Literature of the Restoration," by V. de S. Pinto (1927), pp. 80, 81. I shall refer to this work henceforth simply as " Sir Charles Sedley."

by Sedley were printed in miscellanies or with the plays of other authors during the last three decades of the seventeenth century; one parliamentary speech appeared in the form of a broadside in 1691, and " The Happy Pair " was published in 1702 as a folio pamphlet.

During the eighteenth century no less than six collected editions were published: in 1702, 1707, 1710, 1722, 1776 and 1778. The last three are all in two volumes and profess to be collected editions of the Works in Prose and Verse. They include five plays as well as many poems and a number of pieces in prose. A comparison between them at once shows that those of 1776 and 1778 are merely reprints of that of 1722 with a few very minor variants. The three earlier editions, each in a single octavo, do not include any of the five plays contained in the later collections, but that of 1702 contains an unacted drama called "Beauty the Conquerour: Or, the Death of Marc Antony," which is an unfinished rehandling of Sedley's tragedy of " Antony and Cleopatra," acted at the Duke's House in 1676. No edition of Sedley's works has appeared since 1778, although various lyrics by him have been reprinted during the nineteenth century. Sixteen of the best songs were included by Mr. A. H. Bullen in his " Musa Proterva " (1889), and Sedley's name appeared, I believe, for the first time on the title-page of a book of verse since 1778, when Mr. J. R. Tutin of Hull published a selection of the songs of Suckling, Sedley and Rochester as No. IV of his " Pembroke Booklets " in 1906.

All the eighteenth-century editions include a Preface to the Reader, signed " W. Ayloffe," and it has been generally supposed that Ayloffe was responsible for all of them, or at any rate for those of 1702, 1707, 1710 and 1722.[1] Now Ayloffe in his Preface speaks of his " affinity " to Sedley, whom he describes as his " relation." It is therefore clear that he is William Ayloffe, the second son of a certain Joseph Ayloffe of Brittayns or Breton in Essex, who was admitted to Gray's Inn on January 3, 1687–8.[2] His mother was Frances Ayscough, sister of Anne Ayscough, Sir Charles Sedley's second " wife." He was thus Sedley's nephew by marriage, if such a name can be given to the ceremony of April 1672.[3] He probably owed his first introduction to the town to Sir Charles Sedley,[4] and, being himself a minor author, was a very natural person for Sedley to choose as his literary executor. However, one important fact has escaped the notice of those who have attributed the 1707 and subsequent editions of the works to Ayloffe.

[1] Cf. the following passages :
" 1722, when his works were published by Mr. Ayloffe, a relation of the author's." Biog. Brit.," s.a. Sir Charles Sedley.
" The editor of his works collected in 1707, Capt. Ayloffe." " E. Hood " (*i.e.* Joseph Haslewood, " Gent's Mag.," October 1822).
" Ayloffe edited three editions of his works . . . in 1702 . . . 1707 . . . and 710." Col. W. F. Prideaux in " Notes and Queries," October 16, 1890.
[2] " Register of Admissions to Gray's Inn," ed. J. Foster, London, 1889, p. 339.
[3] See " Sir Charles Sedley," pp. 128–130.
[4] *Ibid.*, pp. 164, 165.

THE
Miſcellaneous Works

Of the Honourable

Sir CHARLES SEDLEY, *Bar*^t

CONTAINING

SATYRS,	TRANSLATIONS,
EPIGRAMS,	ESSAYS, and
COURT-CHARA-	SPEECHES in PAR-
CTERS,	LIAMENT.

Collected into one VOLUME.

To which is added,

The Death of *Marc Antony:*
A Tragedy never before Printed.

---

*Publiſhed from the Original Manuſcripts,
by Capt.* AYLOFFE.

LONDON:
Printed, and ſold by *J. Nutt*, near Stationers
Hall.   1702.

He died unmarried and a lieutenant-colonel of foot in Portugal in 1706.[1] Therefore it is certain that he had no responsibility for any edition after that of 1702, and that the editions of 1707, 1709/10, 1722, 1776 and 1778 have, as far as we know, no authority except where they agree with the volume of 1702 or other editions of individual works which appeared during the poet's lifetime, and which can be ascribed to him on good authority. The edition of 1702, on the other hand, assumes a special importance as the work of a man who was intimate with the poet, and who may be supposed to have had special opportunities of ascertaining his wishes.

It is curious that, although this book is not very rare, there is no copy of it either in the British Museum or the Bodleian Libraries. Its half-title ambitiously proclaims that it contains " The Works of Sir *Charles Sedley*, Bar^t." ; the title-page, however, confines itself to announcing " The Miscellaneous Works . . . containing Satyrs, Epigrams, Court Characters, Translations, Essays, and Speeches in Parliament. Collected into one Volume. To which is added ' The Death of *Marc Antony :* a Tragedy never before Printed.' " Then comes the important statement, " *Published from the Original Manuscripts by Capt.* Ayloffe." There is no reason to doubt the captain's word. It is highly probable that whatever manuscript works the poet had by him at the time of his death passed into Ayloffe's hands, and it is practically certain that the whole of the contents of the edition of 1702 is from Sedley's pen. Ayloffe's Preface is written in a dashing style that suggests the soldier rather than the man of letters. The opening paragraph refers to the prevalence of literary quarrels and the severity of the critics : " Destruction is the Word ; and, as for Quarter, they give none ; these are the bloodthirsty Hussars of *Parnassus*, cut out for the ruine of others, tho' rarely with any great Honour to themselves." An allusion to the great quarrel between the defenders of the Ancients and those of the Moderns [2] naturally follows, and leads to a comparison of the " gallant easie Wit of *Horace* " with that of the " *Normanbys*, the *Dorsets*, the *Rochesters*, and the *Sedleys*." Without any very clear logical connection the writer passes on to a eulogy of the contemporary theatre, citing Congreve's " *Old Batchelour*," and Sedley's own " *Mulberry Garden*," " *Bellamira* " and " *Antony and Cleopatra*," none of which are, however, included in the volume. The next paragraph explains the omission : " 'Tis Pity that the private Institutions of Mechanics shou'd rob the World of having all his Works together ; not that we can in Justice resume what we generously give way." There is no doubt that these words refer to the plays which had been given or sold by Sedley to various booksellers (The Private Institutions of Mechanics), and which they had already pub-

---

[1] Morant's " Essex," ed. 1768, I. 71.
[2] In which Sir Charles Sedley seems to have taken an interest ; see " Sir Charles Sedley," Appendix II, " A Note on Sir Charles Sedley's Library," pp. 324–344.

lished in quarto editions. The editor then informs the reader that
" There are more of his Works which are too well known to the World
to need being mention'd here; and if some of these have seen light,
without his Knowledge, 'twas by the Perfidiousness of some about him,
whom he employ'd to engross what he writ : but being all corrected
by his own Hand, I thought it wou'd not be unacceptable to the World
to see them again, since better drest or otherwise at least, for Sir
Charles Sedley had that Felicity of Thought, that Solidity of Judgment,
that he cou'd alter, but rarely mend." The meaning of this passage
is clearly that Sedley was preparing some kind of collected edition of
such works as were in his hands at the time of his death, and that some
of them had already appeared in pirated editions through the agency
of dishonest amanuenses employed by the poet. The copies which
Sir Charles had corrected for publication seem to have passed into
Ayloffe's hands and to have provided the material for his edition.
After deprecating criticism on moral grounds of anything in the volume
which " suits not with the Gravity of some Nice, or rather Super-
cilious Pretenders to Reformation " (doubtless a reference to the
partisans of Jeremy Collier and such writers as Sir Richard Blackmore),
Ayloffe concludes his Preface with an all too brief personal note in
which he mentions that " the Affinity between Sir *Charles Sedley* and
me gave me the first Honour of his Acquaintance," and pays a high
tribute to his dead friend, whom he describes as a " Man of the first
Class of Wit and Gallantry."

The contents of the 1702 volume are divided into three sections,
each with separate pagination. The first (pp. 1–213) is headed
" *Miscellany Poems* " and is occupied by non-dramatic verse; the
second (pp. 1–24) contains prose works : viz. seven speeches delivered
in the House of Commons and a short " Essay on Entertainments."
The last section (pp. 1–64) is occupied by " Beauty the Conquerour: Or,
the Death of Marc Antony, a Tragedy," with a new title-page containing the true statement " *Never before Printed*." The piece that
follows is an unfinished rehandling of the theme of the author's " Antony
and Cleopatra " on strictly neo-classical lines with a chorus. Of the
" Miscellany Poems " fifty-five are short lyrical or satirical pieces.
They occupy pp. 1–115. The next thirty-five pages (117–152) contain a collection of epigrams in verse, partly original and partly translated from Martial, and headed " Epigrams or Court Characters."
On the remaining pages are found the long poem in heroic couplets
called " The Happy Pair," which appeared separately in the same
year, and a translation (also in heroic couplets) of " The Fourth Book
of Virgil " (*i.e.* the Fourth Georgic).

The publisher of this volume, John Nutt, if we may believe the
testimony of his contemporary and fellow-tradesman, John Dunton,
was a most respectable bookseller. He is described by Dunton as " a
just paymaster and a good Publisher." Dunton also gives him " the
character of being very discreet and obliging, and now gives great

content to those that employ him as any Publisher whatever." [1]
His most famous publication was Swift's " Tale of a Tub," which
appeared in 1704. It is interesting to find that in 1702, Ayloffe's
name appeared on the title-page of another publication of John Nutt's,
" Letters from the Living to the Dead by *Mr* T. Brown, *Capt* Ayloff
etc.," and it may be supposed that he belonged to the circle of men of
letters who were Nutt's regular patrons.

Our first list of Sedley's authentic works will then consist of the
contents of the 1702 volume (which I shall henceforth call A) and the
following dramatic works published during the poet's lifetime : one
act of " Pompey the Great " (4to, 1664), " The Mulberry Garden "
(4tos, 1668, 1675, and 1688), " Antony and Cleopatra " (4tos, 1677
and 1696),[2] " Bellamira or the Mistress " (4to, 1687), all of which can
be attributed to Sedley on good authority.

At this point it is necessary to give some account of works, besides
the plays already mentioned, which were published during the poet's
lifetime. The poetical miscellanies of the Restoration period were
very numerous, and many of them are now exceedingly rare. In a
careful search through those that have been available for the present
work I have found no verse by Sedley in the Miscellanies before 1672.
In this year [3] Hobart Kemp, a bookseller in the New Exchange,
published " A Collection of Poems Written Upon Several Occasions by
Several Persons." No authors' names are printed in this book, but
it contains lyrics which were afterwards ascribed to Sedley, Etherege,
Mulgrave, Buckhurst and others. No less than thirty of these poems
appear again in more or less altered forms among the " Miscellany
Poems " of A.

I have seen four copies of Kemp's Collection (which I shall call K),
three of which contain ascriptions of some of the poems to various
authors in manuscript. They are in the possession of Mr. G. Thorn
Drury, Sir C. H. Firth and Mr. H. F. B. Brett Smith respectively.
The copy without annotations is in the British Museum. In Mr.
Brett Smith's copy (formerly in the Gaisford Collection) nine lyrics
in the First Part are assigned to Sedley. They all reappeared in revised
forms in Ayloffe's edition. One Song in the Second Part, beginning
" *Phillis*, you have enough enjoy'd," is followed by the signature
" W. Smith," but, as this signature is in a different hand from that of
the other annotations, it appears to have no significance. There is a
slight discrepancy between the annotations of Sir C. H. Firth's and
Mr. Thorn Drury's copies. The former assigns thirty-three lyrics to
Sedley and the latter thirty. All the poems assigned to Sedley in

---

[1] "John Dunton's Life and Errors," ed. Bowyer Nichols (London, 8vo, 1818), p. 220.

[2] Prof. Allardyce Nicoll records a quarto edition of 1690 in his " Restoration
Drama." I believe this is due to a mistake in the Brit. Mus. General Catalogue,
which wrongly gives 1690 as the date of a copy of the 1696 edition (11777. c. 93).
(*N.B.*—This mistake has now been corrected in the General Catalogue, 1926.)

[3] See Bibliography, No. 9a.

A

COLLECTION

O F

P O E M S,

Written upon feveral

OCCASIONS,

By feveral

PERSONS.

Never before in Print.

LONDON,
Printed for *Hobart Kemp,* at the Sign of the Ship in
the Upper Walk of the *New Exchange,* 1672.

Mr. Thorn Drury's copy are also assigned to him in Sir C. H. Firth's. The three which are assigned to Sedley in Sir C. H. Firth's copy only have no ascription in Mr. Thorn Drury's, but one (the Song on pp. 56, 57, Part I, beginning " Tell me no more you love; in vain ") was reprinted in a slightly altered form in a periodical called " The Diverting Post " in 1704 (see Vol. II, p. 150). The other two, as far as I know, were never reprinted. They are all ascribed to Sir George Etherege in Saunders's Collection of 1693 and its successors, and there is no reason to doubt the accuracy of this ascription. It may be noticed that of the thirty poems which both Mr. Thorn Drury's and Sir C. H. Firth's copies assign to Sedley, all except two are included in revised forms in Ayloffe's edition. The two poems which were not reprinted by Ayloffe are a " Distich " beginning " Although no Art the Fire of Love can tame," and some lines without title that begin " The painted Apples that adorn " (II. pp. 31, 32). They were also excluded from the later collections that are based on K. Although we cannot accept the evidence of the unknown annotators as conclusive, it seems highly probable that these poems are by Sedley. They are both preceded and followed by authentic pieces, and there are good reasons why both should have been suppressed, the first for its slightness and the second for its inferior quality. One poem which was included by Ayloffe is assigned both in Sir C. H. Firth's and Mr. Thorn Drury's copies to John Sheffield, Earl of Mulgrave. This is the song beginning " Walking among thick shades alone " (No. XXVII in this edition). It is not included in any edition of Mulgrave's works, and, as Ayloffe assigns it to Sedley, I include it among his authentic works in spite of the evidence of the unknown annotators. The annotations in the three copies of K are all in different hands and all apparently belong to the late seventeenth or early eighteenth centuries.

Kemp's Collection formed the basis of a series of verse miscellanies published during the next forty years. In 1672 Thomas Collins and William Cademan of the New Exchange published a " Collection of Poems Written upon several Occasions by Several Persons with many additions never before in Print." This volume is an exact reprint of K, with some additional poems, none of which are, however, ascribed to Sedley either by Ayloffe or any other editor. As in K, no author's names are given. In 1693, Francis Saunders, who had taken over Herringman's old shop at the Sign of the Blue Anchor in the Lower Walk of the New Exchange,[1] published a neat octavo containing " A collection of Poems by *Several Hands* Most of them

---

[1] Francis Saunders and Joseph Knight took over the famous publishing business of Henry Herringman in 1684. Their partnership was dissolved about 1688, and Saunders carried on the business alone until about 1699. Thomas Warren, who printed Saunders's Collection, had been printer to Herringman. (See " A Dictionary of Printers and Booksellers who were at work in England from 1688 to 1725," by R. H. Plomer, Ed. Arundell Esdaile (Bibliographical Society), London, 1922, pp. 262, 302.)

Written by Persons of Eminent Quality." This Collection (which I call S) is based on those of Kemp and Collins, but contains much new matter and omits some of the old. Unlike its two predecessors, it contains a table of contents with the names of most of the authors. Twenty out of the thirty-one lyrics ascribed to Sedley by the unknown annotators of K are assigned to Sedley in the table of S. It is noticeable that among the pieces omitted from S are the two which A does not include, and also that which the annotators of K ascribed to Mulgrave. The text, except for minor differences of spelling and punctuation, is identical with that of K.[1] Saunders's Collection was reprinted in 1695 with a new title-page, and again with many additions by Daniel Browne and Benjamin Tooke in 1701, and the same collection was reprinted by the same publishers in 1702 and 1716. All these volumes reprint exactly the versions which appeared in S. A considerable body of Sedley's verse will thus be seen to have appeared many years before Ayloffe published his edition and to have been actually on the market when A appeared. It is probably to these poems that Ayloffe is referring when he speaks of the works that had " seen light . . . by the Perfidiousness of some about him, whom he employ'd to engross what he writ." They were not, however, the only short pieces by Sedley that appeared during his lifetime. The earliest editions of the famous " Drolleries " and of the " New Academy of Compliments," a curious kind of mixture of a letter-writer's guide, a handbook of etiquette and a miscellany of songs, which went through several editions, appeared about the same time as Kemp's Collection. A pamphlet[2] published in 1675 describes this kind of literature as forming a large part of the library of a young spark of the period : " The *Academy of Compliments, Venus Undress'd, Westminster Drollery*, a *half a dozen plays* and a Bundle of *Bawdy* Songs in *Manuscript*." Several of the Drolleries contain the pretty song sung by Victoria in Act III of "The Mulberry Garden." It also appears in " The New Academy of Compliments " of 1671, together with the lines beginning " As in those Nations where they yet adore," which were to appear both in K and A. The second part of "Westminster Drollery" (12mo, 1672) contains on p. 114 a version of the lively song beginning " Get you gone, you will undo me," which is entirely different from those which appear in K and its successors. Neither the New Academy nor the Drolleries print the names of authors, but the former declares on its title-page that it is compiled by " L. B. Sir C. S. and Sir W. D. and others the Most refin'd Wits of the Age." These initials probably stand for Lord Buckhurst, Sir Charles Sedley and Sir William Davenant, though it is far from probable that these persons had anything to do with the book, except in so far as they unwittingly furnished material for the bookseller's hack who compiled it.

[1] See table after No. 9*e* of my Bibliography (Vol. II, p. 239), where the ascriptions of the various annotators of K and those of the editor of S are given side by side.
[2] " The Character of a Town Gallant," 4to, 1675, pp. 4, 5.

Sedley's next printed work was apparently the Prologue to " Epsom Wells," the famous comedy of his friend Shadwell, in the composition of which he was supposed to have had a share.   The Prologue is said in the Quarto editions to be by " Sir C. S.," and in view of Sedley's alleged connection with the play it is pretty certain that these initials must stand for his name.   It is not, however, included in any of the eighteenth-century editions.   The ascription to Sedley of the sparkling song in Act V, sc. ii, of Etherege's comedy, " Sir Fopling Flutter," is far less likely to be accurate.   This song is sung by the waiting woman " Busy," and begins

> " As Amoret *with* Phillis *sat*
> *One Evening on the Plain.*"

In the margin of the quarto editions there is a printed note stating that the song is " by *Sir C. S.*"   The editor of the 1722 Sedley took these initials to be those of Sir Charles Sedley and reprinted the song among his works.   The Prologue to Etherege's play is, however, by Sir Car Scroop, and it is therefore far more probable that the letters " C. S." stand for Car Scroop than for Charles Sedley.

Anthony à Wood in his list of Sedley's works [1] ascribes to him a comedy called " Tunbridge Wells, or a Day's Courtship," which was acted at the Duke's House and printed by Henry Rogers in 1678. The title-page states only that it is by " A Person of Quality."   Wood is, however, a very unsafe guide even to contemporary bibliography. Langbaine on p. 554 of his " Account of the English Dramatick Poets " (Oxford, 1691) assigns " Tunbridge Wells " with far more likelihood to Thomas Rawlins, a dramatic author who had written a play as far back as 1640.

Obadiah Blagrave's " Wit and Drollery " of 1682 contains the popular song from the " Mulberry Garden " which also appears in the rare " Academy of Complements " of 1684, with another piece which is ascribed to Sedley both by the commentator of K and Ayloffe, beginning

> " *Phillis*, lets shun the common fate."

In the same year Jacob Tonson published the first volume of his well-known collection of contemporary verse, often called " Dryden's Miscellany."   This volume was chiefly made up of translations from the Latin poets, and included a complete version by several hands of Ovid's " Amores."   Translations of three of the elegies are ascribed to Sedley, both in the table and beneath the titles of the individual poems.   There is no reason to doubt Sedley's authorship of these pieces, especially as two of them are also attributed to him in a transcript in a contemporary hand in the British Museum. [2]   They appeared

---

[1] " Athenæ Oxonienses," ed. Bliss, fol., 1820, IV. 731.
[2] Br. Mus. Add. MS. 34, 744, ff. 56, 59.

again in the second edition of Tonson's collection, but were omitted
for some reason from the third, which, however, contains a Prologue
by Sedley which was not included in A, but which appears in the edition
of 1722 and its successors. Curiously enough, the translations from
Ovid were not included in any of the collected editions of Sedley's
works. Dryden seems to have tried to secure Sedley's aid in another
composite translation published by Tonson. In the argument of the
Sixth Satire in the complete Juvenal by Dryden and " other hands,"
which appeared in 1693, the editor states that " Sir C. S. *who cou'd have
done more right to the Author, after a long delay, at length absolutely
refus'd so ungrateful an employment.*" Certainly few other authors
besides Sir Charles had at once the literary skill and the first-hand
knowledge necessary for a successful translator of the terrible " Legend
of Bad Women."

It is possible that a rather boyish copy of verses on p. 165 of " Miscellany Poems and Translations by Oxford Hands " (Anthony Stephens,
Oxford, 1684) may be by Sedley. It is entitled " Upon the Slighting
of His Friends Love," and is followed by the initials C. S. and attributed
in the Contents to Mr. C. S. of Wadham. The only members of
Wadham with the initials C. S. who came up since 1650, according to
the Register,[1] were Charles Sedley (1655–6), Christopher Savery
(1663), Car Scroop (1664) and Charles Standish (1680). Neither
Savery nor Standish is known to have published any verse. Sir
Charles Sedley was certainly " Mr. Charles Sedley " when he came up
to Wadham, for he had not then inherited the title. It is quite
possible that this is a boyish piece written by Sedley when at Wadham,
and given to the " Friend " mentioned in the title. The MS. may
have drifted into the hands of an enterprising bookseller who may or
may not have known that Sedley was now a baronet and a well-known
author. Some colour is lent to this supposition by the fact that there
was probably a copy of Stephens' Miscellany among Sedley's books at
his death.[2]

The rare " Theatre of Complements " of 1688 contains the song
from the " Mulberry Garden " and the lines beginning " As in those
Nations where they yet adore," together with the song " by Sir
C. S." from " Sir Fopling Flutter " and another piece attributed to
Sedley by the compiler of the edition of 1722. In the same year
appeared Mrs. Jane Barker's " Poetical Recreations," the second part
of which is a miscellany of poems by " Several Gentlemen of the
Universities and others." This volume contains on pp. 122–125 a
piece in heroic couplets headed " Upon a Gentlewoman's Refusal
of a Love Letter from one she was ingag'd to. By Sir C. S.," beginning

" Not hear my *Message*, but the *Bearer* shun ! "

---

[1] Gardiner, " Registers of Wadham College," Vol. I.
[2] See " Sir Charles Sedley," Appendix II, pp. 330, 339.

This may be by Sedley, and was attributed to him by the editor of the 1722 edition. The initials, however, could stand for Sir Car Scroop, as in the song in " The Man of Mode."

Eleven other poems which appear in this collection are reprinted as Sedley's in the second volume of the 1722 edition. Of these, seven can be definitely assigned to other authors.

The first, " The Lovers Will " (p. 114) is merely a fragment of Donne's poem " The Will " (" Poetical Works," ed. Grierson, I. 56–58) with a few very slight alterations.

" An Ode " beginning " O Ye blest Pow'rs, propitious be " (p. 137) is assigned both in the contents of " Poetical Recreations," Part II, and beneath the title to " *Mr* R. D. *of* Cambridge." " An Ode of Anacreon Paraphras'd," beginning " I Wonder why Dame *Nature* thus," though not assigned to any author in " Poetical Recreations," is actually by the old cavalier poet, Alexander Brome. It appeared on pp. 22, 23 of his " Songs and other Poems " (3rd ed., enlarged, 8vo, London, 1668). The Song entitled " The Young Lover," though assigned to " *Mr.* Wright " in Poetical Recreations (p. 149), is also Brome's (*op. cit.*, pp. 13, 14). " *Mr.* Wright " is probably James Wright of the Inner Temple, author of the famous dialogue on the theatre, " Historia Histrionica," and some occasional verse.

The lines " To my Much-esteemed Friend Mr. J. N. on his Reading the first line of Pindar " (p. 159) conclude in " Poetical Recreations " with the words *Yours*, J. Whitehall, and are also attributed to *Mr.* Whitehall in the Contents. This must be John Whitehall of the Inner Temple, author of " Miscellaneous Poems with some Remarks on the Death of King Charles II and the Happy Succession of King James II " (London, 4to, 1683).

Another song beginning " *Damon* to *Sylvia*, when alone " (p. 231) is attributed to Mr. Hovenden Walker in the Contents, and the parody of the lines beginning " *Evadne* I must tell you so," headed " The same Song Inverted " (p. 246), is also attributed to Walker both in the Contents and beneath the title. This " Mr. Hovenden Walker, some time of Trinity College, Dublin," must be " H. Walker," who printed a translation of the Elegies of Cornelius Gallus under the title of " The Impotent Lover," published by Benjamin Crayle, the publisher of " Poetical Recreations." This identification is rendered practically certain by the fact that one of the elegies from " The Impotent Lover " reappears in " Poetical Recreations."

In 1689 an anonymous pamphlet entitled " Reflections on our Late and Present Proceedings in England " was published both in London and Edinburgh. It represents the views of a very cautious and moderate supporter of the Revolution, and is reprinted on p. 75 of Vol. I of the 1722 edition. It is also attributed to Sedley in an undated MS. in the Bodleian (Rawl. D. 924, 319), and there is no reason to doubt that it is from his pen.

The next work by Sedley, published after the Revolution, was the

broadside of his famous speech on the Civil List printed in 1691.[1] In
the spring of 1692, Peter Motteux, an industrious literary hack, began
the publication of his " Gentleman's Journal, or the New Monthly
Miscellany," one of the earliest English literary periodicals. Sedley
contributed verses to no less than twelve numbers of Motteux's
journal. None of these poems had been published before except the
lines " To a Devout Young Lady " beginning " Phillis this mighty
zeal asswage," which had already appeared in K and its successors.
Ten of the others (their titles and the first lines with the dates of the
numbers in which they appeared are recorded in my Bibliography of
Sedley's works) were reprinted in A with slight variations. The
eleventh is a Prologue for a comedy called "The Wary Widow or Sir
Noisy Parratt " by Henry Higden, which also appears in the quarto
edition of the play published in 1693 with Sedley's name. It was
reprinted in the 1722 Sedley and in " Dryden's Miscellany " (3rd vol.,
1702) but not in A. Tom D'Urfey, in the dedicatory epistle of his
play " The Intrigues of Versailles, or a Jilt in all Humours," quotes in
full and assigns to Sedley some lines beginning " Scrape, Scrape no
more your bearded Chins," which had already appeared in the
" Gentleman's Journal " of August 1692/3, where they are merely
ascribed to " A Person of Quality." They were to reappear with
some variations in A.

"Poems on Affairs of State " of 1698 has Sedley's name upon its
title-page along with those of Rochester, Dorset, Buckingham and
others. It includes on p. 161 a " Prologue by Sir *Ch* - - - Sedley."
This piece, which also exists in MS. in the British Museum, where it
is headed " to the Stroulers," was probably written by Sedley for a
strolling company of players. It may be remarked that another
Prologue for a strolling company at Cambridge appeared on p. 248
of Gildon's " New Miscellany " of 1701, a volume which contains
verses by Sedley.

In 1700, the Wits who combined to defend themselves against Sir
Richard Blackmore's attack published the mock " Commendatory
Verses." [2] No author's names are printed in this volume, but MS.
notes in the British Museum copy give the names of the writer of each
piece. Sedley is credited with some amusing lines beginning " A
Grave Physician used to write for Fees," which reappear in A with an
extra and highly indecorous couplet.

The last miscellany to publish new poems by Sedley before his death
was Charles Gildon's " New Miscellany " of 1701, which contained
two pieces not previously printed. These are " A Song on the King's
Birthday " and a fine version of Horace's Eighth Ode of the Second
Book, both of which are included in A. They are both ascribed to
" Sir Charles Sidley " in the Table of the " New Miscellany." The
same collection includes two of the poems by Sedley which were

---

[1] See " Sir Charles Sedley," pp. 182, 183.
[2] See *ibid.*, pp. 231, 232.

included in K, and which appear here with slight variants. Curiously enough they are not assigned to any author in the table of the " New Miscellany."

In 1702, the year of the publication of A, John Nutt, the publisher of that volume, also issued " The Happy Pair, A Poem on Matrimony," in the form of a folio pamphlet. The text is distinctly superior to that of A. A volume of " Poems on Affairs of State," dated 1704, contains on p. 438 a very garbled version of Sedley's beautiful song, " Not Celia that I juster am," which surely cannot by any stretch of the imagination be called a Poem on Affairs of State. It may be observed that immediately after it is printed the famous ballad of Dr. Walter Pope, Sedley's old tutor at Wadham, called " The Old Man's Wish." On November 18 of the same year a periodical called " The Diverting Post " printed some unsigned verses entitled " Thirsis to Celia," beginning :

" Tell me no more you love again."

These lines had already appeared in Kemp's Collection (see above, p. xii). They are followed by an exact reprint (also unsigned) of Sedley's poem " Her Answer " (A, p. 28). A later number of " The Diverting Post " (January 13) contains a short piece in octosyllabics, headed " By Sir *Charles Sidley*, written *ex tempore*," beginning " The Noble Man, why he's a thing." These lines were not printed elsewhere either before or after.

In 1704 Nutt published a volume of the second Duke of Buckingham's " Miscellaneous Works " which includes a number of poems by other authors, among which are three ascribed to Sedley. These pieces had not appeared in A. The style of one in particular, " The Royal Knotter," is very suggestive of Sedley's lighter manner. In the absence of any trustworthy external evidence, however, we cannot include either these pieces or the lines in " The Diverting Post " among the authentic works.

" Poems on State Affairs " (8vo, 1705) .has a version of the little squib on William III entitled " A Fable," which was printed as Sedley's in the edition of 1722 and its successors.

We can now add the following to our list of Sedley's authentic works :

The Prologue to " Epsom Wells," " Sir Noisy Parrat " and the " Stroulers."
" Reflections on Our Late and Present Proceedings in England."
The three Elegies from Ovid's " Amores " (" Dryden's Miscellany," 1684).

The pieces in " Poetical Recreations " which cannot be definitely assigned to other authors, and which are attributed to Sedley in the 1722 edition, and the lines in " The Diverting Post " and in the " Buck-

ingham " of 1704, may be regarded as doubtful works, and the poem
by " Mr. C. S. of Wadham " in Stephens' Collection can be included
in the same category.   The poems ascribed to other authors in
" Poetical Recreations," the song in " Sir Fopling Flutter," and
" Tunbridge Wells," can all be definitely rejected from the canon.

We can now compare this list of the authentic works with the
collected editions of 1707, 1709/10, 1722 and their successors.

The edition of 1707, like those of 1709/10 and 1722, was published
by Samuel Briscoe, a well-known bookseller of the early eighteenth
century, who seems to have specialized in collected editions of the
works of the Restoration poets.   John Dunton calls him " reviv'd "
Briscoe, because " after printing for Dryden, Wycherley, Congreve,
&c." he fell into certain " misfortunes " through the attempts of his
enemies to ruin him, but afterwards recovered his prosperity, chiefly,
according to Dunton, by means of his connection with Tom Brown
of Shiffnal, the well-known wit and Grub Street hack, who scored a
great popular success by the publication of his " Letters from the
Living to the Dead," which were printed for Briscoe.   Briscoe was
also responsible for editions of the works of the first Duke of
Buckingham and of Sheffield, Earl of Mulgrave.   It is worthy of
remark that the 1704 edition of Buckingham's Miscellaneous Works
was, like the 1702 Sedley, published by J. Nutt, while the 1715
edition has Briscoe's name on the title-page.   It would therefore seem
probable that Briscoe took over some of Nutt's publications and re-
issued them.   Brown, as Briscoe's literary adviser, may well have
been the editor of the 1707 Sedley.   He probably knew Ayloffe, for
the latter contributed to his " Letters from the Living to the Dead,"
and it is possible that Ayloffe gave him material for a new and enlarged
edition of Sedley's works before he went to Portugal.

The 1707 Sedley professes on its title-page to contain not only the
" Poetical Works of the Honourable Sir *Charles Sedley* Baronet, and
His Speeches in Parliament with *Large Additions never before made
Publick.*", but also " A New Miscelany of Poems by Several of the
Most *Eminent Hands.*", and " A Compleat Collection of All the
Remarkable Speeches in both *Houses of Parliament . . .* from the
Year 1641 to the Happy Union of *Great Britain :* by Several Lords
and Commoners," a list of whose names follows and includes such
curious bedfellows as " the Earl of *Clarendon*," " *Algernon Sidney*,
Esq.," " Mr. *Waller* " and " *Richard Cromwell.*"   Only about one-half
of the volume, indeed, consists of works ascribed to Sedley.   It
begins with an exact reproduction of Ayloffe's Preface.   This is
followed by the whole of the " Miscellany Poems " of A (viz. fifty-
five short pieces, thirty Court Characters, " The Happy Pair " and
" The Fourth Book of Virgil ").   Three other lyrics follow, two of
which belong to the large class of lascivious pieces which were
fathered indiscriminately on the Restoration Wits during the eighteenth
century.   The third is a short piece in heroic couplets entitled " *On*

a Lady that did not love Apples," and is very much in Sedley's manner.

After these pieces come a number of short poems, all of which are preceded by the words " By another Hand," except one which is assigned to " N. Brady D.D." another to " J. Addison," and four which are specially ascribed to Sedley. They include the four pieces assigned to Sedley in the " Buckingham " of 1704.

In the absence of any better authority than Briscoe and his hacks, we can only add the pieces here ascribed to Sedley for the first time to our list of doubtful poems. They are as follows :

" On the *Happy* Corydon *and* Phillis." p. 137.
" On Fruition." p. 139.
" *On a Lady that did not love* Apples." pp. 138, 139.
" Against His Mistress's Cruelty." p. 161.

The prose section of the 1707 edition (which I call B1) contains the seven parliamentary speeches already published in A, followed by a large and miscellaneous collection of " Remarkable Speeches in both *Houses of Parliament : From the Year 1641, to the Happy Union of Great Britain."* Among them are two old scurrilous cavalier satires on the Roundhead Earl of Pembroke, entitled " *The Earl of* Pembroke's *Speech on the Debate of the City's Petition for a Personal Treaty with the King"* and " *The Last Will and Testament of the Earl of* Pembroke." These pieces had already appeared as broadsides in 1648 and 1651 respectively. They were not assigned to any author either in the original editions or in B1. A MS. note in the British Museum copy of the broadside of the earlier piece ascribes it to Samuel Butler. The edition of 1709/10, which I shall call B2, was also published by Briscoe. It was advertised in "The Tatler" of January 10–12, 1709/10. It includes all the contents of the 1707 edition, together with Rochester's famous Mountebank Speech which he is said to have delivered on Tower Hill, and " The State of a Secretaries Place and the Dangers incident to it Writen by Robert Cecil Earl of Salisbury and never Printed before." The texts of the works ascribed to Sedley are identical with those of B1.

We now come to the edition of 1722 in two duodecimo volumes, which with its successors of 1776 and 1778 has usually been accepted as a complete Sedley. This edition was the third published by Briscoe, and I shall therefore call it B3. It opens with a portrait of Sedley " curiously engraved from an original Painting." It is a poor line engraving by Van der Gucht after the oil painting at Knole Park, reproduced in my study of Sedley, and bears only a slight resemblance to the original. The first title-page announces " The Works of the Honourable Sir *Charles Sedley* . . . in Two Volumes, with Memoirs of the Author's Life writ by an Eminent Hand."

The first volume begins with a dedicatory epistle to " The Most

Noble and Illustrious Prince JAMES, Duke of *Chandois*." This is the
first Duke, the famous " princely Chandos " (1673–1744), Pope's
" Timon " and Handel's munificent patron. Briscoe's dedication is
as absurd a piece of adulation as has ever appeared in print. " When
the Works of the *Polite Dead* are published," he informs his patron,
" they belong of right to your Grace, who in the Field of Literature
are *Lord of the Manor*, and whom Nature has made, and whom the
general Voice of Mankind acknowledges to be the *Maecenas* of Universal Learning." This effusion is followed by " Some Account of
the Life of Sir Charles Sedley " (see Introduction to " Sir Charles
Sedley," pp. 5, 6), which is printed in this edition for the first
time.

The first section of this volume (pp. 1–101) contains 105 poems,
original and translated. They include the fifty-five short pieces and
thirty Court Characters ascribed to Sedley in A with " The Happy
Pair," " The Fourth Book of Virgil," the seven additional lyrics
ascribed to Sedley in B1 and B2, and the Prologue to Higden's " The
Wary Widow." There are also ten short pieces which had never
been attributed to Sedley before. One is the Song from " The Man
of Mode," which has been mentioned already and which is probably
by Sir Car Scroop. Another is a pretty song in dialogue beginning

" Prithee tell me, faithless swain,"

which had already appeared in two miscellanies.[1] It is certainly quite
in Sedley's manner, but had never, as far as I can find, been attributed
to him. The little satire, " A Fable," which had appeared in the
" Poems on State Affairs " of 1705, is also reprinted. A rather
commonplace lyric in eight lines beginning " *Celinda,* think not by
Disdain," does not, as far as I know, appear elsewhere. It might be
the work of any minor versifier of the late seventeenth or early eighteenth
century. " Cupid's *Return*," in two irregular stanzas of the " pin-
daric " type, is quite unlike any authentic poem by Sedley both in
form and matter. Of the remaining five pieces it is possible to be
more definite. One is a version of an old mock epitaph on Sir Henry
Leigh of Ditchley, Oxon, who died, according to Aubrey,[2] in 1610/11.
The Aubrey MSS. give a slightly different version of the same piece.[3]
It was probably written before Sedley's birth. The remaining four

---

[1] See Bibliography, Nos. 7 and 8.
[2] Aubrey's " Brief Lives," ed. A. Clark, II. 30.
[3] Aubrey MS., Bodl. 8 f. 91 b. Aubrey's version is as follows:

" Here lies the good old Knight Sr Harry
Who loved well but would not marry.
While he lived and had his feeling,
She did lye & he was kneeling.
Now he's dead and cannot feele,
He doeth lye and she doeth kneele."

The version in the 1722 Sedley (I. 2) is as follows :

THE
WORKS

Of the Honourable
Sir *Charles Sedley,* Bart
In PROSE and VERSE.

In Two VOLUMES.

CONTAINING

The Translations of VIRGIL'S PASTORALS, the
BATTLE and GOVERNMENT of BEES, &c.

WITH

His SPEECHES, POLITICAL PIECES, POEMS, SONGS
and PLAYS, the greatest Part never printed
before, *Viz.*

The HAPPY PAIR.	BELLAMIRA, or, the MI-
ANTONY and CLEOPA-	STRESS, *a Comedy.*
TRA, *a Tragedy.*	The GRUMBLER, *a Co-*
The MULBERRY GAR-	*medy.*
DEN, *a Comedy.*	The TYRANT KING of
VENUS and ADONIS.	CRETE, *a Tragedy.*

With MEMOIRS of the Author's LIFE, writ
by an Eminent Hand.

London : Printed for *S. Briscoe,* at the *Bell-Savage-
Inn* on *Ludgate-Hill,* and Sold by *T. Bickerton,*
in *Pater-Noster-Row,* 1 7 2 2.

had all appeared in Kemp's Collection of 1671–2. They are two lyrics entitled " *A Farewell to* Love " (B3, I. 9), " *To* Phillis " (*ibid.*), and Epilogues to Ben Jonson's " Everyman in His Humour " (B3, I. 19), and to Medbourn's translation of Molière's " Tartuffe " (4to, 1670) (B3, I. 11). " A Farewel to Love " is attributed by the annotator of Mr. Thorn Drury's copy of K to " Capt. Aston." The lines " To Phillis " beginning

" Tho' *Phillis*, your prevailing charms "

had also appeared on p. 122 of " The New Academy of Complements " (1671) in an entirely different version which begins

" *Phillis* though your powerful charms."

Both this lyric and the Epilogues to " Every Man in his Humour " and " Tartuffe " are ascribed by the annotator of Mr. Thorn Drury's and Sir Charles Firth's copies of K to " Ld Buckhurst," that is, Charles Sackville, Sedley's friend, who afterwards became Earl of Dorset. They reappear in C and S, in the latter of which they are merely ascribed " To A Person of Honour." There is every reason to suppose that they are by Dorset, for they appear among his poems in all the eighteenth-century editions. The non-dramatic poems are followed by " Antony and Cleopatra, a Tragedy as it is Acted at the Duke's Theatre," said on its title-page to have been printed " in the year 1617." This is obviously a misprint for 1719, a date which appears on several other title-pages in the second volume and which probably represents the year in which Briscoe began to compile the edition. This " Antony and Cleopatra " is the play which was acted in 1676 and published in quarto in 1677 and 1696, not the " Beauty the Conquerour " of the 1702 volume. The tragedy is followed by a section of prose. It opens with the " Reflections on Our Late and Present Proceedings in England," which had already appeared anonymously in 1689. Next come the seven parliamentary speeches and the " Essay on Entertainments " that had already been printed in A, B1 and B2, followed by the two prose satires on the Earl of Pembroke which had appeared in B1 and B2, but which were not there attributed to Sedley. As these pieces had been printed when Sedley was a boy of ten and twelve, it is quite impossible that they can be from his pen. The rest of the volume is filled up with a prose translation of Cicero's " Oration for M. Marcellus " and a verse

---

" An Epitaph.
Here Sir *Henry Leigh* is lying
With his Doxy kneeling by him ;
When he was alive, and had his feeling,
When she lay down, then he was kneeling.
But now he's dead, and has lost his Feeling,
Now he lies down she is kneeling."

translation of the " Pastorals of Virgil " (*i.e.* the Eclogues), with a separate title-page dated 1719. There is no reason to believe that Sedley had anything to do with either of these translations, which are probably the work of some Grub Street hack employed by Briscoe to fill up the volume.

The second volume opens with a reprint of Ayloffe's " Preface to the Reader," which had already appeared in A, B1 and B2. It is followed by twenty-four short lyrics. Eleven of these had already appeared in Mrs. Jane Barker's " Poetical Recreations " (1688), and six, as we have seen, can be definitely ascribed to other authors and therefore be excluded from the canon of Sedley's works. The other thirteen pieces are of very slight literary merit and might be the work of any rhymester of the age. The most interesting is " *A Pindarique Ode Written in a Garden*" (B3, II. 13), which, in spite of poor technique and absurdly conventional vocabulary, does show a glimmer of the new feeling for landscape which was just beginning to be expressed in English poetry about this time. The lascivious piece entitled " The Fall " is specially labelled " By Sir Charles Sedley." It belongs to the large mass of verse of this kind ascribed to the Restoration Wits during the eighteenth century. It may be remarked that adverse judgments on Sedley's literary ability have sometimes been made on the strength of this group of poems of very doubtful authenticity.[1]

The next section of the second volume contains reprints of " The Mulberry Garden " and " Bellamira " from the Quartos, after which comes a farce in three acts entitled " The Grumbler," with a separate title-page stating that it had never before been printed, and dated 1719. It is a neat translation of " Le Grondeur," a popular French piece by Brueys and Palaprat (produced at the Théâtre Français in 1691). It is not unlikely that Sedley may have amused himself by translating it in his latter years, but, in the absence of any better authority than Briscoe, it cannot be given a place among the authentic works. It is followed by " *Venus* and *Adonis*, or the Amour of Venus," a vigorous poem in heroic couplets, which appears here for the first time. Still more curious is the inclusion of the piece with which the volume closes. This is a play in execrably bad blank verse which is scarcely distinguishable from prose, entitled " The Tyrant King of *Crete*, A Tragedy Never before Printed," with separate title-page dated 1702. It is merely an abbreviated version of Henry Killigrew's " Pallantus and Eudora " (fol., 1653), which had appeared in " a false and imperfect transcript " under the title of " The Conspiracy " as early as 1638. There is no good reason to suppose that Sedley had anything to do with it.[2]

---

[1] *E.g.* in " Rochester and Other Literary Rakes of the Restoration," London, 1902 (by Thomas Longueville), p. 77, where the wretched lines entitled " The Toper " (No. CXXXV of this edition) are quoted as an example of Sedley's lyric verse !

[2] See " Sir Charles Sedley," pp. 280, 281.

It will thus be seen that of the contents of this edition, which has hitherto been considered complete, not more than about two-thirds can be safely assigned to Sedley, while some pieces are undoubtedly spurious. It seems likely that Briscoe desired to bring out a Sedley in two volumes in 1719, and being unable to obtain sufficient copy to fill them, collected odd pieces during the next three years with which he swelled his two duodecimos to the necessary bulk. The contents of the editions of 1776 and 1778 published by T. Davies and J. Ireland respectively do not differ from those of B3 except for a few very slight textual variants.

The following classified list of the contents of B3, B4 and B5 shows how little these editions can be relied upon as complete collections of Sedley's works :

Genuine Works.	*Works of Doubtful Authorship.*	*Spurious Works.*
55 Lyrics.	" The Grumbler."	2 Epilogues and Lyric by Dorset.
30 Court Characters.	" Venus and Adonis."	
" The Happy Pair."	" Oration for M. Marcellus."	Lyric by Sir Car Scroop from " The Man of Mode."
" The Fourth Book of Virgil."	" Virgil's Pastorals."	
Prologue to " Sir Noisy Parrat."	2 Lyrics in Vol. I.	Lyric by Capt. Aston.
7 Speeches.	17 Lyrics in Vol. II.	Epitaph on Sir H. Leigh.
" Upon Our Late and Present Proceedings."		Lyrics by Donne, Whitehall, Brome and Walker in Vol. II.
" Essay on Entertainments."		" The Earl of Pembroke's Speech, etc."
" The Mulberry Garden."		" The Last Will and Testament, etc."
" Bellamira."		" The Tyrant King of Crete."
" Antony and Cleopatra."		

The following genuine works were not printed in any collected edition :

> Translations of three elegies of Ovid in Tonson's Miscellany of 1684.
>
> " Prologue to the Stroulers " in " Poems on Affairs of State," 1698.

The Extempore Lines in " The Diverting Post," 1704, and the lines by " Mr. C. S. of Wadham " in Anthony Stephens' Collection may be added to the list of works assigned to Sedley on doubtful authority.

Very few of Sedley's works exist in manuscript, and none in autograph except the letters printed in " Sir Charles Sedley." There are, however, some transcripts of individual poems and prose pieces in seventeenth-century hands. The lines beginning " As in those Nations where they yet adore," and headed in A, " To Celia," must have been popular, for, besides appearing in several miscellanies, they also exist in two MS. copies, one of which is in the British Museum and the other in the Bodleian. The Bodleian copy is on p. 169 of a quarto volume (West. MS. e. 4) that contains poems by Dryden, Rochester and other contemporary authors. It is of especial interest because of its heading, " To Mrs. Mary Napp," which occurs in none of the printed copies. This is conclusive evidence that the poem was addressed to the well-known actress, Mrs. Knipp ; it also reveals her Christian name, which has not hitherto been known.

The Bodleian also contains a folio miscellany of verse and prose (Rawl. D. 361), on f. 56 of which occurs a manuscript copy of the " Poem to King William on his birthday," printed in A and subsequent editions, beginning

" Behold ye happy Day Againe."

A folio scrap-book among the Rawlinson MSS. (319, D. 924) includes with other seventeenth-century MSS. a transcript of the prose pamphlet " Reflections on Our Present Proceedings in England," which had been published in 1689 and again in B3 and its successors. It consists of nineteen quarto leaves closely written on one side, and the title is followed by the words " By Sir Charles Sedley." This is the only authority, except that of Briscoe's edition, for attributing it to him. On f. 227 of another folio miscellany (Rawl. D. 380) there is a transcript of " A modest Plea for Some Exercises at this time in order to the avoyding of a Land Tax, for the yeare 1694, by the Honble. Sr Cha: Sidley," covering seventeen folio leaves inscribed on both sides. This piece has never, I believe, been printed.

The British Museum MSS. include two of the elegies translated by Sedley from Ovid's " Amores," the lyric addressed " to Mrs. Napp " in the Bodleian MS., the Prologue " to the Stroulers " and the " Pastoral Dialogue between Strephon and Thirsis." The two translations from Ovid are in a folio scrap-book (Add. MS. 34, 744) that contains transcripts of a number of pieces included in " Dryden's Miscellany " of 1684. The first piece of Sedley occurs on f. 56 and is headed " Ovid Bk. 2 Eleg. 5. Taken out of Sir Charles Sedley's and Mr. Oldham's Translations." It is actually a cento made by combining some couplets from the translation of this elegy by Sedley which had appeared in " Dryden's Miscellany " of 1684, with others from another version, by Oldham. On f. 59 *b* there is an exact transcript of the version of the fourth elegy of the third book that was printed as his in " Dryden's Miscellany " of 1684, and which is also ascribed to " Sr Ch: Sedley " here. Another folio volume (Sloane 1009) contains on f. 395 a transcript of the lyric beginning

" As in those Nations, where they yet adore."

This version does not differ materially from the printed versions or the Bodleian MSS., but it does not contain the dedication to "Mrs. Napp" found in the latter. Egerton 2623 is another folio scrap-book, on f. 63 of which occurs a piece headed " Prologue by Sr C. S. Bart to the Stroulers." These lines are printed with slight variants in " Poems on Affairs of State " (8vo, 1698) (see Poem No. LVII). On f. 200 of another MS. miscellany (Harl. 7332) there is a transcript of the shorter version of the " Pastoral Dialogue between Thirsis and Strephon," which first appeared in K, and which, in an enlarged form, was placed by Ayloffe at the beginning of his edition (see Poem No. I). A MS. music-book in the British Museum (Add. MS. 30, 382) bearing the bookplate of Katherine Sedley and the date 1678 (in pencil) contains a fragment of the drinking song, " Drink about till the day find us." The music and words are apparently in the hand of Henry Bowman, a well-known musician, who must have been Katherine's master. Unfortunately the leaf containing the first stanzas has been torn out. Page 91 contains the last lines from " Joyning thus our mirth & Beauty," with a musical setting which will be found in the note to the Poem.

Finally it may be noticed that a manuscript book written by Sir A. Haward in the possession of Mr. G. Thorn Drury ascribes two obscene poems (which were printed in various editions of Rochester's works) to Sedley. They are " Dildeidos a Poem," and some lines beginning " In ye Feilds of Lincoln's Inne." There is no other evidence that they are from Sedley's pen.

The chief difficulty which arises from a comparison of the different texts of Sedley's works is the considerable divergence between the different versions of the same poems published in A and K and the miscellanies that followed it. The explanation of these variants is to be found in the words of Ayloffe which I have already quoted. Ayloffe printed his edition from copies of Sedley's poems " All corrected by his own hand." This must mean that he was making a general revision of all his poems at the time of his death, probably with the object of bringing out a complete edition. Sometimes he would recast an entire poem. The most extreme instance is the piece entitled in K, " *To a Lady who told him he could not Love*," and beginning

> " Madam, though meaner Beauties might,
> Perhaps, have need of some such slight."

On p. 59 of A there is a poem called " The Feigned Love " which has the very similar opening :

> " *Cloris*, tho' meaner Beauties might
> Perhaps, have need of some such Slight."

Out of its twenty-two lines, however, it contains only one other couplet that bears the smallest resemblance to anything in the version in K.

The changes from the text of K which are embodied in A appear to have been made chiefly for artistic, but sometimes for moral reasons. The artistic changes are nearly always improvements. They commonly consist of the elimination of otiose lines or stanzas and the improvement of the rhythm or grammar. Thus the charming lines " To

Cloris " beginning " *Cloris*, I cannot say your Eyes " (No. V) are marred
in the earlier version by an ugly grammatical error in the thirteenth
line which reads :

> " He that both lips and hands adore."

This is neatly mended in A without spoiling the rhyme. The later
version reads :

> " He that does Lips and Hands adore."

In the song (No. II) beginning

> " *Phillis*, let's shun the common Fate "

A omits two very awkward lines :

> " I'le love and hate just where you do,
> And for't no other reason know."

Sometimes the rather free rhythm is regularized in accordance with
the more " correct " standards of the poet's later years. Thus in the
line " *Aurelia* art thou mad " (No. XXVI), " *Aurelia* " becomes Fair
Aminta in order to conform with the trochaic movement of the third
line. Another lyric, " The Complaint " (No. VIII), begins with the
following stanza in K :

> " When *Aurelia* first became
> The Mistress of his heart,
> So mild and gentle was her reign,
> *Thirsis* in hers had part."

The first line is again smoother in A by the insertion of the same
colourless epithet, " fair," before " *Aurelia*."

A far more subtle revision is to be found in the famous song beginning " Not *Celia*, that I juster am " (No. III). In K, the first stanza
reads not ungracefully :

> " Not *Celia*, that I juster am,
> Or better than the rest ;
> For I would change each hour like them,
> Were it my interest."

This is immensely improved in A by the substitution of real beauty
for the mere smartness of the fourth line of K :

> " Not *Celia*, that I juster am
> Or better than the rest :
> For I would change each Hour like them,
> Were not my Heart at rest."

In the earlier version ll. 7 and 8 are clumsy in rhythm and otiose in
sense :

> " Should you my Heart but once set free,
> I should be no more a Slave."

The revision transforms them into two of the finest lines in the lyric
verse of the age :

> " Thy Face I only care to see,
> Thy Heart I only crave."

Compression seems to have been the general rule of the revision,
and most of the later versions are shorter than their counterparts in K.
The only poem that has been expanded is " A Pastoral Dialogue between
Thirsis and Strephon " (No. I), which has only fifty lines in the early
version but is expanded to ninety-six in A.   From this fact and from
the position of the " Dialogue " at the head of A, we may suppose that
Sedley felt that it was more in the taste of his later years than most
of the poems of his youth, and paid special attention to it as a suitable
piece to stand at the head of his collected works.

The corrections made obviously on moral grounds are slight enough,
but provide an amusing commentary on the change that seems to
have taken place in the poet's character after the Revolution.   Thus
the original version of the poem " To Cloris " (No. XXX) ends with
the following couplet :

> " What a Priest says moves not the mind,
> Souls are by love, not words, combin'd."

These lines are omitted from the later version either by Sedley or,
possibly, by Ayloffe, who may not have cared to publish such a
reference to the position of his aunt.   It was probably for a similar
reason that the last lines of " Constancy " (No. IX) were omitted :

> " The passion I have now shall ne're grow less,
> No, though thy own fair self it should oppress ;
> I could e'en hazard my Eternity,
> Love but again, and 'twill a Heaven be."

The Sedley of 1700 seems to have had different ideas about " hazarding
his Eternity " from those held by the companion of Buckingham and
Rochester.

I have chosen to print the text of A in preference to that of K,
in spite of the fact that the latter has a freshness and cavalier freedom
which is, perhaps, slightly toned down in the later versions.   This
consideration is, in my opinion, far outweighed by the arguments that
the revised versions were almost certainly those in which the poet
desired the poems finally to be published, that the alterations are in
the large majority of cases distinct artistic improvements (in spite of
Ayloffe's dictum that Sir Charles " cou'd alter but rarely mend "),
and thirdly, that the versions of A were followed by the eighteenth-
century editions, and have thus become the classic versions of Sedley's
lyrics which, in a few instances at any rate, are familiar to thousands
of readers of modern anthologies.

Where the differences between the two versions are comparatively
slight, they are given as variants in the textual notes ; where, however,

it is impossible to give an adequate idea of the revision in this way, the whole of the earlier version is given in the Explanatory Note on the poem.

I have retained the order in which the poems appear in A, as I suppose it to represent something like the order intended by the poet, except for one slight alteration which enables me to place the three authentic prologues published by Sedley, but not included by Ayloffe, beside the single Prologue which he does include, and at the same time to transfer the little satire on Sir Richard Blackmore (No. LIV) to its natural place beside the other little squib on the medical profession (No. LIII), from which it is separated by the Prologue (LV) in A. I have also placed the three translations from Ovid in the text of "Dryden's Miscellany" of 1684 after the translation of the Fourth Georgic which appears in the text of A. "The Happy Pair," which precedes the latter poem as in A, is given in the text of the Folio edition of 1702. The three authentic plays are all printed from the texts of the first quartos, which are on the whole the best texts in each case, the other quartos being mere page-for-page reprints, which sometimes correct errors, but more often introduce fresh ones. The only serious departures from the texts of the first quartos are the introduction of scene divisions where they are omitted from the originals and where they are obviously required, and a few stage directions where they are necessary for the convenience of the reader; and in the case of "The Mulberry Garden" the abandonment of the absurd division of the prose into short lengths of about the size of blank verse which is found in the quarto editions and is common enough in plays of the period. "Beauty the Conquerour," the unfinished rehandling of the theme of "Antony and Cleopatra," has been allowed to sleep in the decent obscurity of Ayloffe's edition, and "Pompey the Great," of which one unidentified act is by Sedley, has not been reprinted. The prose "Essay on Entertainments" in the text of A has been placed at the conclusion of the authentic works.

The Parliamentary Speeches and prose pamphlets are not included, but an account of them will be found in my Biography of Sedley (pp. 175-201, 303).

The Doubtful Works include, besides the excellent translation of "Le Grondeur" entitled "The Grumbler," forty-six poems which have been ascribed to Sedley during his lifetime and after his death by unknown or untrustworthy authorities. They begin with the two ascribed to him by the unknown annotators of K, and end with those that are first ascribed to him in Briscoe's edition of ¦1722. The "Oration for M. Marcellus," which, if it is by Sedley, is merely a schoolboy exercise, has been omitted.

The texts indicated above have been adhered to throughout except for the silent correction of obvious printer's errors in the originals and for the substitution of the modern *s* for the old long *s*. When emendations involve the addition of words, letters, or stops, what is added is enclosed in pointed brackets ⟨ ⟩. If they involve the omission of a letter or stop, no indication of the omission is given in the text, but the exact reading of the original is given in the textual·notes. The textual notes also record all important divergences from the texts used in this edition which are to be found in other printed or MS. versions. They do not record unimportant variants in spelling or punctuation, or mere printer's errors in later and less trustworthy editions.

I wish to acknowledge the valuable help which I have received in preparing this edition from Mr. G. Thorn Drury, Sir C. H. Firth, Mr. H. F. B. Brett Smith, the Rev. Montague Summers (who kindly allowed me to make use of his MS. notes on " The Mulberry Garden " and " Bellamira "), Mr. W. J. Lawrence, Mr. P. Simpson, Professor G. S. Gordon, Mr. D. Nichol Smith, Professor E. Weekley, and Mr. S. J. Crawford, who read the proofs.

V. DE SOLA PINTO.

Southampton,
  April, 1927.

ERRATA

Vol. I. A Note on the Illustrations:—*For* Mrs. Rinton *read* Mrs. W. Gordon Renton. Ibid. l. 8. *For* father *read* grandfather.

P. xii, l. 2 of second paragraph. *For* 1672 *read* 1673.

P. xviii, quotation from "The Diverting Post." *For* again *read* in vain,

P. 29. "The Indifference" (No. XXXII), l. 7. *For* thrown *read* throw.

Vol. II, p. 240, column 3 (Ascription in K2). *Read* C. S. opposite "Ah, Pardon, Madam," etc., and "Fear not, my Dear," etc., and "no ascription" opposite "Thanks, fair *Urania*," etc.

CONTENTS

Contents

THE PLAYS

LIST OF ILLUSTRATIONS

A NOTE ON THE ILLUSTRATIONS

AFTER the publication of my Life of Sir Charles Sedley, I had the pleasure of meeting Mrs. Rinton of Hollowell Manor, Northants, a descendant of the poet and of the Countess of Dorchester, and of receiving from her much valuable information concerning the family. She drew my attention to the existence of certain portraits which were originally in the Portmore collection at Weybridge, where the Countess of Dorchester lived with her husband, the first Earl of Portmore. These pictures descended to Mrs. Rinton's father, the Rev. Edward Dawkins, great-grandson of Juliana, daughter of the second Earl of Portmore, and grand-daughter of the Countess of Dorchester by the first Earl. The Portmore–Dawkins collection was dispersed at a sale held in 1913, and many of the pictures went to America. Among them was the fine portrait by Kneller, dated 168–, (reproduced as the frontispiece of this volume by courtesy of Messrs. Scott and Fowles of New York, its present owners) which according to family tradition is a portrait of Sir Charles Sedley, the poet. Another was the full-length portrait of a lady also by Kneller, (reproduced as the frontispiece to Vol. II of this edition by permission of Messrs. M. Knoedler of New York) said to be a portrait of the Countess of Dorchester. I have also thought it appropriate to include reproductions of the portraits by Lely in the Hampton Court collection of Frances Stuart, Duchess of Richmond and Lennox, who received the dedication of "The Mulberry Garden," and of Barbara Palmer, Duchess of Cleveland, reputed to have been the original of *Bellamira*.

V. DE SOLA PINTO.

Southampton,
  June, 1928.

POEMS AND TRANSLATIONS

A PASTORAL DIALOGUE BETWEEN
THIRSIS AND *STREPHON*

Thirsis.] *Strephon*, O *Strephon*, once the jollieſt Lad,
That with shrill Pipe did ever Mountain glad ;
Whilome the Foremoſt at our rural Plays,
The Pride and Envy of our Holidays :
Why doſt thou now sit musing all alone,   5
Teaching the Turtles, yet a sadder Moan ?
Swell'd with thy Tears, why does the Neighbouring
    Brook
Bear to the Ocean, what she never took ?
Thy Flocks are fair and fruitful, and no Swain,
Then thee, more welcome to the Hill or Plain.   10

Strep.]   I could invite the Wolf, my cruel Gueſt,
And play unmov'd, while he on all should feaſt :
I cou'd endure that every Swain out-run,
Out-threw, out-wreſtled, and each Nymph shou'd
    shun
The hapless *Strephon*.————

Thir.]   Tell me then thy Grief,   15
And give it, in Complaints, some short Releif.

Strep.]   Had killing Mildews nipt my rising Corn,
My Lambs been all found dead, as soon as born ;
Or raging Plagues run swift through every Hive,
And left not one induſtrious Bee alive ;   20
Had early Winds, with an hoarse Winter's Sound
Scatter'd my rip'ning Fruit upon the Ground :
Unmov'd, untoucht, I cou'd the Loss suſtain,
And a few Days expir'd, no more complain.

Thir.]   E're the Sun drank of the cold Morning-
    dew,   25

I've known thee early the tuskt Boar pursue :
Then in the Evening drive the Bear away,
And rescue from his Jaws the trembling Prey.
But now thy Flocks creep feebly through the Fields,
No purple Grapes, thy half dreſt Vine-yards yields : 30
No Primrose nor no Violets grace thy Beds,
But Thorns and Thiſtles lift their prickly Heads.
What means this Change ?

   Strep.]   Enquire no more ;
When none can heal, 'tis Pain to search the Sore ;
Bright *Galatea*, in whose Mateless Face   35
Sat rural Innocence, with heavenly Grace ;
In whose no less inimitable Mind,
With equal Light, even diſtant Virtues shin'd ;
Chaſt without Pride, and Charming without Art,
Honour the Tyrant of her tender Heart :   40
Fair Goddess of these Fields, who for our Sports,
Though she might well become, negleſted Courts.
Belov'd of all, and loving me alone,
Is from my Sight, I fear, for ever gone.

   Thir.]   Thy Case indeed is pitiful, but yet   45
Thou on thy Loss too great a Price doſt set.
Women like Days are *Strephon*, some be far
More bright and glorious than others are :
Yet none so gay, so temperate, so clear,
But that the like adorne the rowling Year.   50
Pleasures imparted, to a Friend encrease,
Perhaps divided Sorrow may grow less.

   Strep.]   Others as fair, to other Eyes may seem,
But she has all my Love and my Eſteem :
Her bright Idea wanders in my Thought,   55
At once my Poison, and my Antidote.

   Thir.]   Our Hearts are Paper, Beauty is the Pen,
Which writes our Loves, and blots 'em out agen.
Phillis is Whiter than the rising Swan,
Her slender Waſt confin'd within a Span :   60

Charming as Nature's Face in the new Spring,
When early Birds on the green Branches sing.
When rising Herbs and Buds begin to hide,
Their naked Mother, with their short-liv'd Pride,
Cloe is ripe, and as the *Autumn* fair,   65
When on the Elm the purple Grapes appear.
When Trees, Hedg-rows, and every bending Bush,
With rip'ning Fruit, or tasteful Berries blush,
Lydia is in the Summer of her Days,
What Wood can shade us from her piercing Rays ? 70
Her even Teeth, whiter than new yean'd Lambs,
When they with tender Cries pursue their Dams.
Her Eyes as Charming as the Evening-sun,
To the scortcht Labourer when Work is done,
Whom the glad Pipe, to rural Sports invites,   75
And pays his Toil with innocent Delights.
On some of these fond Swain fix thy Desire,
And burn not with imaginary Fire.

Strep.] The Stag shall sooner with the Eagle soar,
Seas leave their Fishes naked on the Shore ;   80
The Wolf shall sooner by the Lambkin die,
And from the Kid the hungry Lion fly,
Than I abandon *Galatea's* Love,
Or her dear Image from my Thoughts remove.

Thir.] *Damon* this Evening carries home his
     Bride,   85
In all the harmless Pomp of rural Pride :
Where, for two spotted Lambkins, newly yean'd,
With nimble Feet and Voice, the Nimphs contend :
And for a Coat, thy *Galatea* spun,
The Shepherds Wrastle, throw the Bar, and Run. 90

Strep.] At that dear Name I feel my Heart re-
     bound,
Like the old Steed, at the fierce Trumpet's sound :
I grow impatient of the least Delay,
No Dastard Swain shall bear the Prize away.

Thir.]   Let us make haſt, already they are met ;   95
The ecchoing Hills their joyful Shouts repeat.

II

SONG

Phillis, let's shun the common Fate,
And let our Love ne'r turn to Hate ;
I'll dote no longer then I can,
Without being call'd a faithless Man.
When we begin to want Discourse,   5
And Kindness seems to taſt of Force,
As freely as we met, we'll part,
Each one posseſt of their own Heart.
Thus whilſt rash Fools themselves undo ;
We'll Game, and give off Savers too ;   10
So equally the Match we'll make,
Both shall be glad to draw the Stake :
A Smile of thine shall make my Bliss,
I will enjoy thee in a Kiss ;
If from this Height our Kindness fall,   15
We'll bravely scorn to Love at all :
If thy Affeſtion firſt decay,
I will the Blame on Nature lay.
Alas, what Cordial can remove
The haſty Fate of dying Love ?   20
Thus we will all the World excel
In Loving, and in Parting well.   22

III

SONG

Not *Celia,* that I juſter am
    Or better than the reſt,
For I would change each Hour like them,
    Were not my Heart at reſt.

But I am ty'd to very thee,   5
  By every Thought I have,
Thy Face I only care to see,
  Thy Heart I only crave.

All that i⟨n⟩ Woman is ador'd,
  In thy dear Self I find,   10
For the whole Sex can but afford,
  The Handsome and the Kind.

Why then should I seek farther Store,
  And ſtill make Love a-new;
When Change itself can give no more,   15
  'Tis easie to be true.

IV

Thirsis no more againſt my Flame advise,
But let me be in Love, and be you wise:
Here end, and there begin a new Address,
Pursue the vulgar easie Happiness:
Leave me to *Amaranta*, who alone   5
Can in my sullen Heart erect her Throne:
I know, as well as you, 'tis mean to burn,
For one who to our Flame makes no return:
But you, like me, feel not those conquering Eyes,
Which mock Prevention by a quick Surprize: 10
And now like a hurt Deer, in vain I ſtart
From her, that in my Breaſt has hid the Dart.
Though I can never reach her Excellence,
Take somewhat in my hopeless Love's defence.
Her Beauty is her not eſteemed Wealth,   15
And Graces play about her Eyes by ſtealth;
Vertue in others, the forc'd Child of Art,
Is but the native Temper of her Heart:
All Charms her Sex so often court in vain,
(Like *Indian* Fruit, which our cold Earth disdain.) 20
In her grow wild, as in their native Air,
And she has all Perfection without Care.

Of Lovers Harms she has the tend'reſt Sense,
That can consiſt with so much Innocense.
Like a wise Prince, she rules her Subjeᶜts so,   25
That neither Want, nor Luxury they know.
None vainly hoping what, she may not give,
Like humble Slaves at small Expence we live :
And I the wretched Comfort only share,
To be the Leaſt whom she will bid Dispair.   30

V

TO CLORIS

Cloris, I cannot say your Eyes
Did my unwary Heart surprize ;
Nor will I swear it was your Face,
Your Shape, or any nameless Grace :
For you are so intirely Fair,   5
To love a Part, Injuſtice were ;
No drowning Man can know which Drop
Of Water his laſt Breath did ſtop ;
So when the Stars in Heaven appear,
And joyn to make the Night look clear ;   10
The Light we no one's Bounty call,
But the obliging Gift of all.
He that does Lips or Hands adore,
Deserves them only, and no more ;
But I love All, and every Part,   15
And nothing less can ease my Heart.
Cupid, that Lover, weakly ſtrikes,
Who can express what 'tis he likes.   18

VI

INDIFFERENCE EXCUSED

Love, when 'tis true, needs not the aid
Of Sighs nor Oaths to make it known ;
And, to convince the cruel'ſt Maid,
Lovers should use their Love alone :

Into their very Looks 'twill ſteal ;   5
  And he that moſt wou'd hide his Flame,
Does in that Case his Pain reveal,
  Silence it self can Love proclaim.

This my *Aurelia* made me shun,
  The Paths that common Lovers tread :   10
Whose guilty Passions are begun
  Not in their Heart, but in their Head.

I cou'd not Sigh, and with cross'd Arms
  Accuse your Rigour and my Fate,
Nor tax your Beauty with such Charms   15
  As Men adore, and Women hate :

But careless liv'd, and without Art,
  Knowing my Love you muſt have spy'd,
And thinking it a foolish Part,
  To set to shew, what none can hide.   20

VII

ORINDA TO *CLORIS*

Cloris, you live ador'd by all,
And yet on none your Favours fall.
A ſtranger Miſtress ne're was known ;
You pay 'em all in paying none.
We him of Avarice accuse,   5
Who what he has forbears to use ;
But what Disease of Mind shall I
Call this, thy hated Penury ?
Thou wilt not give out of a Store,
Which no Profuseness can make poor.   10
Misers, when dead, they make amends,
And in their Wills enrich their Friends ;
But when thou dy'ſt, thy Treasure dies,
And thou canſt leave no Legacies.
What Madness is it then to spare,   15
When we want Power to make an Heir ?

Live, *Cloris*, then at the full Rate
Of thy great Beauty ; and since Fate,
To Love and Youth, is so severe,
Enjoy 'm freely while th' art here.   20
Some Caution yet I'd have thee use,
When e're thou doſt a Servant chuse :
Men are not all for Lovers fit,
No more than Arms, or Arts of Wit :
For Wisdom some respeċted are,   25
Some we see poweful at the Bar ;
Some for Preferment waſte their Time,
And the ſteep Hill of Honour climb.
Others of Love their Business make,
In Love their whole Diversion take.   30
Take one of those ; for in one Breaſt
Two Passions live but ill at reſt :
Be wise, and with Discretion fly
All that take Flame at every Eye.
All sorts with powder'd Coat and Hair ;   35
All that dare more than think thee Fair,
Take one of Love who nothing says,
And yet whom every Word betrays ;
Love in the Cradle pretty'ſt shews.
And when't can speak, unruly grows.   40

VIII

THE COMPLAINT

When fair *Aurelia* firſt became
    The Miſtress of his Heart,
So mild and gentle was her Reign,
    Thirsis in hers had part.

Reserves and Care he laid aside,   5
    And gave a Loose to Love ;
The headlong Course he muſt abide,
    How ſteep so e're it prove.

At firſt Disdain and Pride he fear'd ;
   But they being overthrown,   10
No second Foe a while appear'd,
   And he thought all his own :

He thought himself a happier Man
   Than ever lov'd before ;
Her Favours ſtill his Hopes out-ran,   15
   Yet ſtill he lov'd the more :

Love smil'd at firſt, then looking grave,
   Said, *Thirsis,* leave to boaſt ;
More Joy than all her Kindness gave,
   Her Fickleness will coſt.   20

He spoke, and from that fatal Time,
   All *Thirsis* did, or said,
Appear'd unwelcome, or a Crime
   To the ungrateful Maid.   24

IX

CONSTANCY

Fear not, my Dear, a Flame can never dye,
That is once kindled by so bright an Eye ;
View but thy self, and measure thence my Love,
Think what a Passion such a Form muſt move ;
For though thy Beauty firſt allur'd my Sight,   5
Now I consider it but as the Light
That led me to the Treasury of thy Mind,
Whose inward Vertue in that Feature shin'd.
That Knot be confident will ever laſt,
Which Fancy ty'd, and Reason has made faſt ; 10
So faſt that time, although it may disarm
Thy lovely Face, my Faith can never harm ;
And Age deluded, when it comes, will find
My Love removed, and to thy Soul assign'd. 14

X

THE PLATONICK

Fair *Amaranta*, wert thou not to blame,
To blow the Fire, and wonder at the Flame?
I did converse, 'tis true, so far was mine,
But that I lov'd, and hop'd was wholly thine;
Not hop'd as others do, for a Return,5
But that I might without offending burn.
I thought those Eyes which every Hour enslave
Could not remember all the Wounds they gave:
Forgotten in the Crowd I wisht to lie,
And of your Coldness, not your Anger, die;10
Yet since you know I love, 'tis now no time
Longer to hide, let me excuse the Crime,
Seeing what Laws I to my Passion give,
Perhaps you may consent that it should live:
First then, it never shall a Hope advance,15
Of waiting on you, but by seeming chance;
I at a distance will adore your Eyes,
As awful *Persians* do the Eastern Skies;
I never will presume to think of Sex,
Nor with gross Thoughts my deathless Love perplex;20
I tread a pleasant Path without Design;
And to thy Care my Happiness resign:
From Heaven it self thy Beauty cannot be
A freer Gift, than is my Love to thee.24

XI

TO CELIA

You tell me, *Celia*, you approve,
Yet never must return my Love:
An Answer that my Hope destroys,
And in the Cradle wounds our Joys;

To kill at once what needs muſt die,   5
None would to Birds and Beaſt⟨s⟩ deny.
How can you then so Cruel prove,
As to preserve, and torture Love ?
That Beauty Nature kindly meant
For her own Pride, and our Content;   10
Why shou'd the Tyrant Honour make
Our cruel undeserved Wrack ?
In Love and War th' Impoſtor do's
The Beſt to greateſt Harms expose :
Come then, my *Celia*, let's no more   15
This Devil for a God adore;
Like foolish *Indians* we have been,
Whose whole Religion is a Sin :
Let's lose no Time then but repent,
Love welcomes beſt a Penitent.   20

XII

HER ANSWER

Thirsis, I wish, as well as you,
To Honour there were nothing due,
Then would I pay my Debt of Love
In the same Coin that you approve;
Which now you muſt in Friendship take,   5
'Tis all the Payment I can make;
Friendship so high, that I muſt say,
'Tis rather Love, with some Allay;
And reſt contented, since that I
As well my self as you deny.   10
Learn then of me, bravely to bear,
The want of what you hold moſt dear;
And that which Honour does in me,
Let my Example work in thee.   14

XIII

TO AMARANTA

WHOM HE FELL IN LOVE WITH AT A PLAY-HOUSE

Fair *Amaranta* on the Stage, whilst you
Pitty'd a feigned Love, you gave a true ;
The Hopes and Fears, in every Scene exprest,
Grew soon th' uneasie Motions of my Breast.
I thought to steal the innocent Delight,   5
And not have paid my Heart for a first Sight.
And if I ventur'd on some slight Discourse,
It should be such as could no Passion nurse :
Led by the treacherous Lustre of your Eyes,
At last I play'd too near the Precipice :   10
Love came disguis'd in Wonder and Delight,
His Bow unbent, his Arrows out of sight ;
Your Words fell on my Passion, like those Showers,
Which paint and multiply the rising Flowers ;
Like *Cupid's* self, a God, and yet a Child,   15
Your Looks at once were awful, and yet mild :
Methoughts you blush'd, as conscious of my Flame,
Whilst your strict Vertue did your Beauty blame :
But rest secure, y'are from the Guilt as free
As Saints ador'd from our Idolatry.   20

XIV

THE SUBMISSION

Ah ! Pardon, Madam ; if I ever thought
Your smallest Favours could too dear be bought ;
And the just Greatness of your Servants Flame,
I did the Poorness of their Spirits name ;
Calling their long Attendance Slavery,   5
Your Power of Life and Death flat Tyranny ;
Since now I yield, and do confess there is
No way too hard that leads to such Bliss.

So when *Hippomanes* beheld the Race,
Where Loss was Death, and Conquest but a Face,   10
He stood amazed at the fatal Strife,
Wondring that Love shou'd dearer be than Life;
But when he saw the Prize no longer staid,
But through those very Dangers sought the Maid,
And won her too : O may his Conquest prove,   15
A happy Omen to my purer Love;
Which if the Honour of all Victory,
In the Resistance of the Vanquisht lie,
Though it may be the least regarded Prize,
Is not the smallest Trophy of our Eyes.   20

XV

TO A DEVOUT YOUNG GENTLEWOMAN

Phillis, this early Zeal asswage,
    You over-act your part ;
The Martyrs, at your tender Age,
    Gave Heaven but half their Heart.

Old Men (till past the Pleasure) ne're   5
    Declaim against the Sin ;
'Tis early to begin to fear
    The Devil at Fifteen.

The World to Youth is too severe,
    And, like a treacherous Light,   10
Beauty, the Actions of the Fair,
    Exposes to their sight.

And yet this World, as old as 'tis,
    Is oft deceiv'd by't too ;
Kind Combinations seldom miss,   15
    Let's try what we can do.

XVI

TO CELIA

Princes make Laws, by which their Subjects live,
And the high Gods Rules for the Worship give;
How should poor Mortals else a Service find
At all proportion'd to their heavenly Mind?
Had it been left to us, each one would bring, 5
Of what he lik'd himself, an Offering;
And with unwelcome Zeal perhaps displease
Th' offended Deity he would appease.
All Powers but thine, this Mercy did allow,
And how they wou'd be serv'd, themselves do shew. 10
A rude *Barbarian* wou'd his captiv'd Foe
Fully instruct in what he'd have him do:
And can it be, my *Celia*, that Love,
Less kind than War shou'd to the vanquish'd prove?
Say, cruel Fair, must then my Heart, a Flame, 15
Use for a while Friendship's Disguise and Name?
Or may it boldly like it self appear,
And its own Tale deliver to thy Ear?
Or must it in my tortur'd Bosom live,
Like Fire in unmov'd Flints, and no Light give, 20
And only then humbly send forth a small
Spark, when your self does on that Subject fall?
My Passion can with any Laws comply,
And, for your sake, do any thing, but die. 24

XVII

SONG

Get you gone, you will undo me,
If you love me, don't pursue me,
Let that Inclination perish,
Which I dare no longer cherish;
With harmless Thoughts I did begin, 5
But in the Crowd Love entred in;

I knew him not, he was so gay,
So innocent and full of play ;
At every Hour, in every Place,
I either saw or form'd your Face ;   10
All that in Plays was finely writ,
Fancy for you, and me did fit.
My Dreams at Night were all of you,
Such as till then I never knew :
I sported thus with young Desire,   15
Never intending to go higher :
But now his Teeth and Claws are grown,
Let me the fatal Lion shun ;
You found me harmless, leave me so ;
For were I not, you'd leave me too.   20

XVIII

A DIALOGUE BETWEEN *AMINTAS* AND *CELIA*

Celia.]   *Amintas*, I am come alone,
    A silly harmless Maid,
But whether is thy Honour flown ?
    I fear I am betray'd ;
Thy Looks are chang'd and in the Place   5
    Of innocent Desires,
Methinks I see thy Eyes and Face
    Glow with unusual Fires.

Amintas.]   Sees not my *Celia*, Nature wear
    One Countenance in the Spring,   10
And yet another Shape prepare,
    To bring the Harvest in ?
Look on the Eagle, how unlike
    He to the Egg is found,
When he prepares his Pownce to strike   15
    His Prey against the Ground ;

Fears might my Infant-love become,
   'Twere want of Vigor now
Should Modesty those Hopes benum,
   The Place and You allow.   20

Celia.]   *Amintas,* hold ; What could you worse
   To worst of Women do ?
Ah ! how could you a Passion nurse,
   So much my Honour's Foe ?

Amintas.]   Make not an Idol of a Toy,   25
   Which every Breath can shake,
Which all must have, or none enjoy,
   What Course soe're we take.
Whilst Women hate, or Men are vain,
   You cannot be secure ;   30
What makes my *Celia* then a Pain
   So needless to endure ?

Celia.]   Could I the World neglect for thee,
   Thy Love, though dear it cost,
In some unkind Conceit of me,   35
   Would be untimely lost :
Thou would'st thy own Example fear,
   And every heedless Word,
I chance let fall beyond thy Ear
   Would some new Doubt afford.   40

Amintas.]   If I am jealous, 'tis because
   I know not where you love ;
With me obey Love's gentle Laws
   And all my Fears remove.

Celia.]   Women, like Things at Second-hand 45
   Do half their Value lose,
But whil'st all Courtship they withstand,
   May at their Pleasure choose.

Amintas.]   This were a fine Discourse, my Dear,
   If we were not alone ;   50
But now Love whispers in my Ear,
   There's somewhat to be done.

She said she never would forgive;
  He kissing, swore she shou'd;
And told her, she was mad to ſtrive   55
  Againſt their mutual Good.
What farther paſt, I cannot tell
  But sure not much amiss;
He vow'd he lov'd her dearly well,
  She answered with a Kiss.   60

XIX

SONG

Drink about till the Day find us;
  These are Pleasures that will laſt;
Let no foolish Passion blind us,
  Joys of Love they fly too faſt.

Maids are long c're we can win 'um,   5
  And out Passions waſte the while,
In a Beer-glass we'll begin 'um,
  Let some Beau take th' other Toil.

Yet we will have ſtore of good Wenchcs,
  Though we venture fluxing for't,   10
Upon Couches, Chairs, and Benches,
  To out-do them at the Sport,

Joyning thus both Mirth and Beauty,
  To make up our full Delight:
In Wine and Love we pay our Duty   15
  To each friendly coming Night.

XX

SONG

Love ſtill has somthing of the Sea,
  From whence his Mother rose;
No time his Slaves from Doubt can free,
  Nor give their Thoughts repose:

They are becalm'd in cleareſt Days,   5
   And in rough Weather toſt;
They wither under cold Delays,
   Or are in Tempeſts loſt.

One while they seem to touch the Port,
   Then ſtraight into the Main,   10
Some angry Wind in cruel sport
   The Vessel drives again.

At firſt Disdain and Pride they fear,
   Which if they chance to 'scape,
Rivals and Falshood soon appear   15
   In a more dreadful shape.

By such Degrees to Joy they come,
   And are so long withſtood,
So slowly they receive the Sum,
   It hardly does them good.   20

'Tis cruel to prolong a Pain,
   And to defer a Joy;
Believe me, gentle *Celemene*
   Offends the winged Boy.

An hundred thousand Oaths your Fears   25
   Perhaps would not remove;
And if I gaz'd a thousand Years
   I could no deeper love.   28

XXI

SONG

Phillis, you have enough enjoy'd
   The Pleasures of Disdain;
Methinks your Pride shou'd now be cloy'd,
   And grow it self again:
Open to Love your long-shut Breaſt,   5
And entertain its sweeteſt Gueſt.

Love heals the Wounds that Beauty gives,
    And can ill Usage slight;
He laughs at all that Fate contrives,
    Full of his own Delight;   10
We in his Chains are happier far
Than Kings themselves without 'em are.

Leave then to tame Philosophy,
    The Joys of Quietness;
With me into Love's Empire fly;   15
    And taſte my Happiness:
Where even Tears and Sighs can show
Pleasures, the Cruel never know.   18

XXII

Madam, for your Commands to ſtay,
    Is the mean Duty of a Wretch,
Whose Service you with Wages pay;
    Lovers should at occasion catch,
Not idly wait till it be brought,   5
But with the Deed o're take your Thought;
Honour and Love let them give o're,
Who do their Duty, and no more.   8

XXIII

Awake, my Eyes, at Night my Thought⟨s⟩ pursue
You charming Shape; and find it ever new;
If I my weary Eyes to Sleep resign,
In gaudy Dreams your Love and Beauty shine;
Dreams with such Extasies and Pleasures fill'd, 5
As to those Joys they seem can only yield;
Nor do they yield perhaps, wou'd you allow,
Fair *Amidea*, that I once might know.   8

XXIV

TO CELIA

As in those Nations, where they yet adore
Marble and Cedar, and their Aid, implore :
'Tis not the Workman, nor the precious Wood,
But 'tis the Worshipper that makes the God ;
So, cruel Fair, though Heaven has giv'n you all,　　5
We Mortals (Vertue or can Beauty) call,
'Tis we that give the Thunder to your Frowns,
Darts to your Eyes, and to our selves the Wounds :
Without our Love, which proudly you deride,
Vain were your Beauty, and more vain your Pride ; 10
All envy'd Beings that the World can shew,
Still to some meaner things their greatness owe,
Subjects make Kings, and we (the numerous Train
Of humble Lovers) constitute thy Reign,
This difference only Beauty's Realm may boast,　　15
Where most it favours, it enslaves the most ;
And they to whom it is indulgent found,
Are ever in the surest Fetters bound :
What Tyrant yet, but thee, was ever known
Cruel to those that serv'd to make him one ?　　20
Valour's a Vice, if not with Honour joyn'd,
Beauty a raging Plague, if never kind.

XXV

SONG

I ask not my *Celia* would love me again,
　　In its own Pleasure my Love is o're-paid ;
I'll find such Excuses for all her Disdain,
　　That shortly to Frown I'll make her afraid.

Her Neglect of me, of her self I'll think Care ;   5
   Her Cruelty I her strict Vertue will name ;
When least kind she seems, I'll believe her most near,
   And call her Refusal, but a Virgin's Shame.

Thus all that was wont hertofore to cure Love
   In me shall increase, and stir up the Fire ;   10
I'll make her at last some kind Remedy prove,
   Since all others but increase my Desire.

XXVI

SONG

Fair *Aminta*, art thou mad,
   To let the World in me
Envy Joys I never had,
   And censure them in thee ?

Fill'd with Grief, for what is past,   5
   Let us at length be wise,
And to Love's true Enjoyments hast,
   Since we have paid the Price.

Love does easie Souls despise,
   Who lose themselves for Toys,   10
And escape for those devise,
   Who taste his utmost Joys.

Love should, like the Year, be crown'd
   With sweet Variety ;
Hope should in the Spring abound,   15
   Kind Fears, and Jealousie.

In the Summer Flowers should rise,
   And in the Autumn Fruit ;
His Spring doth else but mock our Eyes,
   And in a Scoff salute.   20

XXVII

SONG

Walking among thick Shades alone,
    I heard a diſtant Voice,
Which, sighing, said, Now she is gone,
    I'll make no second Choice.

I look't and saw it was a Swain,   5
    Who to the flying Wind,
Did of some neighbouring Nymph complain,
    Too fair, and too unkind.

He told me how he saw her firſt,
    And with what gracious Eyes,   10
And gentle Speech, that Flame she nurſt,
    Which since she did despise.

His Vows she did as faſt receive,
    As he could breath 'em to her ;
Love in her Eyes proclaim'd her leave,   15
    That he alone should woo her.

They fed their Flocks ſtill near one Place,
    And at one inſtant met,
He gazing on her lovely Face
    Fell deeper in the Net.   20

She seem'd of her new Captive glad ;
    Proud of his Bondage he,
No Lover, sure a Prospeⅽt had
    Of more Felicity.

But the false Maid, or never lov'd,   25
    Or gave so quickly o're ;
E're his was to the height improv'd,
    Her Kindness was no more.

Even her Dissemblings she let fall,
    And made him plainly see,   30
That though his Heart she did enthral,
    Her own was ever free.

Now, leſt his Care should Pity move,
    She shuns his very Sight;
And leaves him to that hopeless Love,   35
    She did create in Spight.

Her Name I could not make him tell,
    Though vowing him my aid;
He said he never would reveal,
    In Life, nor Death, the Maid.   40

XXVIII

THE FEIGNED LOVE

Cloris, tho' meaner Beauties might
Perhaps have need of some such Slight,
You may those petty Arts despise,
Secure of what is once your Prize;
Ill us'd and scorn'd, we muſt adore,   5
And queſtion not resiſtless Power:
In *Rome*, no Man was known to fly,
Whom the Emperor condemn'd to dye,
The fatal Stroke themselves wou'd give,
Rather than banisht from her live.   10
So to your Empire harsh or kind,
I ſtand by my own choice confind.
I daily saw how others far'd,
Whom the false Hope you gave ensnar'd;
Like foolish Boys at Birds, that catch,   15
Sometimes we thought you in our reach;
And then again, you'd mount and fly
Beyond the compass of our Eye;
Till weary'd with the vain Pursuit,
Like Birds that peck at painted Fruit,   20
The wiser sort their Hopes disclaim,
And beat the Wood for easier Game.

XXIX

ON THE BIRTH-DAY OF THE LATE QUEEN

A SONG

Love's Goddess sure was blind this Day,
  Thus to adorn her greatest Foe,
And Love's Artillery betray,
  To one that wou'd her Realm o'rethrow.

Those Eyes, that form that lofty Meen,   5
  Who could for Vertue's Camp design ?
Defensive Arms shou'd there be seen ;
  No sharp, no pointed Weapons shine.

Sweetness of Nature, and true Wit,
  High Power, with equal Goodness joyn'd   10
In this fair Paradise are met,
  The Joy and Wonder of Mankind.

May her blest Example chase
  Vice in Troops out of the Land,
Flying from her awful Face,   15
  Like pale Ghosts when Day's at Hand.

Long may she Reign over this Isle
  Lov'd and ador'd in foreign Parts ;
But gentle *Pallas* shield the while
  From her bright Charms our single Hearts. 20

May her Heroe bring home Peace,
  Won with Honour in the Field,
And all home-bred Factions cease ;
  He our Sword, and She our Shield.

Many such Days may she behold,   25
   Like the glad Sun without decay;
May Time, that tears where he lays hold,
   Only salute her in his way.

Late, late, may she to Heaven return,
   And Quires of Angels there rejoyce,   30
As much as we below shall mourn
   Our short, but their eternal Choice.   32

XXX

TO CLORIS

Cloris, I juſtly am betray'd,
By a Deſign my self had laid;
Like an old Rook, whom in his Cheat,
A run of Fortune does defeat.
I thought at firſt with a small Sum   5
Of Love, thy Heap to overcome;
Presuming on thy want of Art,
Thy gentle and unpractis'd Heart;
But naked Beauty can prevail,
Like open force, when all things fail.   10
Inſtead of that thou haſt all mine,
And I have not one Stake of thine;
And, like all Winners, doſt discover
A Willingness to give me over.
And though I beg, thou wilt not now;   15
'Twere better thou should'ſt do so too;
For I so far in debt shall run,
Even thee I shall be forc'd to shun.
My Hand, alas, is no more mine,
Else it had long ago been thine;   20
My Heart I give thee, and we call
No Man unjuſt that parts with all.   22

XXXI

THE SOLDIERS CATCH

Room, Boys, room ; room, Boys ; room,
For from *Ireland* we come ;
We have mawl'd the original Tories ;
    We have baffled the League,
    Between Monsieur and Teague,   5
And eclips'd the Grand *Lewis* his Glories.

    They all fly in the Field,
    Their best Garrisons yield,
They stand trembling while we take their Passes :
    Our brave King at our Head,   10
    We fear no Steel nor Lead,
But laugh at their Beads and their Masses.

    If some Blood we have spilt,
    To compound for the Guilt,
In Love's Camp we will do double Duty,   15
    Mankind we will repair,
    With the leave of the Fair,
And pay our Arrears to true Beauty.

    Our worst Noise in the Pit,
    Shall pass all for good Wit,   20
While the Cits and the Bumkins adore us.
    We will pay the Rogues well,
    Their Wives Bellies shall swell,
And the Cuckolds at random shall score us.

    The next Summer for *France*,   25
    We will boldly advance,
Our noble Redeemer shall lead us ;
    We will break the Slaves Chains,
    And drink of their *Champains*,
To the Health of that Heroe that freed us.   30

He hates *Lewis le Grand*,
Like a true English Man,
And ne're will consent to a Treaty,
Till each neighbouring Crown
Have what's juſtly their own,   35
And the French ſtrike sail when th⟨e⟩y met ye.

Since *Elizabeth*'s Reign
No Proteſtant Queen
We have had, but the present God bless her;
Since our *Edward* the Fourth,   40
No brave Prince of such Worth,
But *William* his valiant Successor.

With a Queen so devout,
And a People so ſtout,
A Parliament that will supply 'em,   45
A Cause that is right,
And a King that will fight,
Our Enemies all we defie 'em.   48

XXXII

THE INDIFFERENCE

Thanks, fair *Vrania*; to your Scorn
I now am free, as I was born,
Of all the Pain that I endur'd
By your late Coldness I am cur'd.

In losing me, proud Nymph, you lose   5
The humbleſt Slave your Beauty knows;
In losing you, I but thrown down
A cruel Tyrant from her Throne.

My ranging Love did never find
Such Charms of Person and of Mind;   10
Y'ave Beauty, Wit, and all Things know,
But where you shou'd your Love beſtow.

I unawares my Freedom gave,
And to those Tyrants grew a Slave;
Would you have kept what you had won,   15
You should have more Compassion shewn.

Love is a Burthen, which two Hearts,
When equally they bear their Parts,
With Pleasure carry; but no one,
Alas, can bear it long alone.   20

I'm not of those who court their Pain,
And make an Idol of Disdain;
My Hope in Love does ne're expire,
But it extinguishes Desire.

Nor yet of those who ill receiv'd,   25
Wou'd have it otherwise believ'd;
And, where their Love cou'd not prevail,
Take the vain Liberty to rail.

Whoe're wou'd make his Victor less,
Muſt his own weak Defence confess,   30
And while her Pow'r he does defame,
He poorly doubles his own Shame.

Even that Malice does betray,
And speak Concern another way;
And all such Scorn in Men is but   35
The Smoke of Fires ill put out.

He's ſtill in Torment, whom the Rage
To Detraction does engage;
In Love Indifference is sure
The only sign of perfect Cure.   40

XXXIII

SONG

Who would not gaze away his Heart
    On *Mariana's* Eyes,
Did not her high and juſt Disdain
    The bold Delight chaſtize?

Mirth and Joy she spreads around,   5
    Like the Sun's chearful Light,
When his returning Beams destroy
    The Empire of the Night.

Her Beauty with amazement strikes
    (If with no more) the Old :   10
Her Vertue tempers with Despair
    The Youthful and the Bold.

Her Goodness so disarms her Wit
    Of the offensive part ;
Whilst others only charm the Ear,   15
    She steals the very Heart.

Let us no more defame the Fair,
    But learn to praise again ;
Bright *Mariana's* Worth demands
    A new and nobler Strain.   20

So, to the feather'd Kind, the Spring
    Restores their wonted Voice ;
On ev'ry Bough they sit and sing,
    And court their new-made Choice.   24

XXXIV

THE EIGHTH ODE OF THE SECOND BOOK OF *HORACE*

Did any Punishment attend
    Thy former Perjuries,
I should believe a second time,
    Thy charming Flatteries :
Did but one Wrinkle mark this Face,   5
Or hadst thou lost one single Grace.

No sooner hast thou, with false Vows,
    Provok'd the Powers above ;
But thou art fairer than before,
    And we are more in love,   10

Thus Heaven and Earth seem to declare,
They pardon Falshood in the Fair.

Sure 'tis no Crime vainly to swear,
    By every Power on high,
And call our bury'd Mother's Ghost   15
    A Witness to the Lye:
Heaven at such Perjury connives,
And *Venus* with a Smile forgives.

The Nymphs and cruel *Cupid* too,
    Sharp'ning his pointed Dart   20
On a old Hone, besmear'd with Blood,
    Forbear thy perjur'd Heart.
Fresh Youth grows up, to wear thy Chains,
And the old Slave no Freedom gains.

Thee, Mothers for their eldest Sons,   25
    Thee, wretched Misers fear,
Lest thy prevailing Beauty should
    Seduce the hopeful Heir:
New-marry'd Virgins fear thy Charms
Should keep their Bridegroom from their
        Arms.   30

XXXV

A BALLAD

To the Tune of Bateman.

You Gallants all, that love good Wine,
    For shame your Lives amend;
With Strangers go to Church, or Dine,
    But drink with an old Friend.

For with him tipling all the Night,   5
    You kiss, hugg, and embrace;
Whereas a Stranger, at first sight,
    May kill you on the Place.

There was a rich old Usurer,
   A gallant Son he had;   10
Who slew an ancient Barriſter,
   Like a true mettled Lad.

All in that very House, where Saint
   Holds Devil by the Nose;
These Drunkards met to Roar, and Rant,   15
   But quarrell'd in the close.

The Glass flew chearfully about,
   And drunken Chat went on;
Which Troops had fail'd, and which were ſtout,
   When *Namur* wou'd be won.   20

A learned Lawyer, at the laſt,
   No Tory, as I'm told,
Began to talk of Tyrants paſt,
   In Words both sharp and bold.

He toucht a little on our Times,   25
   Defin'd the Power of Kings,
What were their Vertues, what their Crimes,
   And many dangerous Things.

A Stranger that sat silent by,
   And scarce knew what he meant,   30
O'recome with Wine and Loyalty,
   Did thus his Passion vent:

I cannot bear the leaſt ill Word,
   That lessens any King;
And the bold Man shall feel my Sword;   35
   At that their Friends ſtept in.

The Quarrel seem'd a while compos'd,
   And many Healths there paſt,
But one to Blood was ill dispos'd,
   As it appear'd at laſt.   40

The Counsellor was walking Home,
  Sober, as he was wont,
The young Man after him did come,
  With Sword, that was not blunt.

A Blow there paſt, which no Man saw,   45
  From Cane of Lawyer bold ;
The young Man did his Weapon draw,
  And left the Lawyer cold.

Which Cane held up, in his Defence,
  Was judg'd a Weapon drawn :   50
What needs there farther Evidence,
  Th' Assault was very plain.

At *Hixes*'s Hall, by Jury grave,
  It was Man-slaughter found ;
O what wou'd it have coſt to have   55
  A Pardon from the Crown.

Then learn, my honeſt Country-men,
  To take yourselves the Pence ;
Wisely prevent the Courtier's Gain,
  And save us that Expence.   60

Ye Gallants all, take heed how you
  Come to untimely Ends ;
Juſtice has bid the World adieu,
  And dead Men have no Friends.   64

XXXVI

SONG

Hears not my *Phillis*, how the Birds
  Their feather'd Mates salute ?
They tell their Passion in their Words ;
  Muſt I alone be mute ?
Phillis, *without Frown or Smile*,   5
Sat and knotted all the while.

The God of Love in thy bright Eyes
   Does like a Tyrant reign ;
But in thy Heart a Child he lyes,
   Without his Dart or Flame.   10
Phillis, without ⟨Frown or Smile,
Sat and knotted all the while.⟩

So many Months in Silence paſt,
   And yet in raging Love,
Might well deſerve one Word at laſt   15
   My Passion shou'd approve.
Phillis, without ⟨Frown or Smile,
Sat and knotted all the while.⟩

Muſt then your faithful Swain expire,
   And not one Look obtain,   20
Which he, to sooth his fond Desire,
   Might pleasingly explain ?
Phillis, without ⟨Frown or Smile,
Sat and knotted all the while.⟩   24

XXXVII

ADVICE TO THE OLD BEAUX

Scrape no more your harmless Chins,
   Old Beaux, in hope to please ;
You shou'd repent your former Sins,
   Not ſtudy their Increase ;
Young awkard Fops, may shock our Sight,   5
But you offend by Day and Night.

In vain the Coachman turns about,
   And whips the dappl'd Greys ;
When the old Ogler looks out,
   We turn away our Face.   10
True Love and Youth will ever charm,
But both affected, cannot warm.

Summer-fruits we highly prise,
  They kindly cool the Blood;
But Winter-berries we despise,   15
  And leave 'em in the Wood;
On the Bush they may look well,
But gather'd, lose both taste and smell.

That you languish, that you dye,
  Alas, is but too true;   20
Yet tax not us with Cruelty,
  Who daily pity you.
Nature henceforth alone accuse,
In vain we grant, if she refuse.   24

XXXVIII

SONG

When first *Pastora* came to Town,
  The fresh Desire of every Heart,
Her Innocence so fenc'd her own,
  She laught at *Cupid* and his Dart.

Her Looks might all the World enflame,   5
  Themselves, yet cold as freezing Snow;
Which the bold Hand that thinks to tame,
  Soon with unusual Heat will glow.

As when a Comet does appear,
  We Stars and Moon no more respect;   10
So while *Pastora* guilds our Sphere,
  All former Beauties we neglect.   12

XXXIX

SONG

Smooth was the Water, calm the Air,
  The Evening-Sun deprest,
Lawyers dismist the noisie Bar,
  The Labourer at rest,

When *Strephon*, with his charming Fair,   5
   Cross'd the proud River *Thames*,
And to a Garden did repair,
   To quench their mutual Flames.

The crafty Waiter soon espy'd
   Youth sparkling in her Eyes;   10
He brought no Ham, nor Neats-tongues dry'd,
   But Cream and Strawberries.

The amorous *Strephon* ask'd the Maid,
   What's whiter than this Cream?
She blush'd, and could not tell, she said: 15
   Thy Teeth, my pretty Lamb.

What's redder than these Berries are?
   I know not, she reply'd:
Those lips, which I'll no longer spare,
   The burning Shepherd cry'd.   20

And strait began to hug her:
   This Kiss, my Dear,
Is sweeter far
   Than Strawberries, Cream and Sugar.   24

XL

SONG

The Sun had scarce drunk up the Dew,
   Or underneath the Boughs,
The chearful Birds met, to renew
   Their mutual daily Vows.

Scarce had they paid their Debt to Love,   5
   When *Thirsis* with his Fair,
Enter'd in haste the conscious Grove,
   A lovely loving Pair.

Thirsis began, Why mourns, my Dear ?
    Why does my *Celia* weep,   10
Since all things are propitious here,
    And envious Man asleep ?

Blame not my Tears, the Nymph reply'd,
    Let them for ever flow,
E're *Phœbus* twice his Face shall hide,   15
    I to the Country go.

Let us then snatch at flying Joy,
    Cry'd out the am'rous Swain ;
When cruel Flames an House destroy,
    Who saves not what he can ?   20

If, *Thirsis*, e're we seal our Love,
    We are so loth to part,
The Torment then will double prove,
    And break my tender Heart.

I suddenly must cross the Seas,   25
    To get my self a Name,
For in Love's Camp no Man can rise,
    Who is unknown to Fame.   28

XLI

TO THE KING ON HIS BIRTH-DAY

Behold the happy Day again,
    Destinguisht by the Joy in every Face ;
This Day Great *William*'s Life began,
    Soul of our War, and Guardian of our Peace.

Of three afflicted Realms, the choice,   5
    When on the furious Waves of Faction tost,
They all cry'd out, as with one Voice,
    Save us, Heroick Prince, or we are lost.

So in the gen'ral Deluge met
  Beaſts of all Kinds, whom Nature had made Foes; 10
They did their mutual Hate forget,
  And the bleſt Ark for sacred Refuge chose.

Part of thy Time, and of thy Care,
  Thy Native Country claims, and cannot want.
But we one Movement cannot spare,   15
  (Tho' it be due) without a kind Complaint.

The Sun, who flies around the Earth,
  Painting the Face of Nature where he shines,
Giving to Flowers, and Fruit new Birth,
  Rip'ning for us rich Spice and nobleſt Wines,   20

Permits we shou'd his Absence mourn,
  Tho' for our good, like thee, abroad employ'd,
And that we welcome his Return,
  As if too long by diſtant Climes enjoy'd.

Hail, glorious King, fill all the Mouthes of Fame : 25
  Vertue like thine will fierceſt Envy tame ;
And may thy Life, be laſting as thy Name.

XLII

A DIALOGUE

Mars.]   *Cupid*, I hear thou haſt improv'd
    Thy little Art of War ;
Old Men conceit they may be lov'd,
    And Cripples win the Fair.

False powder'd Beaux at diſtance kill,   5
    And every Fop writes Songs ;
Musick imploys her utmoſt Skill,
    And to thy Camp belongs.

Cupid.]   Great God of War, why shou'd not I
    As well as you advance,   10
And by new Ways make Lovers dye,
    While you bomb Towns in *France*.

William and *Louis* are your Pride,
  Beile Dives, and *Stowel* mine,
Whose Batteries Men can less abide   15
  Than those upon the *Rhine*.

XLIII

OUT OF LYCOPHRON

What shall become of Man so wise,
    When he dies ?
    None can tell
Whither he goes to Heaven or Hell ;
  Or after a few Moments dear,   5
    He disappear,
    And at laſt,
Perish entirely like a Beaſt :
But Women, Wine and Mirth we know,
Are all the Joys he has below :   10
Let us then ply those Joys we have,
'Tis vain to think beyond the Grave ;
Out of our reach the Gods have laid
  Of Time to come th' Event,
And laugh to see the Fools afraid,   15
  Of what the Knaves invent.

XLIV

TO LIBER

⟨From Martial, *Lib*. 8. *Ep*. 77.⟩

Liber, thou Joy of all thy Friends,
  Worthy to live in endless Pleasure :
While Knaves and Fools pursue their Ends,
  Let Mirth and Freedom be thy Treasure.

Be still well dress'd, as now thou art,   5
  Gay, and on charming Objects thinking;
Let easie Beauty warm thy Heart,
  And fill thy Bed when thou leav'st drinking.

Delay no pressing Appetite,
  And sometimes stir up lazy Nature;   10
Of Age the envious Censure slight;
  What Pleasure's made of, 'tis no matter:
He that lives so but to his Prime,
Wisely doubles his short Time.   14

XLV

SONG

Phillis is my only Joy,
  Faithless as the Winds or Seas;
Sometimes coming, sometimes coy,
  Yet she never fails to please;
    If with a Frown   5
    I am cast down,
    Phillis smiling,
    And beguiling,
Makes me happier than before.

Tho', alas, too late I find,   10
  Nothing can her Fancy fix;
Yet the Moment she is kind,
  I forgive her all her Tricks;
    Which, tho' I see,
    I can't get free;   15
    She deceiving,
    I believing;
What need Lovers wish for more?   18

XLVI

TO COSCUS

⟨From Martial,⟩ *Lib.* 9. *Ep.* 7⟨0⟩.

O Times ! O Manners ! *Cicero* cry'd out,
    But 'twas when enrag'd *Catilin* conspir'd
To burn the City, and to cut the Throat
    Of half the Senate, had his Ruffians hir'd :

When Son and Father did the World divide,   5
    And *Rome* for Tyrants, not for Empire fought ;
When slaughter'd Citizens on either side
    Cover'd that Earth, her early Valour bought.

Of Times and Men, why doſt thou now complain ?
    What is it, *Coscus*, that offends thee, say ?   10
Our Laws the License of the Sword reſtrain ;
    And our Prince wills that his arm'd Troops obey :
His Reign, Success, Freedom and Plenty crown,
Blame not our Manners then, but mend thy own.   14

XLVII

SONG

See ! *Hymen* comes ; How his Torch blazes !
    Looser Loves, how dim they burn ;
No Pleasures equal chaſte Embraces,
    When we Love for Love return.

When Fortune makes the Match he rages,   5
    And forsakes th' unequal Pair ;
But when Love two Hearts engages,
    The kind God is ever there.

Regard not then high Blood, nor Riches;
   You that would his Blessings have,   10
Let untaught Love guide all your Wishes,
   Hymen shou'd be *Cupid*'s Slave.

Young Virgins, that yet bear your Passions,
   Coldly as the Flint its Fire,
Offer to *Hymen* your Devotions,   15
   He will warm you with Desire.

Young Men, no more neglect your Duty,
   To the God of Nuptial Vows:
Pay your long, Arrears to Beauty,
   As his chaster Law allows.   20

XLVIII

ON DON *ALONZO*

WHO WAS CUT IN PIECES FOR MAKING LOVE TO
THE INFANTA OF *PORTUGAL*.

How cruel was *Alonzo*'s Fate,
   To fix his Love so high,
That he must perish by her Hate,
   Or by her Kindness dye?

Tortur'd, and mangl'd, cut and maim'd,   5
   If he triumpht o're his Pain,
And with his dying Breath proclaim'd,
   'Twas better than Disdain.

The gentle Nymph, long since design'd
   For the proud Monsieur's Bed,   10
Now to a holy Jayl confin'd,
   Drops Tears with ev'ry Bead.

Tell me, ye Gods, if where a King
   Suffers for Impotence,
True Love be such a fatal thing,   15
   What can be Innocence?

XLIX

SONG

Phillis, Men say that all my Vows
    Are to thy Fortune paid;
Alas, my Heart he little knows
    Who thinks my Love a Trade.

Were I, of all these Woods, the Lord,   5
    One Berry from thy Hand
More real Pleasure would afford,
    Than all my large Command.

My humble Love has learnt to live,
    On what the nicest Maid,   10
Without a conscious Blush, may give
    Beneath the Myrtle-shade.

L

ON A COCK AT *ROCHESTER*

Thou cursed Cock, with thy perpetual Noise,
May'st thou be Capon made, and lose thy Voice,
Or on a Dunghil may'st thou spend thy Blood,
And Vermin prey upon thy craven Brood;
May Rivals tread thy Hens before thy Face,   5
Then with redoubled Courage give thee chase;
May'st thou be punish'd for St. *Peter*'s Crime,
And on *Shrove-tuesday*, perish in thy Prime;
May thy bruis'd Carcass be some Beggar's Feast,
Thou first and worst Disturber of Man's Rest.   10

LI

SONG *A-LA-MODE*

O're the Desert, cross the Meadows,
    Hunters blew the merry Horn ;
Phœbus chas'd the flying Shadows :
    Eccho, she reply'd, in scorn ;
        Still adoring,   5
        And deploring :
Why muſt *Thirsis* lose his Life ?

Rivers murmur'd from their Fountains,
    Acrons dropping from the Oaks,
Fawns came tripping o're the Mountains,   10
Fishes bit the naked Hook⟨s⟩ ;
        Still admiring,
        And desiring :
When shall *Phillis* be a Wife ?   14

LII

OUT OF FRENCH

Dear Friend, I fear my Heart will break ;
In t'other World I scarce believe,
In this I little pleasure take :
That my whole Grief thou may'ſt conceive ;
Cou'd not I Drink more than I Whore,   5
By Heaven, I wou'd not live an Hour.

LIII

THE DOCTOR AND HIS PATIENTS

There was a prudent grave Physician,
Careful of Patients as you'd wish one ;

Much good he did with Purge and Gliſter,
And well he knew to raise a Bliſter ;
Many he cur'd and more he wou'd,   5
By Vomit, Flux, and letting Blood ;
But ſtill his Patients came again,
And moſt of their old Ills complain ;
The Drunkards drank, and spoild their Liver :
Beaux ply'd the Smock as much as ever,   } 10
And got the high Veneral Feaver :
The Glutton cram'd at Noon and Supper,
And doubled both his Paunch and Crupper.
One Day he call'd 'em all together,
And one by one, he askt 'em whether   15
It were not better by good Diet,
To keep their Blood and Humours quiet ;
With Toſt and Ale to cool their Brains,
Than nightly Fire 'em with *Champains* ;
To sup sometimes on Water-grewel,   20
Than drink themselves into a Duel ;
To change their lewd, for sober Life,
And rotten Whore, for sounder Wife ?
They all agreed that his Advice   }
Was honeſt, wholsom, grave and wise ;   25
But not one Man, wou'd quit his Vice ;
For after all his vain Attacks,
They rose and din'd well at *Pontack's* :

The Moral

The Wise may preach, and Satyriſts rail,
Custom and Nature will prevail.   30

LIV

UPON THE AUTHOR OF THE *SATYR AGAINST WIT*

A Grave Physician, us'd to write for Fees,
And spoil no Paper, but with *Recipe's,*

Is now turn'd Poet, rails againſt all Wit,
Except that Little found among the Great;
As if he thought true Wit and Sence were ty'd   5
To Men in Place, like Avarice, or Pride.
But in their Praise, so like a Quack he talks,
You'd swear he wanted for his *Chriſtmas*-box.
With mangled Names old Stories he pollutes,
And to the present Time paſt Actions suits;   10
Amaz'd we find, in ev'ry Page he writes,
Members of Parliament with *Arthur's* Knights⟨.⟩
It is a common Paſtime to Write Ill;
And Doctor, with the reſt, e'en take thy fill;
Thy Satyr's harmless: 'Tis thy Prose that kills, 15
When thou Prescrib'ſt thy Potions and thy Pills⟨.⟩
Go on brave Doctor, a third Volume write,
And find us Paper while you make us S——.   18

LV

PROLOGUE

Since glorious *Dryden* has withdrawn his Light,
Some glimmering Stars relieve our gloomy Night;
Poets of different Magnitudes advance,
In humble Confidence of Song and Dance;
Ballon and Tumblers please, tho' Poets fail;   5
At a ſtrong Back She-Criticks never rail.
When a good Place is void, we all pretend,
Some on their Merit, some their Purse ⟨dep⟩end:
Our Friend can boaſt of neither, yet his Play
He hopes at leaſt may live out his third Day;   10
Adorn him with one Sprig, like *Chriſtmas*-Brawn,
His farther Plea to Bays shall be withdrawn.
In Courts of Law, under Delays we groan,
But here our Poets are too sone undone;
Plays are half seen, half heard, less underſtood, 15
When the dead Warrant issues from the Crowd;
Some are so void of Wit they'll relish none:

Others again like nothing but their own ;
Tho' outwardly they seem to carry it fair,
The Wits are alwayes in a ſtate of War.   20
This Play's so chaſt, so void of Pagan Wit,
It might have been by a Reformer writ ;
Fops, Beauxs and Parsons, shall this Night be safe,
We bring the other Sex to make you laugh.   24

LVI

PROLOGUE ⟨TO EPSOM WELLS⟩

Poets and thieves can scarce be rooted out,
Scape ne're so hardly, they'll have th'other bout ;
Burnt in the hand the Thieves fall to't agen,
And Poets hiſt, cry they did so to Ben——
Like Boys, who have at School too oft been ſtript,   5
They have no feeling in the part that's whipt.
They're for your pity, not your anger, fit,
They're e'en such fools, they wou'd be thought t'have
    wit.
Elsewhere you all can flatter, why not here ;
You'll say you pay, and so can be severe :   10
Judge for yourselves then Gallants as you pay,
And lead not each of you his Bench aſtray :
Let easie Citts be pleased with all they hear,
Go home and to their neighbours praise our Ware.
They with good ſtomachs come, and fain wou'd eat   15
You nothing like, and make them loath their meat ;
Though some men are with Wine, Wit, Beauty
    cloy'd ;
The Creatures are by others ſtill enjoy'd.
'Tis not fair play, that one for his Half Crown
Shou'd judge, and rail, and damn for half the Town.   20
But do your worſt ; if once the Pit grows thin,
Your dear lov'd Masks, will hardly venture in.
Then w'are reveng'd on you, who needs muſt come
Hither, to shun your own dull selves at home :

But you kind Burgers who had never yet,   25
Either your Heads or Bellies full of wit :
Our Poet hopes to please ; but not too well ;
Nor wou'd he have the angry Criticks swell.
A moderate Fate beſt fits his humble mind,
Be neither they too sharp, nor you too kind.   30

LVII

PROLOGUE ⟨TO THE STROULERS⟩

Beauty and Wit so barely you requite   ⎫
That had not Nature joyn'd a dear Delight, ⎬
No Maid wou'd ever Yield, or Poet write⟨.⟩
Yet sometimes Beauty's Lottery sounds a Prize,
And in Alcove the happy Harlot lyes,   5
While but one Wit can to a Laureat rise⟨;⟩
And then a Butt of Sack, and a small Pension,
Is the full summ of his whole Li⟨f⟩e's Pretention.
If not ſtark mad, they'll leave us in the Lurch,
We have but one poor Living in our Church.   10
Hither you come resolving not to like,
And bold-blind Cocks at every Feather ſtrike :
The Language one, another Damns the Plot,
And briskly hits the Poet, ere he Blot.
And pray be Civil my Young Empty *Beaux*,   15
M⟨e⟩re Shew yourselves and only Judge of Shows !
Unbend your Critic Brows, For a Young Wench
As soon may like a Judge upon the Bench,
As one of your Censorious Grimaces,
Let Wit alone and truſt to your sweet Faces.   20
No Man or Woman here expeĉts that you
Should Judge or Write, beyond a *Billet Doux* ;
But if you can, pass by each small Offence,
And ſtrain your Wits to find one Excellence,
Tis much the trueſt, and beſt sign of Sense.   25

LVIII

PROLOGUE TO *THE WARY WIDDOW OR SIR NOISY PARRAT*

Envy and Faction rule this Grumbling Age,
The State they cannot, but they shake the Stage,
This barren trade some woud engross, still hopeing
From our poor Port to banish Interloping :
And like the plodding Lawyers take great care   5
To elbow blooming merit, from the Bar :
In every Age there were a sort of Men,
As you do now, damn'd all was written then.
Thousands before 'em less provok'd their Pride
Then one poor rivall straining by their side,   10
Such vermin Critticks we expect to find,
For Nature knows not how to loose a kind
The stinking Poll Cat, nor the Mole that's Blind.
But against old as well as new to rage,
Is the peculiar Phrensy of this Age.   15
Shackspear must down, and you must praise no more
Soft *Desdemona*, nor the Jealous *Moor :*
Shackspear whose fruitfull Genius, happy Wit
Was fram'd and finisht at a lucky hit
The Pride of Nature, and the shame of Schools,   20
Born to Create, and not to learn from Rules ;
Must please no more, his Bastards now deride
Their Fathers Nakedness they ought to hide,
But when on Spurs their *Pegasus* they force,
Their faded Muse is distanc'd in the Course :   25
All that is now has been before tis true,
And yet the Art, the Fashion may be new :
Tho' old Materials the large Pallace raise,
The skillfull Architect deserves his praise.
If nothing please, you are not nice, but sick,   30
'Tis want of stomack, ever to dislike.
On our Past Poets, petty Juries sit,

The Living sink beneath your present spite,
As if this were the doomsday of all wit.
But *Beaus* and *Ladies* for your selves be wise   35
You'l break our Lottery if none draw a Prize⟨.⟩
For this one night, do as kind Lovers use⟨,⟩
Tye up strict Judgement and let fancy loose.   38

EPIGRAMS : OR, COURT CHARACTERS

Carmina vix placeant Romæ si displicet Author ;
Docta premit Livor, stulta favore vigent.

LIX

TO MAXIMINA

⟨From Martial,⟩ *Lib.* 2. *Ep.* 41

Ovid, who bid the Ladies laugh,
    Spoke only to the Young and Fair ;
For Thee his Council were not safe,
    Who of sound Teeth has⟨t⟩ scarce a Pair ;
    If thou thy Glass, or Me believe,   5
Shun Mirth, as Foplings do the Wind ;
At *Durfey's* Farce affect to grieve ;
    And let thy Eyes alone be kind.
Speak not, tho't were to give Consent ;
    For he that sees those rotten Bones,   10
Will dread the⟨ir⟩ monumental Scent,
    And fly thy Sigh's like dying Groans.
If thou art wise, see dismal Plays,
    And to sad Stories lend thy Ear ;
With the afflicted, spend thy Days,   15
    And laugh not above once a Year.

LX

TO SEXTUS

⟨From Martial,⟩ *Lib.* 2. *Ep. 55.*

I Offer Love, but thou Respect wilt have ;
Take, *Sextus*, all thy Pride and Folly crave ;
But know, I can be no Man's Friend and Slave.   3

LXI

TO NYSUS

How shall we please this Age ?   If in a Song
We put above six Lines, they count it long ;
If we contract it to an Epigram,
As deep the dwarfish Poetry they damn ;
If we write Plays, few see above an Act,   5
And those lewd Masks, or noisie Fops distract :
Let us write Satyr then, and at our ease
Vex th' ill-natur'd Fools we cannot please.   8

LXII

TO CLASSICUS

⟨From Martial,⟩ *Lib.* 2. *Ep. 69.*

When thou art ask'd to Sup abroad,
    Thou swear'st thou hast but newly din'd ;
That eating late does overload
    The Stomach, and oppress the Mind :
But if *Appicius* make a Treat,   5
    The slend'rest Summons thou obey'st,
No Child is greedier of the Teat,
    Then thou art of the bounteous Feast.
There thou wilt drink till every Star
    Be swallow'd by the rising Sun :   10

Such Charms hath Wine we pay not for,
  And Mirth, at others Charge begun.
Who shuns his Club, yet flies to ev'ry Treat
  Does not a Supper, but a Reck'ning hate.   14

LXIII

TO SEXTUS

⟨From Martial,⟩ *Lib.* 2. *Ep.* 38.

What Business, or what Hope brings thee to Town,
  Who can'st not Pimp, nor Cheat, nor Swear, nor
    Lye ?
This Place will nourish no such idle Drone ;
  Hence, in remoter Parts thy Fortune try.
But thou hast Courage, Honesty, and Wit,   5
  And one, or all these three, will give Thee Bread :
The Malice of this Town thou know'st not yet ;
  Wit is a good Diversion, but base Trade ;
Cowards will, for thy Courage, call thee Bully,
  Till all, like *Thraso's*, thy Acquaintance shun ;   10
Rogues call thee for thy Honesty a Cully ;
  Yet this is all thou hast to live upon :
Friend, three such Vertues, *Audley* had undone ;
  Be wise, and e're th'art in a Jayl, be gone,
Of all that starving Crew we saw to Day   15
None but has kill'd his Man, or writ his Play.

LXIV

TO POSTHUMUS

⟨From Martial,⟩ *Lib.* 2. *Ep.* 12.

That thou dost *Cashoo* breath, and Foreign *Gums*,
Enough to put thy Mistress into Fits ;
Tho' *Rome* thy Hair, and *Spain* thy Gloves perfumes,
Few like, but all suspect, those borrow'd Sweets :
The Gifts of various Nature come and go,   5
He that smells always, well does never so.

LXV

TO SCÆVA

⟨From Martial, *Lib.* 1. *Ep.* 54.⟩

If *Scæva* for more Friends thou care,
   Which thy great Merit cannot want ;
For me an humble Place prepare,
   That I am new, make no complaint,
Thy deareſt Friends were Strangers once, like me,⎫ 5
Like them, in time, I an old Friend may be,   ⎬
If thou no want of friendly Vertues see.   ⎭ 7

LXVI

TO SERTORIUS

If thou do'ſt want a Horse, thou buy'ſt a Score,
   Or if a Piece of Wine, thou'lt have a Tun ;
Swords, Belts, or Hats, does any Cheat bring o're ;
   At his own Rate thou wilt have all or none.
Whil'ſt out of Wantonness thou buy'ſt so faſt,   5
Out of meer Want thou wilt sell all at laſt.

LXVII

TO CLOE

⟨From Martial, *Lib.* 3. *Ep.* 42.⟩

Leave off thy Paint, Perfumes, and youthful Dress,
And Nature's failing Honeſty confess ;
Double we see those Faults which Art wou'd mend,
Plain downright Ugliness wou'd less offend.   4

LXVIII

TO CANIDIUS

Thou ſtrutſt, as if thou wert the only Lord ;
  When we all know of such there is an House,
Where I might sit, cou'd I the Price afford,
  And Child has now three Earldoms out at use,
High Expeſtation does attend good Seed,   5
Yet none will buy a known Jade, for his Breed ;
Boaſt not too much thy mighty Pedigree,
Were they alive, they'd be asham'd of Thee.   8

LXIX

TO SEPTIMUS

Thro' servile Flattery thou doſt all commend :
Who cares to please, where no Man can offend ?

LXX

TO FLAVIUS

Thou quibleſt well, haſt Craft and Induſtry,
  Flatt'reſt great Men, laugh'ſt at their Enemies,
Rally'ſt the absent, art a pretty Spy,
  Yet for all this in Court thou doſt not rise ;
Thou play'ſt thy Court-game booty : I'm affraid   5
Th'aſt promis'd Marriage, when thy Fortune's made,
And so thou dar'ſt not thrive upon thy Trade.

LXXI

TO CANDIDUS

⟨From Martial,⟩ *Lib.* 2. *Ep.* 43.

All Things are common amongst Friends, thou say'st;
   This is thy Morning and thy Ev'ning-song,
Thou in rich Point, and Indian-Silk art dress'd
   Six foreign Steeds to thy Calash belong,
Whil'st by my Cloaths the Ragman scarce wou'd
     gain;   5
   And an uneasie Hackny jolts my Sides;
A Cloak embroider'd intercepts thy Rain,
   A worsted Camblet my torn Breeches hides;
Turbots and Mullets thy large Dishes hold,
   In mine a solitary Whiting lies;   10
Thy Train might Fire the impotent and old,
   Whil'st my poor Hand a *Ganimede* supplies:
For an old wanting Friend thou'lt nothing do, ⎫
Ye⟨t⟩ all is common among Friends we know; ⎬
Nothing so common, as to use 'em so.   ⎭   15

LXXII

TO GAURUS

⟨From Martial,⟩ *Lib.* 2. *Ep.* 89.

That thou dost shorten thy long Nights with Wine,
   We all forgive thee, for so *Cato* did;
That thou writ'st Poems without one good Line,
   Tully's Example may that Weakness hide;
Thou art a Cuckold, so great *Cæsar* was;   5
   Eat'st till thou spew'st, *Antonius* did the same;
That thou lov'st Whores, *Jove* loves a bucksom Lass;
   But that th'art whipt, is thy peculiar Shame.   8

LXXIII

TO THRASO

Whil'ſt thou sit'ſt drinking up thy Loyalty,
   And rail'ſt at Laws, thou doſt not underſtand,
Ador'ſt the Miniſters, who know not ⟨thee⟩,
   Sel'ſt thy long Freedom for a short Command,
The Power thou aim'ſt at, if o're thee one have,   5
   In a rich Coat th'art but a ranting Slave.

LXXIV

ON COSCUS

⟨From Martial,⟩ *Lib.* 2. *Ep.* 77.

Coscus, thou say'ſt my Epigrams are long;
   I'd take thy Judgment on a Pot of Ale:
So thou may'ſt say the Elephant's too ſtrong,
   A Dwarf too short, the Pyramid too tall;
Things are not long, where we can nothing spare;   5
But, *Coscus*, even thy Diſticks tedious are.

LXXV

TO BITHINICUS

⟨From Martial,⟩ *Lib.* 2. *Ep.* ⟨26⟩.

That thy Wife coughs all Night, and spits all Day;
   Already thou believ'ſt thy Fortune made,
Her whole Eſtate thou think'ſt thy suddain Prey;
   She will not dye, but wheedles like a Jade.   4

LXXVI

TO MAXIMUS

⟨From Martial,⟩ *Lib.* 2. *Ep.* 53.

Wou'd'st thou be free, I fear thou art in jest;
But if thou wou'd'st, this is the only Way,
Be no Man's Tavern, nor Domestick Guest;
Drink wholsom Wine, which thy own Servants draw;
Of knavish *Curio*, scorn the ill-got Plate,   5
  The numerous Servants, and the cringing Throng:
With a few Friends on fewer Dishes eat,
  And let thy Cloaths, like mine, be plain and strong;
Such Friendships make, as thou may'st keep with ease,
Great Men expect, what good Men hate to pay;   10
  Be never thou thy self in pain to please,
But leave to Fools, and Knaves, th' uncertain Prey.
  Let thy Expence with thy Estate keep pace;
Meddle with no Man's Business, scarce thy own;
  Contented pay for a Plebeian Face,   15
And leave vain Fops the Beauties of the Town.
If to this Pitch of Vertue thou can'st bring
Thy Mind, th'art freer than the *Persian* King.   18

LXXVII

TO JULIUS

Thou swear'st thou'lt drink no more; kind Heaven
    send
Me such a Cook or Coach-man, but no Friend.

LXXVIII

TO FLAVIA

When to thy Husband thou didst first refuse
  The lawful Pleasures of thy charming Bed;
Men did his Pipe, and Pot, and Whores accuse;
  On his meer Lewdness the whole Fault we laid:

Into thy House thou took'st a deep Divine,   5
  And all thy Neighbours flockt to hear him Preach;
The cheated World did in thy Praises joyn,
  The wiser sort yet knew thy wanton Reach,
From Sundays-crowds thou did'st thy Gallants chuse,
And, when they fail'd thee, the good Doctor use.   10

LXXIX

TO SERGIUS

Thou'lt fight, if any Man call *Thebe* Whore:
That she is thine, what can proclaim it more.

LXXX

THE MAIDENHEAD

⟨From Martial, *Lib.* 1. *Ep.* 58.⟩

Cloris, the prettyest Girl about the Town,
  Askt fifty Guineas, for her Maidenhead;
I laught, but *Cascus* paid the Money down,
  And the young Wench did to his Chamber lead.
This Thrift my eager *Catso* did upbraid,   5
  And wisht that he had grown 'twixt *Cascus* Thighs;
Get me but half what his got him, I said,
  And to content thee, I'll ne'er stick at Price.   8

LXXXI

TO QUINTUS

Thou art an Atheist, *Quintus*, and a Wit,
  Thinkst all was of self-moving Attoms made,
Religion only for the Vulgar fit,
  Priests Rogues, and Preaching their deceitful
    Trade;

Wilt drink, whore, fight, blaspheme, damn, curse and
   swear : 5
  Why wilt thou swear, by G——, if there be none ?
And if there be, thou shou'd'ſt his Vengeance fear :
  Methinks this Huffing might be let alone ;
'Tis thou art free, Mankind besides a Slave,
  And yet a Whore may lead the⟨e⟩ by the Nose, 10
A drunken Bottle, and a flatt'ring Knave,
  A mighty Prince, Slave to thy dear Soul's Foes,
Thy Luſt, thy Rage, Ambition and thy Pride ;
He that serves G——, need nothing serve beside. 14

LXXXII

ON *ARRIA* AND *PŒTUS*

⟨From Martial, *Lib*. 1. *Ep*. 13.⟩

When *Arria* to her *Pœtus* gave the Steel,
  Which from her bleeding Side did newly part ;
From my own Wound, she said, no Pain I feel :
  And yet thy Wound will ſtab me to the Heart. 4

LXXXIII

TO MILO

⟨From Martial, *Lib*. 2. *Ep*. 64.⟩

One Month a Lawyer, thou the next wilt be
  A grave Physician, and the third a Prieſt ;
Chuse quickly one Profession of the three ;
  Marry'd to her, thou yet may'ſt court the reſt.
Whil'ſt thou ſtand'ſt doubting, *Bradbury* has got 5
  Five Thousand Pound, and *Conqueſt* as much more ;
W—— is made B——, from a drunken Sot :
  Leap in, and ſtand not shiv'ring on the Shore ;
On any one amiss thou can'ſt not fall,
Thou'lt end in nothing, if thou grasp'ſt at all. 10

LXXXIV

TO SABINUS

Surly and Sour thou dislik'st Mankind ;
　But most thou hat'st the Company thou'rt in ;
Seest all their Faults, but to thy own art blind :
　Yet still thou cry'st, When shall we meet agen ?
Thou can'st not sit at Home, what should'st thou
　　read ?   5
　For all are Fools, thou know'st that ever writ.
What should'st thou do abroad ? this Age does breed
　A sort of Vermin, have not half their Wit.
Thou hat'st the World, hate Flesh and Devil so,
And, for a blessed End, to *Burnet*'s go ;   10
But, for thy Misery, th'art an Atheist too.

LXXXV

ON PHRINE

Phrine, as odious as Youth well can be,
　The Daughter of a Courtier in high Place,
Met with a b—— Mass, that cou'd not see ;
　His Blindness she, and that excus'd her Face.
Were she not ugly, she wou'd him despise ;   5
Nor wou'd he marry her, if he had Eyes.
To their Defects, they're for the Match in debt,
And, but for Faults on both sides, ne're had met. 8

LXXXVI

TO BASSA

⟨From Martial, *Lib.* 1. *Ep.* 90.⟩

That I ne're saw thee in a Coach with Man,
　Nor thy chast Name in wanton Satyr met ;
That from thy Sex thy liking never ran,
　So as to suffer a Male-servant yet.

I thought thee the *Lucretia* of our time :   5
    But, *Bassa*, thou the while a *Tribas* wert,
And clashing ——, with a prodigious Crime,
    Did&t a&t of Man th' inimitable part.
What *Odipus* this Riddle can untye ?
Without a Male, there was Adultery.   10

LXXXVII

TO SCILLA

Storm not, brave Friend, that thou had&t never yet
    Mi&tress nor Wife that others did not ——,
But, like a Chri&tian, pardon and forget,
    For thy own Pox will thy Revenge contrive.   4

LXXXVIII

ON SEXTUS

⟨From Martial, *Lib.* 2. *Ep.* 44.⟩

When I had purcha&t a fresh Whore or Coat,
    For which I knew not how to pay,
Sextus, that wretched covetous old Sot,
    My ancient Friend, as he will say ;
Le&t I shou'd borrow of him, took great care,   5
    And mutter'd to himself aloud,
So as he knew I cou'd not chuse but hear
    How much he to *Secundas* ow'd,
And twice as much he paid for Intere&t,
    Nor had one Farthing in his tru&ty Che&t :   10
If I had ask'd, I knew he wou'd not lend ;
'Tis new, before-hand, to deny a Friend.

THE

Happy PAIR :

OR, A

POEM

ON

MATRIMONY.

By the Honourable
Sir *CHARLES SIDLEY*, Baronet.

LONDON:
Printed for *John Nutt*, near *Stationers-Hall*,
M DCC II.

LXXXIX

THE HAPPY PAIR: OR, A POEM, &c.

When firſt the World from the black Chaos rose,
    And Infant-Beauty did the Frame compose;
When Heav'n and Man possess'd one ſtate of Mind,
    And the pure Globe, like its *CREATOR*, shin'd:
When frce from Sin the noble Mortal ſtrove   5
    To Rival God in his return of Love.
When damning *PRIDE*, that Architeſt of Hell,
    Made not, as yet, his Tempted Soul Rebel.
When plunging Avaricc no Birth had found,
    Nor tore the precious Entrails of the Ground;   10
Then then the new Inhabitant was bleſt,
    Ease watch'd his Heart, and Peace secur'd his
        Breaſt;
No Earthy Thought tainted his gen'rous Mind,
    That World th' Almighty gave him, he declin'd;
His God-like Image made him upwards move;   15
    He liv'd below while his Soul dwelt above.
Riches were things too weak t' enslave his Sense,
    The Daz'ling Di'mond wanted Influence.
Pearls, like the Common Gravel, he contemn'd,
    And what we count a God, he thought no Friend. 20
With heat of Love he flam'd upon his Mate,
    And on the green Swarth without dowry sate:
Circling her snowy Neck, he sought her Heart;
    A fi'ry Lover, free from Fraud, or Art.
The Objeſt of his reſtless Thoughts, was *Bliss*,   25
    And that he found in one Embrace, one Kiss:
One Clasp, one Hugg, one eager Glance was more,
    Than Worlds of Pearl, or heaps of Golden Ore.

He prais'd his priz'd Affection next his God,
    And   thought   his   Wife   the   second   Chiefest
    Good;   30
The   Heav'n-born   Dame   brought   to   his   longing
    Arms
    Her Soul, her Beauty, and resistless Charms.
Her Breast an equal active Fire did move,
    She lost the thoughts of Empire in his Love.
The splendid Stile of Empress she despis'd,   35
    The World a Cypher to the Man she priz'd:
Her crouding Wishes *him* alone persu'd,
    No sep'rate Greatness cou'd her Love delude:
Her *Intellectuals* pure, knew how to scan
    That Great and Independent Monarch, Man;   40
That little, but more weighty World Refin'd,
    More *apt*, and suited to her Heav'nly Mind.
She understood, that all that Good we name,
    Was nicely wrapt and folded up in him.
Oh Fate! from whence proceeds the hidden Cause, 45
    That we at *LOVE*, that glorious Passion, pause!
Was it with *Adam's* Innocence betray'd,
    Or, by his Lapse, a Malefactor made?
Or have our own acquir'd Excesses been
    So daring, to determin it a Sin?   50
What shou'd at once proclaim us Blest and Great,
    We fly, and court the Land-mark of our Fate.
Like murm'ring full-mouth'd *Isra'lites* we stand,
    And run on Rocks, to shun the Holy Land.
From hence the baffl'd World has been inverst,   55
    Princes involv'd in War, and People Curst;
Friends to their Confidents Estrang'd, and those
    Whom Fathers Got, to tender Fathers Foes.
Hence Lands United to themselves, divide,
    And cease their Strict Alliance, tho' Ally'd.   60
Hence hot debates grow in Domestick Pow'rs,
    The Man's unkind, the cheated Woman Low'rs.
Man, like the sordid Earth, from which he sprung,
    Corrupts his Soul by a base heap of Dung:

Forgetting the Celestial Form he bore,   65
  He values not the Woman, but her Store :
Extends his treach'rous Pledge to golden Charms,
  And joins his hands to none but spangled Arms.
He Weds her Jewels, and her Amber-Chains
  But her Rich Self (that merits all) Disdains :   70
Her Face he praises, but he courts her Ears,
  Catching the glitt'ring Pendants that she wears :
Each Eye no longer he esteem's a Star,
  Than flaming Rubies h⟨u⟩ng upon her Hair :
And judging Love, without her Gold, a Curse,   75
  He scorns her Vertue, and adores her Purse.

The Woman too no less Debas'd than he,
  Gives not her self, but for *GRATUITY* ;
Sooth's like a Merchant, with inveagling Art,
  Demands her *JOINTURE*, and keeps back her
    Heart.   80
On *Terms* and *Articles*, with Pride proceeds,
And Seals her cold *Affections* to her Deeds :
Stands off and Treat's like an Imperious State,
  And baulks her Happiness, to be made Great :
Proclaims her Fortune of a goodly Size,   85
  And he that offers most, obtains the Prize.

Both Sexes now deprave their Noble Kind,
  While sordid Avarice corrupts the Mind.
Never consult poor Vertue when they choose.
  But for a painted Cloud, the Goddess lose.   90
Divine content they count a finer Cheat,
  A Dish for Ornament, but no true Meat :
A meer Romance, an idle Dream of those,
  Who wanting Wealth, think to disguise their Woes.
A *Mountebank*, that only boasts of Cures ;   95
  But cannot work th' Effects his Cant assures.
The vain deluded Atheist thus denies
  A Supreme Essence, hid from Human Eyes :
Because his Sense can't apprehend a God,
  Religion's Sottish and her Zealots Mad.   100

But look, a Marry'd and a happy PAIR,
　　Are now like Revelations, *Strange* and *Rare* :
But if we reason from the Ages gone,
　　There scarcely was a happy Match, but One.

We mind not now the Merits of our Kind,　　105
　　Curious in Gold, but to the Persons Blind.
The Man ne'er minds his Love, for Money still
　　Is the base thirsted Object of his Will.
Upon condition of a promis'd Store,
　　He'll hugg a thing that crawls upon all Four.　110
Bring him an Old Rich Corps with grim *Death's Head*,
　　He'll Swear she's Young, and her Complexion Red.
Or if you cou'd bring one without a Face,
　　He'll praise her conq'ring Eyes, and charming
　　　Grace.
The *Woman* too, by such Affections led,　　115
　　Contemns the *Living*, to embrace the *Dead*.
And rather than not Covet, basely bold,
　　Would wed a Coffin, were the Hinges Gold.
Nature's Apostate, active Youth she Scorns,
　　Will long for Oxen, if you gild their Horns.　120
Say he's Deform'd, has neither Eyes nor Nose,
　　Nay, nothing to bespeak him Man, but Cloaths,
Strait she reply's he's Rich, so passes down ;
　　There's nothing ugly, but a poor Baboon.
Thus might she clasp a loathsom Toad in Bed,　125
　　Because he bears a Pearl within his Head.
And gilded Pills, tho' bitter, may delight
　　The liquerish Lust of wav'ring Appetite.
But still tho' *Wealth* their griping Senses Feasts,
　　At most, they're but concatenated Beasts.　　130
For as they scorn all consonance of Soul,
　　A mutual Hatred must their Peace control.
And this stands fix'd, what with my Love won't suit,
　　Appears Deform'd, and strait commences Bruit.
To various Climes of Tempers each are thrown,　135
　　The Frigid coupled to the Torrid Zone ;

Like Curs of different Nature, in a Chain,
  They're link'd in Fear, and wear their Bonds in
    Pain.
Perhaps a cold Respect they both may shew,
  As Impious Men to a kind Demon do.   140
Who when some skulking Wealth he does unfold,
  Honour and dread him for their New-found Gold.
But view, unrobe the bosom of Disguise,
  Observe the strange aversion of their Eyes :
With palpitations of Regret They Twine,   145
  Like Oil and Water their false Loves combine.
With feign'd Embrace they seem Love's Joys to crave,
  But with their Bed, converted to a Grave :
And whilst their backward Hearts like Load-stones
    meet,
  They wish their Linnen were their Winding-
    sheet.   150
He, like the Bear of Love, her Body Clips,
  Instead of pressing, bites her glowing Lips.
She, like a wounded *Otter*, flings and Rails,
  Fires with her Tongue, and combats with her Nails.
Hell and Confusion seize the Place around,   155
  Nothing but mutual Frenzy's to be found.
They both launch out into a Sea of Strife,
  A clam'rous Husband, and a brawling Wife.
The whole Armado of their Thoughts combine,
  On each side Summon'd, they in Consort join.   160
He arms Revenge, she meets him with Disdain,
  And to't they rush, like Storms upon the Main.
She to her shrill loud Clamours, takes recourse,
  Stamps, and invokes the Clergy for Divorce ;
Detests the Light by which his Face she saw,   165
  Curses the Bands, and Execrates the Law.
Directs to Heav'n her folded Hands with Pray'rs,
  And pouring down a flood of briny Tears ;
Hopes that kind Justice wou'd her grief behold,
  Pity an injur'd Lover, tho' a Scold :   170
That Death wou'd snatch him from the loathsom Bed,
  And Heav'n restore the Will which *she* betray'd,

He with Distraction and with Rage grows blind,
  Curses the Sex, and Damns all Woman-kind:
Accuses Heav'n that such a Monster made,   175
  A Fury in deceitful Masquerade.
A gaudy Phantom, that deludes the Sight,
  A Devil with the Coverture of Light;
Blasphemes, and by his Passion cast so far,
  Destroys himself by Persecuting her: 180
Abjures his Faith sworn to a legal Bed,
  Hates her, and lays another by his Side;
Profusely lavishes, her Right, each Kiss,
  And wracks her with the sight of wrongful Bliss.
She grows provok'd upon the dismal Change,   185
  And turns Dishonest, to retort Revenge:
The breach of Chastity she makes her Play,
  Plagues him all Night, and Cuckolds him all Day.

This must be then the issue, where our Love,
  Does not together with our Nuptials move.   190
Possessions can't for fickle Joy provide.
  When Love the end of Living, is Destroy'd.
Alas! we're all mistaken in the Kind,
  A happy Man is measur'd by the Mind.
Suppose him born to all the Pomp of Life;   195
  Admit he's match'd to Beauty in a Wife,
These are but Pageants, which a while may please,
  They may Divert him, but procure no Ease.
That Grandeur is no compound of our Bliss,
  The rugged Bosoms of the Great confess.   200
The gilded Monarch's Sable stands within,
  His Glory to his Troubles, but a Shrine:
His Cares, his Jealousies, Nocturnal Frights,
  Imbitter all his Joys and false Delights.
His toiling Head with Grief a Crown must bear,   205
  Whilst he still starts and grasps, to hold it there.
And thus all Princes to this Hell we trace,
  They Reign without, and are but Kings by Place.
But lest ambitious Maids in Scorn relate,
  This is the utmost Tyranny of Fate;   210

That such Seditious disagreeing Pairs,
  Are scarcely known in Centuries of Years.
We'll grant, (which yet no less Misfortune breeds)
  The Woman loves the Golden Man she Weds.
We'll think she brings with her Estate a Mind,   215
  Pure as her Sterling, from it's Dross Refin'd.
Yet this is so unlikely to succeed,
  It Murders what it first design'd to Feed.
He strait concludes her Passion a Pretence,
  Condemns her Soul, and lays the Crime on
    Sense.   220
Argues, she only chose to be his Bride,
  To serve and gratify her costly Pride.
But still we'll give this Topick larger Law,
  We'll say an equal Passion both does draw.
We will suppose them both enclin'd to Love.   225
  We'll call her *Venus*, and we'll stile him *Jove*;
Yet through the Tides of Business in his Head,
  He must neglect, and at length slight her Bed.
His peeping Passion, like a feeble Sun,
  Mingled with Show'rs of Rain, will soon be
    gone.   230
And if perhaps there's left some poor Remains,
  Like Northern Gold, 'tis in penurious Veins.
Diffus'd and scatter'd o'er the barren Land,
  Amidst vast heaps of Lead and worthless Sand.
This must be then a sad Reward of Love,   235
  When he thus senseless of her Choice do's prove.
Her Am'rous Courage ne'er can long be *bold*,
  That finds herself out-rival'd by her Gold.
Both their Affections to the Deep are sent,
  He sinks through Weight, and she through Dis-
    content.   240
Their Riches then shew their defect of Pow'r,
  That can't create what Want do's oft procure.
In thought of Wealth, he can't Intomb his Smart,
  When sullen Love preys on his stubborn Heart.
If crouded Chests and glutted Coffers can   245
  Restore Contentment to the anxious Man ;

Possess'd of those, if he from Pain is free,
   A troubled, may be call'd a quiet Sea:
Because there's Pearl and Amber on the Shoars,
   And thus it's ſtrangely Silenc'd when it Roars. 250

But 'twere, methinks, an easie Task to prove
   There's no such Curse, as Mercenary Love;
True Fire the Hearts oth' Wealthy seldom breed,
   They may through Care, but not Affeĉtion bleed.
Their Tenures, Lands, their Rents, and Quarter-
     days,   255
   In their Diſtraĉted Heads ſtrong Faĉtions raise.
And whensoe'er poor simpering Love peeps in,
   He's by that boiſtrous Crowd beat out agen:
Cræsus is ſtill perplex'd to guard his Store;
   Fears 'twill be less, labours to make it more. 260
Thus what he hoard's by the excess of Gain,
   Starves his lean Joy, but feeds his pamper'd Pain.
When Love with kind Caresses he should please,
   He forms Indentures, draws a cautious Lease;
On naſty Acres all his Speeches run,   265
   His Heart's a Tumult, like a Market-Town.
And when in Bed he shou'd Embrace his Spouse,
   Like a Dull Ox, he's ſtill amongſt the Cows;
Chew's all the Night upon the next fair Day,
   How much this Horse, how much that Load of
     Hay.   270
No thought but that of Cattle, yoaks his Heart,
   His Soul's the Driver, and himself the Cart.
Nothing but Buz and Noise, his Fancy seize,
   His Head's the Hive, his busie Thoughts the
     Bees.
In vain the Wife do's for the Husband Mourn, 275
   Whilſt she's the Burthen, and her Love the Droan.
Love, like a cautious fearful Bird, ne'er builds,
   But where the Place Silence and Calmness yields:
He slily flies to Copses, where he finds
   The snugging Woods secure from Blaſts and
     Winds.   280

Shuns the huge Boughs of a more ſtately Form,
  And Laughs at Trees tore up with ev'ry Storm.
The pleasant Nightingale can ne'er be won,
  To quit a Temp'rate Shade, to scorch i'th' Sun ;
In some low Grove, he sings his Charming Note ⟨,⟩ 285
  And on a Thorn tunes the sweet Warbling Throat.

We'll take a Ruſtick Couple for our Scenes,
  Who Love, and know not what Ambition means :
Who such an even competence possess,
  What may support, but not diſturb their Bliss. 290
See how unmov'd they at all Changes ſtand,
  Shipwrecks at Sea, and Earthquakes on the Land :
The Fraud of Courts, the Knavish Toil of Clowns,
  A Monarch's Favour, or his pointed Frowns,
Concern them not ; they but themselves abuse, 295
  In valuing that they ne'er intend to use.
Each to the other proves a solid Bliss,
  Rich in themselves no want of Happiness.
Like *Ægypt*, in whose Land all Plenty grows,
  Each others Bottom is their beſt Repose. 300
When clam'rous Storms, and pitchy Tempeſts rise,
  Cheek clings to Cheek, and swimming Eyes to Eyes :
When jarring Winds and dreadful Thundres Roar,
  It serves to make 'em Press, and Love the more.
Immortal Beings thus themselves Cajol, 305
  Spurn ſtinking Sense, and feed upon the Soul.
Here let us leave them bathing in pure Joy,
  Whom envious Man, nor Fate can e'er deſtroy.
Here let 'em live to share all Wealth and Pow'r,
  As Greatness can't love less, they can't love
    more. 310
To the Divineſt State of things they drive,
  Like Pilgrim-Angels, on the Earth they live,
Kind Nature gave them, Fortune bore no part,
  Love join'd their Souls, and Heav'n seal'd each
    Heart. 314

XC

THE FOURTH BOOK OF VIRGIL

⟨Translation of the Fourth Georgic.⟩

Next I will sing ethereal Dews refin'd,
The heavenly Gift of Honey to Mankind ;
Let not *Mecænus* this small Part despise,
Nature is always wonderful and wise ;
But mind, while I the Laws, Birth, Wars relate,   5
And sing the Leaders of this winged State ;
The Subjects humble, but not so the Praise, ⎫
If any Muse assist the Poets Lays,   ⎬
Or invok'd *Phœbus* his small Labours grace, ⎭
First for your Bees, a Seat and Station chuse,   10
Shelter'd from Winds, and where no Cattle use ;
For they in Winds cannot bring home their Food :
Nor let the Dew from off the Flowers be trod
By Sheep or Goats ; let no young Heifer in,
With wandring Feet to crush the rising Green ;   15
Suffer no greedy Wood-pecker to live,
Nor spotted Lizard, near you fruitful Hive ;
Nor *Progne's* Race admit, who long since stain'd
Her feather'd Bosom, with her bleeding Hand ;
Lest in their Bills they bear the Swarm away   20
To their devouring Nests a cruel Prey.
But let clear Fountains, mossy Pools be near,
And a small Brook his murmuring Passage wear
Between the grassy Banks ; let the Hives be
O'ershaded by some Palm or Olive-tree ;   25
That when new Kings first lead their Troops abroad,
And the glad Youth forsake their dark aboad ;
They on the neighbouring Banks may shun the Heat,
Or find on shady Boughs a cool Retreat.
Whether the sluggish Waters make a Pool,   30
Or in weak Streams, with gentle Murmur rowl,

Throw in some Boughs and Stones where they may
    stand,
And to the Summer's Sun their Wings expand.
If by East Winds, disperst in their short flight,
They headlong on the Water's Surface light.   35
Let Cassia's spicy Shrub be ever nigh,
With verdant Thyme and fragrant Savory;
And near some Fountain, on well water'd Beds,
Let early Violets raise their Purple Heads:
And let your Hives, whether of Barks of Trees,   40
Or bending Osier have small Passages,
Le⟨s⟩t Cold condense, or Heat the Honey warm,
For both Extreams may equally do harm.
Nor is't in vain; so artfully they line
Their Cells with Wax, Herbs, Leaves and Flowers
    joyn,   45
Closing with certain Glue, their Outlets, which
For that small use excels *Idean* Pitch.
If Fame say true, sometimes they under Ground
Make themselves Nests, sometimes their Swarms are
    found
In the dark Vaults of hollow Pumices,   50
Or in the rotten Trunks of aged Trees.
To stop the gaping Crannies of their Hive,
Of Leaves and Mud a yielding Paste contrive.
Let no dire Yew, her baneful Shadow spread
Near their small House; no filthy Crabs grown
    red   55
In crackling Flames, infect the Neighbouring Air;
No odious smell of Mire, no Fen be near.
Echo, that babbling Nymph, be far away,
And hollow Caves that with last Accents play,
When under Ground the Sun makes Winter fly,   60
And with his fruitful Light expands the Sky.
They spread o're every Forest and dark Wood,
Sip of each Stream, and taste of every Bud:
Then back with Vernal Sweets, refresht they come,
New build and people their beloved Home.   65

Next in their artful Combs fresh holes they drill,
Which with tenacious Honey soon th⟨e⟩y fill.
When thou look'ſt up, and seeſt 'em all above,
In a thick Cloud before the Weather move,
Through yielding Skies cutting their liquid Way, 70
No more they mean in their own Homes to ſtay,
But fly to the next Water or green Wood,
For there they'll swarm, if not by Art withſtood.
Press then each Herb of grateful smell and taſte,
Before 'em Mint and Honey-suckles caſt. 75
Let Brass and Old *Cybile's* Cymbals beat,
Till to their Medicin'd Hives, they all retreat;
But if adventurous Kings for Empire ſtrive,
Or civil Wars divide the faſtious Hive,
The Vulgars Hearts thou early maiſt perceive, 80
Trembling for Rage; and through the buzzing
    Hive,
A broken Noise, like that of Trumpet's sound,
Till the hoarse Warlike Call the Camp go round:
Then shine their Wings, and each bold *Warrior*
Whets in his Mouth, and shakes his brandisht
    Spear; 85
About their King and his Pavillion all
The Braveſt flock, and for th' Battle call.
At his Command in the early Spring they fly
Out of their Hives, and in the open Sky,
Meet in thick living Clouds, headlong they fall; 90
Not faſter from a freezing Cloud the Hail,
Nor drops the Acorn from the shaken Oak.
The Kings their Camp and Squadrons overlook,
Diſtinguisht by illuſtrious Wings they go,
And mighty Courage in small Bodies show; 95
So brave to fly no King was ever found
Till half his Hoſt lay breathless on the Ground,
These Tempeſts of their Mind, this mighty Rage,
A little Duſt thrown up, will soon asswage:
But if both Kings return, the Vanquisht slay; 100
The conquering Monarch let the Swarm obey;

One bright with various Spots, shining like Gold
(For of the two sorts there are) this beſt and bold
In Looks and Courage, gay with glittering Scales;
Deform'd with Sloth, the other poorly trails   105
A gross inglorious Paunch; as of the Kings,
Their Nations, Shape, are different, and their Wings;
Those foul and russet, like the Duſt appear,
New Spit on by some thirſty Traveller;
These are all bright like Lumps of shining Gold,   110
And equal Spots their painted Backs unfold;
These are the nobleſt kind, from such thou maiſt
Sweet Honey press, and of the smootheſt taſte,
Not only sweet and clear, but such as may
The roughness of unpleasing Wines allay: 115
But when the Swarms fly wanton in the Air,
And to forsake their empty Hives prepare,
Thou may'ſt with ease the Wanderers recall,
Clip their King's Wings; the Labour is but small.
No great Attempt, if he once lag behind,   120
No airy March, no Flight will be design'd:
From various Flowers let grateful Odors rise,
And place the Garden's God before their Eyes:
Plant Thyme and Pines, from lofty Mountains torn,
About their House: Let Hinds, to labour born,   125
Set deep, and water well the fruitful Shade:
And now did not my ending Task perswade
To slack my Sails, as to my Port I ſteer,
Perhaps the Art of Gardening I'd declare,
And rosie Harveſts of the *Pæſtan* Year,   130
How their broad Leaves new water'd Endives rear,
Green Parsly-beds, slow Daffadils, and how
The bending Cucumbers to Belly grow;
Nor the *Achantus* wou'd in silence pass,
Y⟨ew,⟩ Mirtles, nor th' Ivies dire embrace;   135
For I under *Tarentums* lofty Towers,
On yellow Fields, where slow *Galasus* pours
He⟨r⟩ fruitful Stream, remember to have known
A good old Man; some Acres of his own

He did possess, but neither fit to breed   140
The useful Heifer, or the Flock to feed,
No Purple Vines his naked Elms adorn,
But his poor Soil was overgrown with Thorn,
Roots he preferr'd, and Pot-herbs of his own.
To all the Pomp and Riots of a Crown.   145
When late returning from his Work abroad,
He did with unbought Fare his Table load.
In the new Spring he cropt the earliest Rose,
And the first Apples ripen'd on his Boughs;
When even Rocks with cold fierce Winter cleaves,   150
And every Stream his icy Chain receives,
He the soft Sprigs of yielding Bearsfoot binds,
Chides the late Summer, and slow Western Winds:
He first made fruitful Bees his early care,
Had many Swarms, whose Combs much Honey
    bear: 155
As many Blossoms as the Spring display'd,
So much ripe Fruit his grateful Autumn paid:
He cou'd transplant large Elms and make 'em grow,
And to a tastful Plum, improve the Slow:
And Plants remove, such as might then afford   160
A grateful Shade to his small chearful Board.
To treat those things at large I here want room,
And therefore leave 'em to some Muse to come;
And now proceed the Natures to declare,
Which *Jove* himself did on the Bees confer   165
As a Reward, for following the shrill
Sound of *Cybile's* Priests on *Ida's* Hill;
Till by their tinkling Cymbals they were led,
Where Heaven's new exil'd King th⟨e⟩y found and fed.
Their off-spring they alone in common rear,   170
And their small City in like Houses share;
Under eternal Laws they wisely live,
Each knows his little Cell, and loves his Hive;
Mindful of Winter, in the Spring takes pains,
To swell the publick Stock with private Gains.   175
Some Food provide, and by appointment scour,

O'er every Meadow, and each opening Flower.
Others at home their induſtry imploy ;
Tears of *Narcissus*, the too lovely Boy,
And lighteſt Gums f⟨ro⟩m Barks of Trees they
    take,   180
The firm Foundation of their Combs to make ;
Those form the Wax, while these brood o're the
    young ;
Others the Cells with liquid Neƈtar throng ;
Some watch abroad, and of the Gates take care,
Observe Clouds, Rains, and Tempeſts in the Air ;   185
Of the returning Swarm the loads receive,
Or force the idle Drones out of the Hive :
Hotly the Work is ply'd through all their Cells,
Fragrant with Thyme, the new-made Honey smells ;
And as the Cyclops, when they Thunder mold,   190
Of melting Wedges, some the Bellows hold,
Draw in the Winds, and force 'em out again,
From the dark Womb of the Bulls nine-fold Skin :
Others dip hissing Metals in the Lakes,
With their huge massy Anvils *Ætna* shakes :   195
In tuneful Strokes, their high-rais'd hammers fall :
Some turn with nimble Tongs the glowing Ball.
So if small things I may with great compare,
Cecropian Swarms in their close Work-house fare ;
Deſire of Gains sollicites all Degrees,   200
And makes 'em ply their several Offices ;
Care of the Town and Combs the Elder take ;
And with *Dædalian* Art new Houses make ;
The Younger late at Night with Labour worn,
And laden Thighs, from their days Task return.   205
Among the Wildings, and fat Teils they feed,
Pale Violets, and the Osier's bending Reed ;
All the same Labour, and same Reſt partake.
Soon as 'tis Day out of their Hives they break ;
And when th' Evening calls 'em from abroad,   210
Alike refresh themselves with Reſt and Food ;
The House is fill'd with their returning Hum ;

But when into their inward Rooms they come,
A Sacred Silence reigns throughout the Hive,
And all with Sleep their wearied Limbs relieve.   215
In threatning Show'rs from Home they will not fly,
Nor trust, when East-winds blow, the low'ring Sky,
But from their Walls, safe, short Excursions make,
And from the near'st Spring their Water take.
With little Stones they poise their flight,   220
As reeling Barks by Ballast are kept right.
'Tis strange this sort of Life shou'd please 'em so,
Where kindly Joys of Sex they never know;
To *Venus* never sacrifice, nor breed,
With glad short Pangs, the Youth that must succeed;   225
But gather from sweet Herbs, and Flowers their young,
Choose Kings, and such as to his Court belong;
Their little Cells, and Realms of Wax repair;
Sometimes on Flints, their labouring Wings they tear:
Under their Load, some generously expire,   230
Of Flowers, and Honey, through too great desire.
Though their Lives seldom seven Years exceed,
Their Kind's immortal, deathless is their Breed:
The ancient House and Families survive,
And a long faithful Pedigree derive.   235
Not *Egypt*, *Lydia*, nor *Hidaspis* Shore,
Their Monarch more obsequiously adore;
While he is safe, they all are of one Mind,
But if he fail, Faith Laws no longer bind;
On their own Stores tumultuously they fall,   240
And of their Combs, destroy themselves the Wall;
He keeps them all in order, and in awe.
Him they admire, and guard, observe, obey,
Oft bear him on their Shoulders through the Air;
And a brave Death pursue in Arms and War.   245
Some by these Signs, and these Examples taught,
Bees to partake of the eternal Mind have thought,
And of Ethereal Race; *Jove* runs through all,

High Heaven, deep Seas, and the Earth's massy Ball;
Hence Cattle, Men, all Animals receive   250
When th⟨e⟩y are born, the Souls by which they live,
And when dissolv'd, to him return, none dye, ⎫
To their first Elements the grosser fly,   ⎬
Th' etherial Parts ascend their native Sky.   ⎭
But if their little Stores thou car'st to sieze,   255
And force the Sacred Treasure of thy Bees,
First from thy Mouth large draughts of Water spout,
Then, with thy Hand extended, smoak 'em out.
Twice they have Young, two Harvests in a Year,
One when the lovely *Pleiades* appear,   260
And their new Light above the Ocean show;
The other when those Stars feel Winters blow,
And to moist Northern *Pisces* leave their Place,
Hiding in stormy Seas their sullen Face.
With the least hurt provok'd, they arm for fight,   265
And dart a painful Venom where they light:
Fixt in the Veins their Sting and Soul they leave,
And often perish by the same Wound they give.
But if thou seest a cold hard Winter near,
And their low Minds, their sickly State declare,   270
Who doubts to spare their Stores, or will delay
To burn fresh Thyme, or cut some Wax away?
Oft on their Combs, the unseen Lizards light,
And buzzing Moths disturb 'em in the night;
Or sluggish Drones (on others Toil that thrive)   275
Or Wasps with their unequal Arms arrive.
Some filthy Worm gets in, or Spider sets
At their Hive's Mouth, her loose and deadly Nets.
The more they are exhausted, still the more
Their wasted Stock they labour to restore.   280
But if, perhaps (as Life will on the Bees
Bring our Distempers) with some new Disease
They languish, which no doubtful Signs declare, ⎫
A horrid paleness will their Looks impair,   ⎬
And dusky Colours their sick Bodies wear.   ⎭ 285
Then bear they out great Numbers of the Dead,

And in long Pomp, sad Funerals they lead,
Or dully hang, clincht in each others Feet,
At the Hive's Mouth, or to their Cells retreat,
Through cold or hunger, for their Work unfit.   290
Whispers and Murmuring rise, as when a Breese
Of Southern Winds breath on the bending Trees,
Or troubled Seas in ebbing Tides retire,
Or Forges labour with imprison'd Fire.
To burn *Galbanean* Fumes I would perswade,   295
And through fresh Pipes let Honey be convey'd ;
So to reſtore 'em to their Strength and Food.
To mix the Juice of Galls, perhaps were good.
Dry'd Roses, and new Wines half boil'd away,
Cluſters of Raisins, Thyme, and Centaury.   300
There is a Flower, which we in Meadows find,
And call'd *Amello* by the Country Hind ;
By those that seek it, easie to be known,
Each single Root a many Branches crown ;
Yellow the Flowers, but to the numerous Leaves,   305
The darker Purple of the Vi'let cleaves ;
With it the Altars of the Gods are crown'd,
Rough to the Taſte, in fruitful Vallies found
By Shepherds, that near winding *Mella* dwell.
Boil this sound Root in generous Whit⟨e⟩-   310
    wine well,
Then Osier-pipes with the new Diet fill.
But shou'd the whole Stock fail, and none remain,
Whence a new Progeny might rise again,
'Tis time, the fam'd Invention to unfold,
Of the *Arcadian* Shepherd, how of old,   315
From the bruis'd Blood of Heifers new slain, Bees
Have taken Life, and swarm'd out by degrees
Here the whole Story shall at large have place.
While the long Fame, I to its Author trace :
For where the People of *Canopus* dwell,   320
And fruitful Waters of fat *Nilus* swell ;
On whose smooth Bosom painted Vessels ride,
Where-e're it borders on rich *Persia's* Side ;

Or with seven Mouths do's the plain Country drown,
As far as from parcht *India* rowling down,   325
Egypt's green Soil, with fruitful Slime to mend;
All the vast Region on this Art depend.
A Place contracted for that use they chuse,
And the low House with narrow Walls inclose:
Of well-wrought Tyles, four Windows they contrive
To the four Winds expos'd, that may receive   331
The Light obliquely; then they choose a Steer,
Whose bending Horns proclaim his Second Year;
On him they seize, and stop his struggling Breath
At Mouth, and Nostrils, beating him to death.   335
With his bruis'd Entrals his warm Hide they fill,
And thus inclos'd, they leave him for a while:
Fresh Boughs, Thyme, Cassia's on his sides they throw,
E're Western-winds first on the Waters blow;
E're Nature with fresh Colours paints the Fields,   340
Or on House-tops the airy Swallow builds.
The clotted Blood and dissolv'd Bones, the while
Ferment, and into wondrous Creatures boil,
Who without Feet at first their Voices try,
And with new Wings in little Parties fly;   345
Till they at last break forth, as when a Shower
Hot Summers Clouds on the parch'd Mountains pour,
Or as the Arrows from the *Parth⟨i⟩an* Bow,
When twanging Strings first send 'em on the Foe.
What, God, my Muse? who first this Secret
   taught,   350
Or was it the high Flight of Human Thought?
The Shepherd *Aristæus* (as Fame says)
Losing his Flock, through Famine and Disease,
Forsook *Thessalian* Temple, and dismay'd, ⎫
Ran to the Sacred River's utmost Head,   ⎬ 355
And thus his Moan to his bright Parent made: ⎭
Mother, *Cyrene*, Mother who dost keep
Thy watry Court beneath this Crystal Deep,
Why dost thou say I am of heavenly Race,
And sprung from Great *Apollo*'s hot Embrace,   360

Since Fate pursues me thus ?   Is this thy Love ?
Why doſt thou bid me hope a Seat above,
Since in this Life that little Fame decays,
Which I by Herds and Gardens thought to raise ?
With thy own Hand my thriving Woods deſtroy, ⎫ 365
Devouring Fire againſt my Stalls employ,   ⎬
Burn my full Barns, if I too much enjoy,   ⎭
Cut down my Vines, and blaſt my coming Years, ⎫
Since my small Fame offends a Mother's Ears.   ⎬
His Voice *Cyrene* through her Waters heard,   ⎭ 370
While round her Nymphs *Milesian* Fleeces card ; ⎫
Drymo and *Xantho*, *Ephyre* the Fair,   ⎬
Her Neck half cover'd with her flowing Hair ;   ⎭
Cydïpe and *Lycoris*, one a Maid,
The other rising from *Lucina's* Aid ;   375
Clio and *Beroe*, both Ocean-born,
Whom well-wrought Gold and painted Skins adorn ;
Bright *Deiopea*, *Arethusa*, now
No more a Huntress with her Spear and Bow ;
To these *Clymene* sings of *Vulcan's* Care,   380
Defeated by the amorous God of War :
From *Chaos* she the Loves of Gods relates.
Pleas'd with these Tales, while the soft Flax abates
From their swift Spindles, the Nymph hears again,
Nearer and nearer ſtill her Son complain,   385
All rise aſtonisht from their green Abode ;
But *Arethusa* firſt above the Flood
Lifts her bright Head : The Cryſtal Waters bow'd,
And spying him afar, 'Twas not in vain,
Siſter, she said, we heard a Voice complain ;   390
Sad *Ariſtæus*, once thy Care and Joy,
See at thy Father's Spring the weeping Boy : ⎫
By Name he calls thee Cruel and Unkind.   ⎬
Fear and Amazement, seiz'd *Cyrene's* Mind, ⎭
Let him, she said, he may behold th' aboads,   395
And tread the Threshold of his kindred Gods. ⎫
At his command the wondring Rivers spread,   ⎬
And a new Passage for his Entrance made.   ⎭

The Waters like a Mountain ſtood on Heaps,
While he into their yielding Bosom leaps :   400
Down to the bottom, where amaz'd he sees
His Mother's Realm and Cryſtal Palaces :
And as he goes, admires the sounding Groves,
And hidden Lakes, thro' which the Water moves
With such amazing Force, and under Ground   405
Beholds the Rivers that our World go round ;
Phasis and *Lycus,* and the sacred Head
Whence the deep Waters of *Enipeus* spread ;
Whence *Aniena* and fam'd *Tyber* flow,
The ſtony *Hypanis, Mysus* and the *Poe,*   410
Than which no River runs a swifter Race
To his old Father *Neptune*'s moiſt Embrace.
Into her inmoſt Seat while they withdrew,
And of each other took a nearer View,
The Nymphs clear Fountains for their Hands pre-
      pare,   415
And curious Towels of the fineſt Hair :
Some with full Cups, with Banquets some attend,
While in rich Smoak *Panchæan* Gums ascend :
Take this full Bowl of Wine, *Cyrene* cries,
And to the Ocean pour the Sacrifice :   420
To *Neptune* firſt, Father of all she Prays ;
Then Nymphs inhabiting the Woods and Seas ;
Pure Nectar thrice upon the Fire she throws,
And thrice the auspicious Flame up to the Cieling
      rose :
Embolden'd by the Omen, thus she spake,   425
A Prophet dwells in the *Carpathian* Lake ;
Green *Proteus,* whom a wondrous Coach conveighs,
And scaly Horses draw through yielding Seas :
His own *Palene* on th' *Emathian* Shore
He visits : Now him, all we Nymphs adore,   430
And aged *Nereus* self ; for well he knows
What is, what was, what Fate will next expose :
So *Neptune* has decreed, whose Herds and Flocks
He feeds beneath the Ocean's craggy Rocks :

Him thou muſt seize, my Son, and bind him well,   435
Till thy Misfortune's Cause and Cure he tell :
For uncompell'd he nothing will declare,
Nor can his Heart be touch'd with humane Prayer.
When thou haſt seiz'd him, chain, or use him worse,
His Shifts will fail before the God-like Force :   440
My self, when the Sun climbs the middle Sky,
Plants scorch, and Cattle to their Coverts fly,
Will bring thee where the aged Prophet lies
Dissolv'd in Sleep and Sloth, and easie for surprize.
When thou haſt seiz'd and bound him, every
     Shape   445
And frightful Form he'll vary, to escape ;
One while he'll seem a Dragon, or tusk'd Boar,
Then shake his yellow Mane, and like a Lyon roar ;
Then crackle like a kindling Flame, or slide
Out of thy Chains like a declining Tide :   450
The more he varies Forms, my Son, the more
Urge thy Success, and never give him o're,
Till vext through all his Forms, that Shape he keep
Which firſt he wore when he lay down to sleep.
This said, she with *Ambrosia* scents the Room,   455
And 'noints his Body for the time to come,
The Steam Divine on his loose Tresses dwells,
And every Nerve which active Vigor swells.
Worn in a Mountain's side there is a Cave,
Where beat by ceasless Winds the Waters rave ;   460
And into crooked Bays the Currents glide,
Of old a Port where Vessels us'd to ride :
Within lies *Proteus*, with high Rocks inclos'd.
In ambush here her Son the Nymph dispos'd :
For her Retreat a diſtant Cloud she wove ;   ⎫465
Now *Syrius* scorcht the *Indians* from above,   ⎬
And through the middle Sky swift *Phœbus* drove :⎭
Herbs wither'd at his touch, and to the Mud,
His thirſty Beams drank up the boiling Flood ;
When *Proteus* rising from the Waves repair'd   470
To his old Cave ; on him the watry Herd

Of Sea-born Monſters their Attendance pay, ⎫
And in glad Leaps shake the salt Dews away. ⎬
Around the Shore the sleepy Sea-calves lay ; ⎭
He, like a Herdsman on some Hill that lives,   475
When Night the lazy Cattle homeward drives,
And bleating Lambs the hungry Woolf provoke,
Reviews and tells 'em over, from his Rock :
Seeing his time, the bold Youth on him rush'd,
And with new Chains the aged Prophet crush'd.   480
He on the other side trys every Shape,
And dreadful Form, whereby he might escape :
One while a Monſter, Flame, and then a Flood.
Finding himself through all his Shifts pursu'd,
Wearied' o'ercome, his former Shape he took,   485
And with a Humane Voice at laſt he spoke :
Bold Youth, who bid thee to our Cave repair ?
What would'ſt thou learn ? he said, What mak'ſt
    thou here ?
Proteus, thou know'ſt no Man can thee deceive,
Deceive not others by the Gods high Leave ;   490
Ruin'd, undone, I come to know of thee,
What was the Cause, what is the Remedy.
Here the green Prophet caſt a dreadful Look,
He ſtar'd, he gnasht his Teeth, and big with Fate
    thus spoke :
Some powerful God with no light Wrath pursues   495
Thy fatal Crime ; now injur'd *Orp⟨h⟩eus* shews
His fierce Revenge, he this Contagion sent,
For his loſt Wife too small a Punishment :
Unhappy Nymph, who while she headlong fled
Thy foul Pursuit, on a loathed Serpent's Head   500
Trod unawares, which then she could not see
For the long Grass, and for worse Fears of thee :
For equal, Nymphs the *Dryades* with shrill
Complaints and Shrieks the neighbouring Mountains
    fill.
The Towers of *Rhodope*, the *Gætan* Race,   505
The rough Inhabitants of Warlike *Thrace* ;

Pangæum, Hebrus, Orithyia, all,
With their united Grief lament her Fall:
He on bleak Sands, soothing his vain Desire,
Wanders alone, and with his mournful Lyre   510
Feeding his Grief, pining himself away,
With her begins, with her he ends the Day.
The Jaws of *Tænarus,* Infernal Gates,
Dark Groves he paſt, where dismal Terrour waits;
To Ghoſts, and their dread King, does fearless
    sue,   515
And Minds that never yet Compassion knew:
Charm'd with his Voice the airy People throng
About the Youth, and liſten to his Song;
Thick as small Birds to their dark Coverts fly,
When th' Evening comes, or the tempeſtuous Sky   520
Pours down a Storm.
Mothers with Husbands, and the breathless Shades
Of once great Heroes, Boys, and riper Maids,
Unmarry'd Youth whom their fond Parents mourn'd,
Before their Face t' untimely Ashes turn'd.   525
All these with filthy Mud, rank ugly Weeds,
Such as alone infernal Water breeds,
Styx does nine times surround the House of Fate,
And Snake-hair'd Furies in Amazement sate.
Cerberus three Mouths were dumb, *Ixion*'s Wheel, 530
And Winds that move it at, his Song, were ſtill.
Now he returning, had all Dangers paſt,
And freed *Eurydice* beheld at laſt
The upper Sky again, following behind, unseen,
So far obeying the infernal Queen;   535
Here Love, Rage, Joy, to a short Madness drive,
Th' impatient Lover, (could those Gods forgive,
How small a Fault!) here fatally he ſtaid,
Rashly forgetting the Agreement made:
With the firſt Glimpse of fresh Ethereal Light,   540
On his dear Wife he turn'd his longing Sight:
Here vanish'd all his Labour, and their Law
Those unrelenting Powers negleĉted saw.

Three Peals of Thunder shook th' infernal Coast,
Orpheus, she cry'd, was ever Love so croſt ?   545
How are we both by thy rash Passion loſt ?
Fate puts me back, and my declining Sight
Feels the cold Hand of Death and endless Night.
Farewel, farewel for ever, now I go
Plung'd deep in Darkness, to the World below ;   550
Stretching to thee, (dear Cause of all my Harms)
No longer thine, alas ! my helpless Arms.
And at that Word from his diſtraĉted sight,
Like Smoak mixt with thin Air, she took her flight,
Ne'r to return again.   At the dear Shade   555
In vain he catcht, and much he wou'd have said,
Too late : For surly *Charon* wou'd no more
Permit his Passage to the *Elysian* Shore.
His Wife twice loſt, ah, Whither shou'd he move ?
With what soft Prayer invoke the Powers above ?   560
Or with what Tears the Shades ? cold in the Boat,
On the dark Lake she did already float.
'Tis said seven Months he did his Loss deplore
On the bleak Rocks of *Strymon's* Desart-shore ;
Singing this sad Event of too much Love,   565
He soften'd Tygers and made Forreſts move.
As in some Poplar Shade the Nightingal,
In mournful Strains, does her loſt Young bewail,
Whom some course Hind has newly torn away
From their warm Neſts, unfeather'd as they lay.   570
Night after Night, upon some Bough she sits, ⎫
And her sad Note no Moment intermits,   ⎬
Which every Field and echoing Grove repeats :⎭
Nor Love, nor Marriage charm'd his reſtless Mind ;
Alone he wanders, where the Northern Wind   575
Beats upon snowy *Tanais* chilling Shoar,
Where Ice ne're fails, and ceasless Tempeſts roar ;
There his loſt Wife he mourns in doleful Strains,
And of the Gods and their vain Gift complains.
The fierce *Sithonian* Women thus despis'd,   580
As they the Feaſt of *Bacchus* solemniz'd,

Full of their God, and boiling with disdain,
Scatter'd his bleeding Limbs through all the Plain.
From his firm Neck his gory Head thus torn,
Down the swift Stream of rapid *Hebrus* born,   585
Shriekt out, Ah poor *Eurydice*, and dy'd,
The echoing Banks *Eurydice* reply'd.

   This said, he plung'd into his watry World,
About his Head the foaming Billows curl'd.
Her anxious Son divine *Cyrene* chears,   590
Here end thy Grief, she said, and needless Cares :
This was the Cause of all thy Woe, the Crime,
For which the Nymphs, Companions of her prime,
Whom she in sacred Dances us'd to lead,
Among thy Bees that dire Contagion spread.   595
With Prayers and Sacrifice their Wrath appease :
Napæan Nymphs invok't, forgive with ease.
Take four curl'd Bullocks of thy largest breed,
Whom now the Hills of green *Lycæus* feed ;
As many untam'd Heifers ; and for these   600
Four Altars in their Sacred Temples raise :
Then from their wounded Throats let out the Blood,
And leave their Bodies in some shady Wood.
Soon as the ninth *Aurora* gilds the Skies,
To *Orpheus* drowzy Poppeys sacrifice,   605
With a black Lamb ; then view the Grove again ;
Eurydice, with a Calf newly slain
Thou shalt appease.   Without delay he goes ;
All she commands immediately he does :
Comes to the Temple, does the Altars raise ;   610
Four mighty Bulls of wondrous Bulk he slays,
As many Heifers that ne'r felt the Yoke,
When from the *East* the ninth *Aurora* broke :
He Worships *Orpheus*, to the Grove he goes ;
When lo a strange and wondrous Sight arose.   615
From the Bulls Entrails Bees were found to hum,
And met in Swarms from out the putrid Womb :
In moving Clouds to the next Tree they go,

And hang like Cluster'd Grapes upon a bending
   Bough.
While thus of Plants, Tillage, and Herds I sung,   620
With *Cæsar*'s thundring Arms *Euphrates* rung.
Just Laws he for the willing World ordain'd;
By God-like Acts his Claim to Heaven maintain'd.
Me all that while proud *Naples* did embrace,
Fam'd for th' inglorious Arts of lazy Peace: 625
Full of the Loves of Shepherds, bold and young,
Under the Beechen Shade, thee, *Tityrus*, I sung.   627

TRANSLATIONS FROM OVID'S AMORES PRINTED IN " DRYDEN'S MISCEL-LANY," 1684

XCI

BOOK I

Elegy the Eighth

He Curses a Bawd, for going about to debauch his Mistress.

There is a Bawd renown'd in *Venus* Wars,
And dreadfull still with honourable scars :
Her youth and beauty, craft and guile supply
Sworn Foe to all degrees of Chastity.
Dypsas who first taught Love sick Maids the way   5
To cheat the Bridegroom on the Wedding day.
And then a hundred subtile tricks devis'd,
Wherewith the Amorous Theft might be disguis'd.
Of Pigeons-blood, squeez'd from the panting heart,
With Surfeit-water to contract the part,   10
She knows the Use : whilst the good man betray'd,
With eager Arms huggs the false bleeding Maid.
Of herbs and Spells she tries the Guilty Force,
The poyson of a Mare that goes to Horse.
Cleaving the Midnight Air upon a Switch,   15
Some for a Bawd, most take her for a Witch.
Each Morning sees her reeling to her Bed,
Her Native Blew o'ercome with drunken red.
Her ready Tongue ne'er wants an usefull lie,
Soft moving words, nor Charming flattery.   20

Thus I o'erheard her to my *Lucia* speak,
Young *Damon's* Heart wilt thou for ever break ?
He long has lov'd thee, and by me he sends
To learn thy motions, which he ſtill attends.
If to the Park thou go, the Plays are ill ;   25
If to the Plays, he thinks the Air wou'd kill.
The other day he gaz'd upon thy Face,
As he wou'd grow a Statue in the place ;
And who in deed has not ? like a new Star,
Beauty like thine ſtrikes Wonders from afar.   30
Alas, methinks thou art ill dreſt to night,
This Point's too poor ; thy Necklace is not right.
This Gown was by some botching Taylor made,
It spoils thy Shape ; this *Fucus* is ill laid.
Hear me, and be as happy as thou'rt fair,   35
Damon is rich and what thou want'ſt can *spare.*
Like thine his Face, like thine his Eyes are thought,
Wou'd he not buy, he might himself be bought.
Fair *Lucia* blusht ; It is a sign of Grace,
Dypsas reply'd, that Red becomes thy Face.   40
All Lovers now by what they give are weigh'd,
And she is beſt belov'd that is beſt paid.
The Sun-burnt *Latines,* in old *Tatius* Reign,
Did to one man perhaps their love reſtrain.
Venus in her *Aeneas* City rules,   45
And all adore her Deity, but Fools.
Go on, ye Fair, Chaſte onely let such live,
As none will ask, and know not how to give.
How prettily you frown⟨!⟩   But I'll speak on,
Hear me, another day 'twill be your own.   50
Vertuous *Penelope* is said t'have try'd,
With a ſtrong Bow, each luſty Lover's side.
Nor did *Lucretia* kill herself for rage,
But love of *Tarquin,* in that colder Age.
To the young Prince she vow'd, ne'er more to joyn 55
In dull Embraces with her *Collatine.*
To keep her word she dy'd——
Life ſteals away, and our beſt hours are gone,

E'er the true Use, or worth of them, be known.
Things long neglected of themselves decay,   60
What we forbear time rudely makes his prey.
Beauty is best preserv'd by Exercise,
Nor for that Task can one or few suffice.
Wou'dst thou grow rich, thou must from many take⟨;⟩
From one 'twere hard continually to rake.   65
With out new Gowns, and Coaches, who can live?
What does thy Poet, but new Verses give?
A Poet, the last thing that Earth does breed,
Whose Wit, for sixpence, any one may reade.
Him that will give, to *Homer* I prefer,   70
To give is an ingenious thing I swear.
Despise not any can a present make,
It matters not from whom, but what we take.
Nor with the sound of titles be thou caught,
For nothing can with empty Names be bought.   75
Hang the poor Lover, and his Pedigree,
The thriving Merchant, or fat Judge give me.
If any beardless Stripling ask a Night,
And think thee paid with mutual delight;
Bid him go earn thy price among the men,   80
And when he has it, come to thee again.
Love truly none, but seem in Love with all,
And at old friends to thy new Lover rail.
Sometimes deny, 'twill Appetite procure;
The sharp-set Hawks will stoop to any Lure.   85
Then grant again, lest he a habit get
Of living from thee, but be sure thou let
No empty Lover in: murmur sometimes,
And as first hurt, reproach him with thy Crimes.
Seem jealous, when thou'st been thy self to blame, 90
'Twill stop his mouth, if thou the first complain.
All thou hast done be ready to forswear,
For Lovers Oaths fair *Venus* has no Ear,
Whilst he is with thee, let some Woman bring
Some *Indian* stuff, or Foreign pretious thing;   95
Which thou must say thou want'st, and he must buy,

Though for it six months hence in Gaol he lye.
Thy Mother, Sister, Brother, and thy Nurse,
Must have a pull each at thy Lover's Purse.
Let him from Rivals never be secure,   100
That hope once gone, Love will not long endure.
Shew him the presents by those Rivals sent,
So shall his bounty thy request prevent.
When he will give no more, ask him to lend,
If he wants money, find a trusting Friend.   105
Get hangings, Cabinets, a Looking-glass⟨,⟩
Or any thing for which his word will pass.
Practise these Rules, thou'lt find the benefit;
I lost my Beauty e'er I got this wit.
I at that word stept from behind the door,   110
And scarce my Nails from her thin Cheeks forbore.
Her few Grey hairs in rage I vow'd to pull.
And thrust her drunken eyes into her Skull.
Poor in a Dungeons bottom mayst thou rot,⎫
Dye with a blow with thy beloved Pot,   ⎬ 115
No Brandy and Eternal thirst thy Lot.   ⎭

XCII

BOOK II

Elegy the Fifth

To his false Mistress.

Cupid, begon! who wou'd on thee rely,
And thus at every moment wish to dye?
Death is my wish, when on thy guilt I think,
(Thy faithless guilt) at which I fain wou'd wink.
False Maid, thou various torment of my life,   5
Thou flying pleasure, and thou lasting grief;
No doubtfull Letters thy lost faith accuse,
Nor private gifts, thou mightst with ease excuse
Such proofs, one word of thine might overcome;

Why is my cause so good, and thou so dumb ?   10
Happy's the man that's handsomely deceiv'd,
Whose *Miſtress* swears and lies, and is believ'd.
Those Eyes beheld thee, when thou thoughtſt me
In books and signs (nor yet in those alone)
Conveying the glad message of thy Love   15
To that gay, vain, dull Fopp that sate above.
I knew the Language soon, what could be hid
From Lovers Eyes of all ye said or did ?
When others rose, I saw thee Dart a kiss,
The wanton prelude to a farther bliss :   20
Not such as Wives to their cold Husbands give,
But such as hot Adulterers receive.
Such as might kindle frozen appetite,
And fire even waſted nature with delight.
What art thou mad, I cry'd, before my face,   25
To ſteal my wealth, and my new Rival grace ?
I'll rise and seize my own upon the place.
These soft endearments should not farther go,
But be the secret treasure of us two,
How comes this third in for a share I'd know ?   30
This, and what more my grief inspir'd, I said ;
Her face she cover'd with a Conscious red :
Like a Cloud guilded by the rising Sun,
Or Virgin newly by her Love undone.
Those very blushes pleas'd, when she caſt down   35
Her lovely Eyes, with a disdainfull frown.
Disdain became her, looking on the Earth,
Sad were her looks, but Charming above mirth.
I could have kill'd my self or him, or her,
Scarce did my rage her tender Cheeks forbear :   40
When I beheld her Face my anger cool'd,
I felt myself to a mere Lover fool'd.
I, who but now so fierce, grow tame and sue,
With such a kiss we might our Love renew.
She smil'd and gave me one might *Jove* disarm,   45
And from his hand the brandisht Thunder charm.
'Twas worse than Death, to think my Rival knew

Such Joys as till that hour to me were new.
She gave much better kisses than I taught,
And something strange was in each touch me-
thought.   50
They pleas'd me but too well, and thou didst tongue,
With too much art and skill, for one so young :
Nor is this all, though I of this complain,
Nor should I for a kiss be so in pain :
But thine cou'd never but in Bed be taught,   55
I fear how dear thou hast thy Knowledge bought.

XCIII

BOOK III

Elegy the Fourth

To A Man that lockt up his Wife.

Vex not thy self and her, vain Man, since all
By their own Vice, or Vertue stand or fall.
She's truely chaste and worthy of that name,
Who hates the ill as well as fears the shame :
And that vile Woman whom restraint keeps in   5
Though she forbear the Act, has done the Sin.
Spies, Locks and Bolts may keep her brutal Part,
But thou'rt an odious Cuckold in her heart.
They that have Freedom use it least, and so
The power of ill does the design o'erthrow.   10
Provoke not Vice by a too harsh restraint,
Sick men long most to drink, who know they may'nt.
The fiery Courser, whom no Art can stay
Or rugged force, does oft fair means obey :
And he that did the rudest Arme disdain,   15
Submits with Quiet to the looser rein.
An hundred Eyes had *Argos*, yet the while
One silly Maid did all those Eyes beguile.
Danae though shut within a brasen Tower,

Felt the male virtue of the Golden shower :   20
But chaste *Penelope*, left to her own will
And free disposal, never thought of ill ;
She to her absent Lord preserv'd her truth,
For all th'Addresses of the smoother Youth.
What's rarely seen our fancy magnifies,   25
Permitted pleasure who does not despise ?
Thy Care provokes beyond her Face, and more
Men strive to make the Cuckold, than the Whore.
They're wondrous charms we think and long to know,
That in a Wife inchant a Husband so :   30
Rage, Swear and Curse, no matter, shee alone
Pleases who sighs and cryes I am undone ;
But could thy Servants say we have kept her chaste ?
Good Servants then but an ill Wife thou hast.
Who fears to be a Cuckold is a Clown,   35
Not worthy to partake of this lewd Town :
Where it is monstrous to be fair and Chaste,
And not one Inch of either Sex lies waste.
Wouldst thou be happy ? with her ways comply,
And in her Case lay Poynts of honour by :   40
The Friendship she begins wisely improve,
And a fair Wife gets one a world of Love :
So shalt thou wellcome be to Every treat,
Live high, not pay, and never run in debt.   44

THE

Mulberry-Garden,

A

COMEDY.

As it is Acted by
His MAJESTIE'S SERVANTS
AT THE
THEATRE-ROYAL.

Written by the Honourable
Sir *CHARLES SIDLEY*.

LONDON,
Printed for *H. Herringman*, at the Sign of the *Blew Anchor* in the
Lower walk of the *New Exchange*.   1668.

EDITOR'S PREFACE

Source and Analogues. The opening of " The Mulberry Garden " is imitated fairly closely from that of Molière's " L'Escole des Maris " (produced at the Théâtre du Palais Royale, June 24, 1661). From this play Sedley seems to have taken the hint of the contrast between *Sir John Everyoung* and *Sir Samuel Forecast*, who correspond to *Ariste* and *Sganarelle*. There is, however, very little borrowing from the French play after the first scene, and Sedley's rambling plot diverges very considerably from Molière's closely knit fable. The motif of a contrast between a rational and an irrational treatment of women or children was probably suggested to Molière by Terence's " Adelphi " (160 B.C.) and the same notion provides the basis for Shadwell's " The Squire of Alsatia " (1668).

The mixture of romantic scenes in riming couplets with realistic scenes in conversational prose connects this play with Sir George Etherege's first comedy, " The Comical Revenge, or Love in a Tub " (1664), where the same combination is found. There are other points of resemblance to Etherege's works. *Sir John Everyoung's* visit to the Widow's house with the fiddlers is not unlike *Sir Frederick Frollick's* similar escapade in " The Comical Revenge," and *Estridge's* marriage to *Wildish's* cast mistress is perhaps suggested by the trick played by *Sir Frederick* on *Sir Nicholas Cully* in the same play. The visit of *Victoria* and *Olivia* to the Mulberry Garden, and their encounter with *Estridge* and *Modish* there, is closely paralleled in Etherege's second play, " She Wou'd If She Cou'd " (produced February 1667/8), where *Ariana* and *Gatty* indulge in a similar frolic in the same place.

The incident of the cudgelling of Sir Samuel Forecast is connected by Genest [1] with the chastisement administered by Sedley's orders to the well-known actor Edward Kynaston. The story is told both by Pepys in his Diary (ed. Wheatley, VIII. 217) and William Oldys in his MS. notes on Sedley (printed in " Sir Charles Sedley," Appendix I, p. 318). According to Pepys, Kynaston's offence was that on Saturday, January 1, 1668/9, he acted a part in a lost play by the Duke of Newcastle called " The Heyresse," " in abuse to Sir Charles Sedley," which probably means that Kynaston turned the part into a caricature of Sedley's mannerisms. For this he was " exceedingly beaten by two or three " and was unable to act for some days. Oldys gives no date and does not mention " The Heyresse." He says Kynaston resembled Sedley very closely in " the Shape and Features " and had

---

[1] " Some Account of the English Stage," by Rev. J. Genest, I. 80, 81, 93.

" Lac'd clothes " made exactly like a suit that Sir Charles habitually wore. For this he was " well can'd : Sir Charles his Emissary pretending to take Kynaston for Sr Charles quareld with him in St James's Park for some private Misusage and beat him for Sr Charles." It seems to me quite unnecessary to suppose, as Lord Braybrooke did (in a note on the passage in Pepys), that Pepys and Oldys refer to two different incidents. The " Lac'd clothes " were probably worn in " The Heyresse." As the caning of Kynaston took place over eight months after " The Mulberry Garden " was produced, the cudgelling of Forecast could not have been suggested by that incident. Genest suggests that " It was perhaps meant by Sidley as a hint to Kynaston. Kynaston was, however, far from taking the hint and proceeded to greater liberties with Sir Charles." If this is true, Kynaston must have been aping Sedley for a long time before the baronet took his revenge. It seems to me far more probable that Sedley, casting about for a humorous method of punishing Kynaston, took a hint from his own play.

In his recent edition of " The Poems of Richard Lovelace " (Oxford, 1925), Mr. C. H. Wilkinson, following a suggestion of Mr. Thorn Drury, notes that *Eugenio* may possibly be intended as a portrait of Lovelace. Like Lovelace he is a fugitive and later imprisoned. Like Lovelace's his mistress is called *Althea*. In Act III, sc. i (ll. 11–14) he says

> " The strictest Prison, I have freedom thought,
> And been on Scaffolds without terrour brought.
> But these few words (*Althea* is a Bride)
> More wound my Soul, than can the world beside."

We may compare this passage with Lovelace's

> " Stone Walls do not a Prison make,
> Nor I'ron bars a Cage ; "

which occur in a poem addressed " To Althea." In l. 82 of the same scene, *Eugenio* says

> " Though Love possess, Honour must rule my heart ; "

and in Act I, sc. iv (ll. 25–28) Diana says to Althea

> " On thee *Eugenio* did his Life bestow,
> To me *Philander* did his service vow ;
> Yet both for Honour have these ties despis'd,
> And now are fled, or must be sacrific'd."

Both these passages call to mind Lovelace's " Song to Lucasta, *Going to the Warres* "

> " I could not love thee (Deare) so much,
> Lov'd I not Honour more."

If *Eugenio* can indeed be identified with Lovelace, we seem to have here an interesting proof that the " heroic " strain in Restoration drama owed something to the English cavalier tradition as well as to foreign sources.

Date of the Action. There is a considerable incongruity not merely between the styles of the romantic and realistic parts of " The Mulberry Garden," but also apparently between the dates at which they are supposed to be enacted. There is no doubt that the events which take place in the romantic scenes are supposed to happen at the time when General Monk was in London just before the Restoration, that is, in February 1659/60. Eugenio and Philander are cavaliers who are in hiding and have apparently taken part in a recent insurrection. Such a royalist insurrection actually occurred under the leadership of Sir George Booth in Cheshire just before the Restoration, and was accompanied by movements in Kent and Sussex of which Sedley would know, and in which he may have been implicated. In the prose scenes we find also that the Puritans are in power until the end of the play, when the " General declares like an honest man." However, there are several expressions in these scenes which belong to the life of a later period. There is a reference to the game of Ombre, which only came in after the Restoration. We hear several times of the playhouse and the acting of plays, as though the theatre was a regular public entertainment, which it was certainly not till after the king's return, and, what is still stranger, Wildish speaks of " a friend at court " when there was no such thing as a court, and of a " bishop " giving a Church living when the bishops were in exile or retirement, and had no power in the Established Church. The most probable explanation of these incongruities would seem to be that Sedley wrote a play about the events immediately preceding the Restoration very soon after that event took place. It was, doubtless, a play in rimed verse and of a romantic and sentimental character. At a later date he may have added realistic scenes in prose in order to adapt it to the taste of an age which had been accustomed to a new sort of comedy by Etherege and Dryden, and introduced into these scenes the language of the Restoration court rather than that of the Protectorate.

Topography. The real Mulberry Garden was a famous Restoration pleasure-ground. It derived its name from a garden of mulberry trees planted by James I with the object of promoting an English silk industry. It stood on the site of Buckingham Palace and part of its grounds, and adjoined St. James's Park. Charles I granted it to Lord Aston, who sold it to Sir George Goring, the famous Cavalier General. During the Civil War it was occupied by Speaker Lenthall, and under the Commonwealth it became a place of public entertainment. Goring returned to his house at the Restoration, and one of the other buildings on the estate became a tavern and was kept by a person called Coleby. It is first mentioned as a public resort by Evelyn under the date of May 10, 1654, when he had been there with Lady Gerrard and remarks that it is " now the only place about the town for persons of the best quality to be exceedingly cheated at ; Cromwell and his partisans having shut up and seized on Spring Gardens." [1] Ludlow in his Memoirs mentions that Charles II frequented it, " drinking healths at a debauch " there, and Pepys visited it several times. The first was after seeing Sedley's play on May 20, 1668, when he was greatly disappointed, finding only " a rascally whoring, roguing sort of people : only a wilderness here that is somewhat pretty but rude." He seems to have enjoyed it better when he went there three months later when he spent " 18s," and on April 5, 1669, he found " a good deal of company " there " and we mighty merry." The famous writer in " The Gentleman's Magazine " of February 1745 said that he used " to eat tarts " with Dryden and Mrs. Reeve, the actress, in the Mulberry Garden, " when our author advanced to a sword and chadreux wig." By 1709, when Dr. King wrote his " Art of Cookery," [2] Buckingham House, the predecessor of the present Buckingham Palace, had been built over part of the site of the Mulberry Garden by John Sheffield, Duke of Buckingham, who married Sedley's grand-daughter. The last record of it is found in a Report to the Lords of the Treasury dated February 25, 1672, which describes it as " containing about four acres twenty-two perches," over part of which stands more than half of Buckingham House. It is referred to in many contemporary comedies as a resort of lovers, harlots and young sparks. Etherege laid the graceful second scene of " She Wou'd If She Cou'd " there, and he had been anticipated by the Duke of Newcastle, who had already put " The Mulberry Garden " on the stage in Act II, sc. i, of his " The Humorous Lovers " (March 1667).

Stage History. On January 11, 1667/8, Mrs. Knipp, the well-known actress of the King's House, had a chat with Pepys at a performance of " The Wild Goose Chase," and told him among other items of theatrical gossip " of a play shortly coming on the stage, of Sir Charles Sidly's, which, she thinks, will be called ' The Wandering Ladys,' a comedy that she thinks will be most pleasant." The play that Mrs. Knipp referred to was undoubtedly " The Mulberry Garden," the earlier title of " The Wandering Ladys " probably referring to the exploits of Victoria and Olivia. On May 7, 1668, preparations for the production of Sedley's play seem to have started in earnest. On that day Pepys called for Mrs. Knipp at the King's House and drove her to her lodgings, " and thither comes Bannister with a song of her's, that he hath set in Sir Charles Sidly's play, which is, I think, but very meanly set ; but this he did, before us, teach her, and it being but a slight silly short ayre, she learnt it presently." The song in question is almost certainly the famous lyric in Act III. sc. ii. of " The Mulberry Garden " beginning " *Ah*, Cloris ! *that I now could sit*." As this song is sung by Victoria, we may infer that Mrs. Knipp

[1] Evelyn's " Diary," ed. Dobson, II. 71.
[2] " A princely palace on that site does rise,
Where *Sedley's* noble muse found mulberries."

was cast for that part. On May 18 " The Mulberry Garden " was at last staged, and Pepys gives the following account of the first performance : " Thence to my tailor's, and there did find Mercer come with Mrs. Horsfield and Gayet according to my desire, and there I took them up, it being almost twelve o'clock, or a little more, and carried them to the King's play-house, where the doors were not then open ; but presently they did open ; and we in, and find many people already come in by private ways, into the pit, it being the first day of Sir Charles Sidly's new play, so long expected, ' The Mulberry Garden,' of whom being so reputed a wit all the world do expect great matters. I having sat here awhile, and eat nothing to-day, did slip out, getting a boy to keep my place ; and to the Rose Tavern, and there got half a breast of mutton, off of the spit, and dined all alone. And so to the play again, where the King and Queen, by and by, come, and all the Court, and the house infinitely full. But the play when it come, though there was here and there a pretty saying, and that not very many neither, yet the whole play had nothing extra-ordinary in it at all, neither of language or design, insomuch that the King I did not see laugh, nor pleased, the whole play from the beginning to the end, nor the company ; insomuch that I have not been less pleased at a new play in my life, I think. And which made it the worse was, that never was worse musick played—that is, worse things composed, which made me and Captain Rolt, who happened to sit near me, mad. So away thence, very little satisfied with the play. . . ."

In spite of Pepys's adverse criticism, " The Mulberry Garden " seems to have been a successful acting play. Pepys went to see it again on May 20, " and cannot be reconciled to it, but only find here and there an independent sentence of wit and that is all." On June 29 he saw it a third time with his wife. There is no other record of performances, but it was probably revived in 1675 and 1688, when quarto editions were published. The names of the original caste have not been preserved, but, as we have seen, it is pretty certain that Mary Knipp was *Victoria*. It is possible that Nell Gwynne may have been *Olivia*, as she and Mrs. Knipp frequently acted together. In March 1666/7 they had appeared together as *Florimel* and *Asteria*, and in Dryden's " The Maiden Queen," and in June 1669 as *St. Catherine* and *Nakar* in " Tyrannic Love." It is true that Pepys heard on July 13 that Buckhurst had induced her to leave the King's Company and become his mistress, but she seems to have returned soon after, for on November 9, according to Pepys, she was acting again in " The Indian Emperour." Mrs. Margaret Hughes, after-wards Prince Rupert's mistress, who may also have had a liaison with Sedley himself (see " Sir Charles Sedley," p. 127), the sisters Anne and Beck Marshall, Mrs. Corey, Mrs. James, Mrs. Boutell, Mrs. East-land, Mrs. Knight, Mrs. Uphill and Mrs. Weaver were actresses belonging to the Company at this time from whom the other female characters would be drawn. The male members of the Company included such famous veterans as Michael Mohun and Charles Hart, who may well have been cast for *Everyoung* and *Forecast*. The other men would be selected from Nicholas Burt, John Lacy, Richard Baxter, William Cartwright, Robert Shatterall, and William Wintershall.

Sir Peter Lely pinxit   Emery Walker ph.sc.

Frances Stuart
Duchess of Richmond

By Gracious permission of His Majesty the King

TO

HER GRACE

THE

DUTCHESSE

OF

RICHMOND AND *LENOX*

Madam,

  Tis an unquestion'd Priviledge we Authors have of [1
troubling whomsoever we please with an Epistle Dedica-
tory, as we call it, when we print a Play: Kings and
Princes have never been able to exempt either themselves
or their Favourites from our Persecution. I think your [5
Grace (for a Person of so great Eminence, Beauty,
Indulgence to Wit, and other Advantages that mark you
out to suffer under Addresses of this Nature) has scap't
very well hitherto. For I do not remember your Name
yet made a Sanctuary to any of these Criminals: But, [10
Madam, your time is come, and you must bear it patiently.
All the favour I can shew you, is that of a good Executioner,
which is not to prolong your pain. You see, Madam,
here the unhappiness of being born in our time, in which
to that Vertue and Perfection, the Greeks and Romans [15
would have given Temples and Altars, the highest thing
we dare dedicate, is a Play or some such Trifle. This
that I now offer to your Grace, you were so kind to when
it was in loose Sheets, that by degrees you have train'd
it up to the confidence of appearing in Print before you: [20
And I hope you will find it no hard matter to pardon a
Presumption you have your self been accessory to, especially
in one that is intirely,

MADAM,

Your Graces Devoted and

Obedient Servant,

CHARLES SIDLEY.

DRAMATIS PERSONÆ

Sir John Everyoung.
Sir Samuel Forecast.
Harry Modish.
Ned Estridge.
Jack Wildish.
Snappum.
Eugenio.
Philander.
Horatio.
Officer and Assistants.
Servant to Sir *Samuel Forecast.*
Musicians and Dancers.
Prentices, and Sedan-men.
Diana.⎫
Althea.⎭⟨*Forecast's* Daughters.⟩
Widow Brightstone.
Victoria.⎫
Olivia. ⎭⟨*Everyoung's* Daughters.⟩

PROLOGUE

New Poets (*like fresh Beauties come to Town*)
Have all that are decay'd to cry 'em down,
All that are envious, or that have writ ill:
For Wits and Heroes fain wou'd, dying, kill.
Like Statesmen in disgrace, they ill endure   5
A better conduct should our good procure:
As an old Sinner, who in's youth has known
Most Women bad, dares venture upon none.
Our Author, seeing here the Fate of Plays,
The dangerous Rocks upon the Coast of Praise,   10
The cruel Critick and malicious Wit,
Who think themselves undone if a Play hit:
And like those Wretches who on shipwracks thrive,
Rage if the Vessel do the Storm out-live,
By others loss he stood a while forewarn'd,   15
But against tempting hope no man is arm'd:
Amongst great Gamesters, when deep play is seen,
Few that have money but at last come in:
He has known many with a trifling sum,
Into vast Fortunes by your favours run: 20
This gives him confidence to try his Fate,
And makes him hope he is not come too late;
If you'le undo him quite, like Rooks begin
And for this once in cunning let him win
He hopes the Ladies at small faults will wink,   25
And a new Poet, a new Servant think.

THE MULBERRY GARDEN

ACT I. SCENE I

Sir John Everyoungs *House stands.*

Enter Sir John Everyoung, *and Sir* Samuel Forecast.

Ever. Well, for all this heat, let's every one
govern his own Family as he has a mind to't; I never
vex my self that your Daughters live shut up as if
they were in *Spain* or *Italy*; nor pray don't you trouble
your self that mine see Plays, Balls, and take their   [5
innocent Diversion, as the Custom of the Country,
and their age requires.

Forec. They are my Neeces, as they are your
Daughters, and I'le tell you, you spoil 'um with your
own Examples: youth may well be allow'd to be   [10
stark mad, when they see age so Extravagant: is that
a Dress for my elder Brother, and a Reverend Justice?

Ever. Yes, and a properer than your little Cuffs,
Black Cap, and Boots there, for a Gentleman.

Forec. Of Eighteen I confess, but not of   [15
Fifty.

Ever. Yes, though he were as old as any before
the Flood; and for my part I'le not bate a Riband
for all the whole Tribe of you can say: you know
your self every Fool wou'd fain be thought wise;   [20
and why an old man shou'd not desire to be thought
young, I see no Reason: as long as I am whole at
heart, I'm resolv'd my Cloaths shall n'ere betray me.

Forec. There's no need on't, your face does it
sufficiently; Come I'm asham'd to see you every   [25
day set out thus powder'd, and trim'd like an old

Player, to act a young Prince; your Periwig I like very well, it serves to keep your bald pate warm, but that flirting Hat there looks as it were made rather for your Wit than your Head.   Pray which is   [30 most *a-la-mode*, Right Reverend Spark?—Points, or Laces?   Girdle, or Shoulder-Belts? what say your Letters out of *France*?

Ever.   Lord, what pains you take to Quarrel at my Dress and Mirth, as if age were not tedious   [35 enough already, but we must adde neglect of our selves, and moroseness toward others: Children now adays are not so fond of their Parents, that we need use any Art to make 'um hate us.

Fore.   Well, go then, and carry your Daugh-   [40 ters abroad, and break their Bellies with Sillabub, 'tis the greatest kindness you can do 'um now; As you have bred 'um, you may e'ne keep 'um to your self, and save their Portions; I believe no body will be very fond of a Hide-Park Filly for a Wife; nor   [45 an old Boy that looks like a Pedlar's Pack for a Father-in-Law: But now I think on't, you are such a Spark, they'd lose their Reputations with you if they had any.

Ever.   For ought I see good Brother, they stand as fair in the opinion of the world as yours, and   [50 have done nothing but what I like very well.

Fore.   What do you count is nothing, to be all day abroad, to live more in their Coach than at home, and if they chance to keep the House an Afternoon, to have the Yard full of Sedans, the Hall full of   [55 Footmen and Pages, and their Chambers cover'd all over with Feathers and Ribands, dancing and playing at Cards with 'um till morning.

Ever.   Why, where's the hurt of all this?

Fore.   O no hurt at all; but if they were my   [60 Daughters I should be looking for Cradles and Nurses, I shou'd be sorry to hear *Diana* or *Althea* went abroad without some discreet body to look after them, or were at home indeed without imploying their time

in some piece of Huswifry, or at least some good   [65
Book.

Ever.   You and I shall never hit it, for now I
think those women who have been least us'd to Liberty,
most apt to abuse it, when they come to't.

Fore.   O this fine believing Gentleman, I   [70
should laugh heartily to see him a Grand-father without a Son-in-Law.

Enter to them Victoria *and* Olivia.

Vict.   Sir if you don't use the Coach your self, my
sister and I wou'd go abroad this Afternoon.

Ever.   Take it Children, but don't keep the   [75
Horses out too late.

Fore.   What! never ask 'um whither they're
going? by your favour I'll put that Question to 'um;
Come hither *Victoria*, what visits do you intend this
Afternoon?   [80

Vict.   None Sir, we were only going a Rambling.

Fore.   A Rambling, methinks that word sounds
very prettily i'the mouth of a young Maid; next
time I ask 'um whither they're going, I believe they'l
answer me, To drink a Bottle or two : but whither   [85
pray?

Olivia.   For that Sir we shall take counsel of the
weather, either up into the City, or towards the
Park.

Fore.   What, none but you two?

Oliv.   We intended to call on my Cousins   [90
Althea and *Diana.*

Fore.   They took Physick this morning, and are
not well, you'l but lose your labour.

Vict.   Sir they sent for us but an hour ago.

Fore.   You had better go without 'um, they   [95
are all undrest, to stay for 'um would but make you
lose the sweet of the Evening.

Ever.   Brother, what are you jealous of them too?
I assure you they are no men in womens cloaths.

Fore. I am not jealous of 'um, but since [100
you'd have it so, I'de as lieve they'd keep away.

Ever. And I'de as lieve you'd keep away, till you
underſtand your self better; what? you think your
Daughters, like your Money, never safe, but under
Lock and Key; who wou'd you have 'um con- [105
verse with, if not with their Relations?

Fore. With those that are a kin to 'um in manners
and behaviour, such as they may learn some goodness
of; I see nothing they can learn here but vanity.

Vict. Siſter they begin to be angry, come [110
let's leave 'um till the ſtorm be over. [*Exeunt.*

Fore. What are they gone? I warrant if we had
been reading a Play, or Romance, we shou'd not have
been rid of 'um so soon; but I'le spoil their sport at
my House. [115

Ever. A precious Design, and worthy of your
Gravity! But if you do Brother, I'le tell you one
thing, you'l go near to spoil a match at cross purposes:
farewel. [*Exeunt.*

SCENE II

Modish *his Chamber.*

Enter Henry Modish *and* Ned Eſtridge.

Mod. Good morrow, *Ned,* I thought I had left
you too deep engag'd laſt night to have been here
thus early.

Eſtr. Why you sneak'd away juſt as the Sport
began, like a half-bred Cock that ſtrikes a Stroke [5
or two briskly, and then runs.

Mod. Faith, I had so many Irons in the fire for
to day, I durſt not run the hazard of a disorder laſt
night: but you know my Heart was with you.

Eſtr. You wou'd not have repented it, if [10
your whole Body and Soul had been with us; *Jack*

Wildish sent for a dozen more of Champaigne and a
Brace of such Girls, as we shou'd have Made Honour-
able Love to, in any other Place; and Sir *John
Everyoung* was in the pleasanteſt Humour, I'de [15
give a piece I cou'd repeat the Satyr he made of the
Country.

Mod. It wou'd be good News to his Daughters,
for they say, now and then in a morning he is of
another mind.   [20

Eſtr. That's only while his head akes, they need
not fear him; he swears hee'l n'er ſtir beyond *Hide-
Park* or *Colebys* at fartheſt, as long as he has an Acre
left, they shall all come to him: 'tis a pleasant old
Fellow, he has given me a hundred pounds for [25
my Gray beard, and is to ride himself this day month
twice round the Park, againſt a bay Stone-horse of
Wildishes, for two hundred more.

Mod. Methought *Wildish* and you were very
intimate, pray how long have you been [30
acquainted?

Eſtr. Faith, about a week or so, times a thing
only necessary for the Friendship of vulgar Spirits:
O here comes the Gentleman we were speaking of;
now *Jack*, what small Petticoat do you come [35
from?

Enter *Wildish*.

Wild. E'ne such another as you are going to now
with all this Bravery: those Cravats that design the
Right Honourable, I'le lay a piece will be rumpl'd by
a worse Woman than they were washt, yet afore [40
night.

Mod. Wou'd all the world were of his mind, we
Young men shou'd pass our time well.

Wild. O never the better for that; such Mounsieurs as you by your Feathers are known to be [45
Birds of prey, and though you catch nothing, you
scare all; Besides, every good man is not acquainted

with this Principle among you, that you can be in Love with nothing but your selves, and may be jealous of his Wife, when indeed you come [50 innocently to take a view of your persons from Head to feet in the great Glass; comb out your Periwig, shake your Garnitures, and be gone.

Eſtr. What, doſt think we have no other way of Entertainment? No Discourse, *Jack*? [55

Wild. Yes, a little now and then about their dress, Whether their Patches be too many or too few, too great or too small, whether her Hankerchief Be *Point de Venie* or *Rome*; and having left behind you some proof of your ability in the Mode, return [60 to shew your selves at the laſt Aɕ of a Play.

Mod. I dare swear, *Jack*, thy Acquaintance puts thee to none of these Criticisms, a plain Gorget and a black Scarf are all their varieties; and are you well Miſtress? and what Company have you kept [65 lately? thy moſt familiar Queſtions. But Raillery apart. Say it were a mans Fortune to prevail upon one of these thou believeſt so impregnable Forts, and to be receiv'd where never any but your self came so near as to be deny'd; were not that a Conqueſt? [70

Wild. As great as that of a place not tenible can be; the present Plunder indeed is somewhat, but upon the firſt Siege you muſt look to be driven out: a Ladies heart is a kind of Fortification that is easier surpris'd by being well man'd, and makes ever [75 the ſtrongeſt resiſtance of it self.

Eſtr. 'Tis true, *Modish*, for I have ſtill observ'd, that when one of these persons of Honour does a little forget her self, though at firſt through a secret Sympathy, and invincible inclination (as they call [80 it) for one particular Man, she ever after loves the whole Sex the better for it.

Wild. Right; for these good Creatures, Women, are like Cats, if once made tame, any one may play with 'um; if not, there's no coming near 'um. [85

Mod. Thou think'st thou hast maul'd 'um now; Why I tell thee, *Jack*, a Hector is not readier to pick a Quarrel with a sawcy Creditor, and swear he will never pay the Rascal, then a man is to have one with his Mistress towards the latter end of an Amour; [90 especially if it amount to a handsom occasion of leaving her, 'tis the kindest thing she can do then: what think you, *Estridge*?

Estr. Faith, I'm of your mind, yet I have known some unconscionable Ladies make their Servants [95 wait as long for a just Exception, and almost as impatiently, as they did for the first Favour.

Wild. Favour and Exception, Gentlemen, are words I don't meet with in seven years, where I go, my piece makes my Complement when I come [100 in, and my Excuse when I go away; and 'tis ever well taken too: I have all the day to bestow upon my business, the night upon my Friends, whilst you are kissing the Cards at *Ombre*, or presenting Oranges at a Play-house.   [105

Estr. Thou never knew'st it seems what 'twas to be in Love then.

Wild. No faith, I never let the Disease run on so far, I always took it in time, and then a Bottle of Wine or two, and a she Friend is an approv'd [110 Remedy; there are men in the world though, who in that Distemper prescribe some serious Employment, continual Exercise, spare Diet, and the like; but they are Philosophers, and in my opinion make the Remedy worse then the Disease.   [115

Estr. I do confess your's is the pleasantest Cure, if it be one; but I doubt it only gives a little ease for the present, and like small Beer in the Morning after a merry bout over night, doth but make us the worse afterwards.   [120

Mod. I now, you talk to him of what he under-stands, What you do tell him of Love for? who by his own confession never knew what it was.

Wild. No, but I guess this same Love you speak
of, Gentlemen, to be much like Longing in [125
Women, a phantaſtical appetite to some one thing
above all others, which if they cannot get, the Lover
miscarries of his passion, and the Lady of her little
one; or if they do, are both quickly satisfi'd, and it
becomes for ever after very indifferent, if not [130
loathsom.

Eſtr. Well, *Modish*, I perceive we shall do no
Good on him, let's take him to the Mulberry-Garden,
and see what the Ladies can do.

Wild. You shall excuse me, I have a small [135
Ramble of my own for an hour or two this Afternoon: and so your Servant.   [*Exit.*

Mod. 'Tis time we were going, I warrant they
have walk'd every foot of the Garden, twice over by
this time: They are mad to know, whether [140
their Friends in Town have dealt faithfully with 'um
of late, concerning the Mode.

Eſt. These Country Ladys for the firſt month
take up their places in the *Mulberry Garden*, as early
as a Citizens Wife at a new Play.   [145

Mod. And for the moſt part are as easily discover'd; they have always somewhat on, that is juſt
left off by the Better Sort.

Eſt. They are the Antipodes of the Court; for
when a Fashion sets there, it rises among [150
them.   [*Exeunt.*

SCENE III

⟨*The Mulberry Garden.*⟩

Enter Victoria *and* Olivia.

Vict. Siſter, whatever the matter is, methinks we
don't see half the Company that us'd to meet here
anights, when we were laſt in Town.

Oliv. 'Tis true, but methinks 'tis much better than the long Walk at home: for in my opinion [5 half a score young men, and fine Ladies well drest, are a greater Ornament to a Garden, than a Wilderness of Sycamores, Orange, and Lemmon Trees; and the ruſtling of rich Veſts and Silk Petty-coats, better Musick than the purling of Streams, [10 Chirping of Birds, or any of our Country Entertainments: and that I hope the place will afford us yet, as soon as the Plays are done.

Vict. Siſter, what wou'd you give to see *Eſtridge* come in now? [15

Oliv. 'Tis impossible, he wou'd not miss his Devotion to the Park, for all I could give, such an Evening as this: besides the two Garnitures he brought out of *France* are Soil'd; his Feather broke, and he has been so out of humour these two days, [20 there's no enduring him; he loſt his Money too laſt night I hear; and losing Gameſters are but ill company.

Vict. Fye Siſter, you make him a saver with a look; and Fine, in but thinking he is so: you [25 deserve not so compleat a Servant, but I hope you'le be as obliging to his face, as you are severe to him behind his back.

Oliv. The only way to oblige moſt men is to use 'um thus, a little now and then; even to their [30 faces, it gives 'um an Opinion of our wit; and is consequently a Spur to theirs: the great pleasure of Gaming were loſt, if we saw one anothers hands; and of Love, if we knew one anothers Hearts: there would be no room for good Play in the One, . [35 nor for Address in the Other; which are the refin'd parts of both. But what would you give to see *Horatio*?

Vict. To see *Horatio*, as I knew him once, I would all other happiness renounce;   40
But he is now anothers, and my aim

Is not to nourish, but to sta⟨r⟩ve my flame :
I dare not hope my Captive to regain,
So many Charms contribute to his Chain.
Althea's Slave, let false *Horatio* live,　　　　　　45
Whilst I for freedom, not for Empire strive.

　　Oliv.　Fye Sister leave this Ryming at least.

Enter to them Estridge *and* Modish.

　　Est.　Ladys, it is our wonder to find any body here
at this time of Day, and no less our Happiness to
meet with you ; all the world is at the Park,　[50
where we had been our selves, but that we saw your
Livery at the Gate.

　　Vict.　I pray let us not keep you here Gentlemen,
your Mistresses will curse us, and your selves too,
by and by, if the Garden shou'd not fill.　　　　[55

　　Est.　If we wish any company, Ladies, 'tis for
your sakes, not our own.

　　Mod.　For my part I wou'd ne're desire a Garden
fuller than this is now ; we are two to two, and may
be hand to hand when you please.　　　　　　[60

　　Oliv.　I don't know what you think, but in my mind
the More the Merrier, especially in these places.

　　Est.　I, for show, Madam, but it happens in
great Company, as at Feasts, we see a great deal,
and fall to heartily of nothing, and for the most　[65
part rise hungry : and 'tis with Lovers, Madam, as
with great bellied Women, if they find what they
long for, they care not whether there be any thing
else or no.

　　Vict.　What in love already ? sure the air of　[70
this place is a great softner of mens hearts.

　　Mod.　How can it chuse, having so many Lovers
sighs daily mixt with it ? but 'twere a much better
quality in't, Madam, if it could incline Ladies to
believe, and look with pity on those flames they　[75
raise.

　　Oliv.　'Tis too early to make Love this two Hours.

Flames and Pity wou'd sound much better in the
Evening.

Mod. 'Tis not with love, Madam, as with   [80
meaner Arguments; I might entertain you with my
passion for an age, and yet have as much left for anon,
as if I had not spoke one word; the Sea is easier
emptied then a Lovers breaſt.

Oliv. What say you, Sir, is this your opinion   [85
too?

Eſt. Yes faith, Madam, and I think a Lover can
no more say at once, what he hath to say to his Miſtress,
than a man can eat at once for his whole life time.

Oliv. Nay, if it be so endless, I should beg   [90
of my Servant, when ever I have one, e'ne to keep
it to himself for altogether.

Eſt. There you betray your ignorance, with
your pardon, Madam; to see the fair *Olivia*, and
not love her, is not more impossible, than to love   [95
her, and not tell her on't. Silent Lovers you may
read of, and in Romances too, but Heavens forbid
you shou'd e're meet with any.

Oliv. If they knew how little they were like to
get by being otherwise, I'm confident I shou'd   [100
meet with none else.

Eſt. Well, Madam, I perceive Love, like Wine,
makes our Discourse seem extravagant to those that
are not wound up to the same height: But had you
any spark of what I feel, I should have had   [105
another Answer.

Oliv. Why, what Answer?

Eſt. Nay, I know not, but some pretty one, that
love wou'd have devis'd for you; No more to be
imagin'd by you now, than what you shall talk   [110
of next in your sleep. In the mean time, Ladies,
will you do us the honour to eat Syllabubs?

Oliv. Siſter, let's go, so they'l promise to say
nothing but what they think to us when we are
there.   [115

Mod.   You may do what you please, *Ned*, but 'tis a liberty I dare not use my self to, for fear of an ill habit.

Eſtr.   You are very confident of our good opinion, Ladies; I believe there are few women in Town   [120 wou'd accept of our Company on these terms.

Vict.   Faith, Siſter, let's bate 'um that circum-ſtance, Truth is a thing meerly necessary for witnesses, and Hiſtorians, and in these places doth but curb invention, and spoil good Company; We will   [125 only confine 'um to what's probable.

Mod.   Content, and I dare swear 'twill be better for all Parties.   [*Exeunt.*

SCENE IV.   *Sir* Samuel Forecaſts *House.*

Enter Althea *and* Diana.

Dian.   We two, or none; may of our Stars com-
        plain,
Who afford us nothing to share but pain;
Each bears her own, and th'others portion too;
This cruel wonder can high friendship do.

Alth.   To us how cheap might they have joy
        allow'd,   5
Since both had had what they on each beſtow'd!
But yet thy loss I rate above my own.
Fate on thy Love till now did never frown:
Philander thee above the world did prize,
Thy Parents saw him almoſt with thy Eyes: 10
All things so prosperous were, thou cou'dſt not guess,
An Accident to wound thy happiness.
I wretched Maid, have but a passion loſt,
Which if none else, my Parents wou'd have croſt:
My lowly hopes do but a ſtep descend,   15
Whilſt thine, from their full height do head-long bend:
This hour that promis'd all, can nothing pay,
And *Hymen* ſteals his lighted Torch away.

Dian.   Ah, dear *Althea*, let not thou and I
Contend who moſt exceeds in misery ;   20
It is a dismal ſtrife, since were my own
Less, I'de share thine till they were equal grown.
Curse on Ambition, why shou'd Honour take
A present back agen, that Love did make ?
On thee *Eugenio* did his Life beſtow,   25
To me *Philander* did his Service vow ;
Yet both for Honour have those ties despis'd,
And now are fled, or muſt be sacrific'd.
Unkind *Philander*, had Love fill'd thy breſt
With half those flames thou haſt so oft expreſt,   30
They had consumed in their purer fires
All other thoughts, and thou wou'dſt never mind,
Who were for Kings, and who for Slaves design'd.
Alth.   The noble sense they show of the sad Fate
Of their dear Country, sets a higher rate   35
Upon their Love ; for who that had a grain
Of Honour in him, cou'd endure the Reign
Of proud Usurpers, whose Relentless will,
Is all the Law by which men spare or kill ;
And his true Prince in Banishment behold,   40
Worthy of more than Fortune can with-hold ;
These monſtrous with the crimes of prosperous Fate,
The other shining in his adverse State,
So that each ſtroke of Fortune does but seem
A ſtep for his Heroick mind to climb,   45
Till he has got above her reach, and then
The Vertue she has try'd she'l love agen ?
Though I muſt truly mourn their ill success,
I cou'd not wish *Eugenio* had done less.
Dian.   Had their high Vertue the leaſt doubt
    endur'd,   50
Even with their death it had been cheaply cur'd :
But this brave Aċt is but to me and you,
A dangerous proof of what before we knew.
Alth.   Though their true worth to us before were
    clear,

This Act has made it to the world appear; 55
None ever with that obstinacy lov'd,
But they were pleas'd to see their choice approv'd:
No joy compleat to worthy minds can seem,
Which is not height'ned by the worlds esteem.

    Dian. My heart, *Althea*, does less grieve it
    has 60
Ventur'd it's treasure in so lov'd a cause,
Then that *Philander* did not let me know
The danger he was like to undergo.

    Alth. Sister, though Laws of Decency refuse,
We shining Swords and glittering Armour use; 65
Yet a decision of what's right or wrong,
As well as mens, does to our minds belong;
And we best show it when we most approve
Those men that fight in Quarrels which we love:
Though they of Courage have the ruder part, 70
The Vertue may become a womans heart,
Though not her hand; and she that bravely dares
Expose her Love, sure for her life not cares.
I knew *Eugenio* must that hazard run,
Nor could consent he should the danger shun; 75
And had *Philander* the like thoughts of you,
He without doubt had dealt as freely too.

    Dian. I must confess my love could never yield,
That he agen shou'd win it in the field:
Let me the greatness of your mind admire, 80
Whilst I deplore the greatness of my fire,
A fire which lends no light, but that which serves
To shew how much what I expos'd deserves,
How much he hazards, and how far I am
From vent'ring him for the whole voice of Fame, 85
Whose danger had I known, my Eyes, alas!
Had wept a Sea, he wou'd have fear'd to pass;
But we so long of what is past complain,
As if no further mischief did remain,
As if Fate here had her whole malice spent, 90
And all the Arrows from her Quiver sent.

Alth.   When Fate wou'd harm where Vertue does
     protect,
She does her guilt and impotence detect ;
She can but rob the Vertuous of that rest,
She must restore again with interest,   95
And all the danger of these Heroes past,
Must needs consider their high worth at last.
    Dian.   What we desire, how fain we wou'd believe,
And wish that Fortune knew not to deceive ?
But she profusely to some presents makes,   100
And as unjustly from some others takes.
I fear she's so much to their worth in debt,
She'l nothing pay, because the whole's too great :
Like Tyrants wealth, her Bounties still appear,
Who give to few, what they from many tear.   105
    Alth.   In the mean time I fear our cruel friends
Will not consult our liking, but their ends :
I know they'l press I should *Horatio* wed,
And promise thee unto some Strangers bed.
    Dian.   They may such Matches as they please
     provide,   110
But here I vow, I'le never be a Bride
To any but *Philander*; in that Heart
He taught to love, none else shall have a part.
    Alth.   I the like Vow to my *Eugenio* make,
Which Fates worst malice shan't have power to
     break ;   115
As Trees expos'd to Storms take deeper root,
Than those that do in peaceful Valleys sprout :
So in all Noble minds, a virtuous Love
By opposition does the firmer prove.
    Dian.   'Tis fit, *Althea*, I now take my leave,   120
Whilst you prepare *Horatio* to receive.
    Alth.   Farewel, *Diana*, and be sure you do
Nothing unworthy of your Love and Vow.   [*Ring.*
                    Exeunt Diana *and* Althea *severally.*

ACT II. SCENE I

⟨*Sir Samuel Forecaſt's House.*⟩

Enter Sir Samuel Forecaſt, Althea, Jack Wildish,
and Olivia.

Fore. Daughter, we are much beholding to *Horatio*,
The Portion I can give with you does not deserve a
man of paſt half his Fortune ; Six thousand pounds a
year, an Eſtate well Wooded, and I am told very
improveable, it makes me young again to think   [5
on't : *Eugenio* I never lik't, and as things ſtand now,
am right glad we had no more to do with him ; but
that I am one whose Affeċtion and good will to the
State has sufficiently manifeſted it self, I might be
thought to have a hand in their Design, and so   [10
have been put in the Tower, and had my Fortune
seiz'd on : *Eugenio* shall never call a Child of mine,
Wife, as long as I live.

Wild. But, Sir, your zeal to the Cause has put
you above those apprehensions.   [15

Fore. You say right, Mr. *Wildish*, but we cannot
be in this case too secure ; and I am resolv'd *Althea*,
to take off all suspition, shall out of hand marry with
Horatio.

Alth. Sir, I hope you will allow me some   [20
time to dismiss *Eugenio* from my thoughts.

Wild. And, pray Sir, what prejudice, what Exception have you to *Eugenio* ?

Fore. Originally this only, his Father made a
Purchase of some Land, that lay next hedge to   [25
mine, and gave a thousand pounds more than it was
worth, only to buy it over my head : Think no more
on him upon my blessing, he is not the man he was ;
he had an Eſtate, 'Tis now sequeſter'd, he dare not
show his Head ; and besides, I would not have   [30
a Son-in-Law of his principles, for six times his

fortune; I shou'd be sorry to see any Child of mine
solliciting her Husbands Composition at a Committee.

Alth. Had I once had the relation of a Wife [35
to *Eugenio*, I should have thought nothing a trouble
that had become my Duty, and cou'd as chearfully
have shar'd an honourable Suffering, as the moſt
flourishing condition.

Fore. I charge you never receive visit, or [40
Message from him more, and tell your Siſter *Diana*,
'tis my pleasure she quit all Correspondence with
Philander. They are both dangerous persons. [*Turns
to* Wildish.] These young Wenches, Mr. *Wildish*,
have less Forecaſt than Pigeons, so they be [45
billing, they look no farther; n'ere think of building
their neſts, nor what shall become of their little ones.

Wild. Sir, I think they're i'th' right, let 'um
encrease and multiply, and for the reſt, truſt him
that set 'um a work.   [50

Fore. Mr. *Wildish*, you are a merry Gentleman;
but I'le tell you, Mrs. *Althea*, as I have given you
Life, I'le take care you shan't make it miserable.

Alth. Sir, the happiness of life lies not in wealth,
in Title, or in shew, but in the mind, which is [55
not to be forc'd; and we are not the less Slaves for
being bound in Chains of Gold: A marriage with
Horatio may make me appear happy to the envious
world, but like those deſtructive Arts, which, while
they seem to aid, consume our native Beauties, [60
indeed muſl prey upon my inward peace.

Fore. I'le warrant you peace within, and without
too; *Horatio* is a well natur'd proper Gentleman, and
one that loves you.

Wild. Now there Sir *Samuel* I'm on your [65
side, for so the Fan be play'd with, the hand kiſt;
in fine, the passion handsomly discharg'd, 'tis no
great matter who does it. As Children cry after
their old Nurses, but 'till they are acquainted with

their new : so young Ladies regret the loss of one [70
Servant, but till they have got the same familiarity
with another; which, by the way, is seldom long
firſt.

Enter a Servant.

Serv. Sir, there's a man out of *Pater-Noſter Row*
with Stuffs. [75
Fore. Bid him carry 'um into the next Room.
Come *Althea*, let's in and look upon 'um.

[*Ex.* Althea, *and Sir* Samuel.

Manent Wildish *and* Olivia.

Oliv. We Women are ever sure of your good word,
Mr. *Wildish*; when you have a Miſtress, I hope
she'le deserve it from you in particular, and [80
have in perfeƈtion all those good qualities you so
liberally beſtow upon the whole Sex, in your
Discourse.

Wild. Why, Madam, I thought you had underſtood Raillery; faith I have so good an opinion [85
of the Sex I am asham'd to own it but to one of them
in private; this is only the way of talking I have
got among my Companions, where when we meet
over a Bottle of Wine, 'tis held as great a part of wit
to rallee women handsomly behind their back, [90
as to flatter 'um to their Faces.

Oliv. But why do you make us poor women the
subjeƈt of your mirth ?

Wild. You are grown of late so uncharitable, and
villainous hard-hearted, are incompass'd with so [95
many difficulties, as decency, honour, and reputation,
that we men that love our pleasure, begin to hate you
worse than Beggars do a Coach with the Glasses
drawn up, despair of Relief, and fall a Railing.

Oliv. And if some kind-hearted wretch do [100
chance to relieve one of you, like Beggars you tell it
presently, and send more; I warrant y'are fine Fellows,

a woman is well helpt up, that has one of you to her Servant.

Wild. Nay don't put me in among 'um, I [105 am a meer Apostate, though not resolute enough to endure the Martyrdoms of being continually laught at by half a score of 'um: all that I have done of late, has been meer compliance, as Papists go to Church for fear of the penalty. [110

Oliv. Pray, Sir, to what fair Saint do we owe your Conversion?

Wild. Faith there are many in the World now wou'd make you guess this half hour, telling you first the colour of her hair, her age, her Country, [115 and perhaps the first Letter of her name; But I hate that way of fooling—'tis your self—whom I love.

Oliv. Impudent fellow! don't you expect I shou'd forbid you the house, or at least, for punishment of such rudeness, condemn your guilty [120 passion to eternal silence and despair? what! men have liv'd years in Desarts for their Mistresses sake, and yet have trembled when they spoke of love; which you venture at with as little Ceremony, as you'd ask me how I slept last night. [125

Wild. I know not what Romances order in this case, I n'ere thought it would be mine, and so ha'n't much study'd it; but prithee don't baulk a young Beginner; 'tis my first fault, and so been't too severe, I shall relapse else beyond Redemption. [130

Oliv. Well, I'm content for once your ignorance shou'd plead your pardon.

Wild. Nay Mrs. *Olivia* consider me a little further; I have lost the pleasures of mirth, of Wine, and Company; all things that were before [135 delightful to me, are no longer so; my Life is grown but one continu'd Thought of your fair self: and is a pardon all that I must hope for?

Oliv. Come, leave your fooling, your old humour does better with you, a thousand times, then [140 this whining Love. As there are some Perfumes so strong, that they lose that name with most: So Complements may be so gross, that they become injurious.

Wild. Why here's it now; there are so many cheats in this Trade of Love too, that like [145 Beggars, the true go unreliev'd, because we meet with now and then a counterfeit: on my life Mrs. *Olivia* the plenty I have ever liv'd in, puts me as much out of countenance to ask a Charity of this kind, as I cou'd be, should Fortune constrain [150 me, to intreat one of the other; and wou'd not trouble you, cou'd my pain admit redress from any but your self.

Oliv. Sure, Mr. *Wildish*, you wou'd think I had an excellent opinion of my self, or an implicite [155 Faith in whatever you say, shou'd I believe all this now.

Wild. If I told a Chirurgion, I had broke my leg, do you think he wou'd not take my word?

Oliv. Yes sure.

Wild. Why shou'd not you take it then for a [160 wounded Heart? they are neither of 'um matters to brag on; and I wou'd no more lead the life of a Lover if I were free, then I wou'd that of a sick man if I were well.

Oliv. Methinks the sick men, as you call [165 'um, live so like the well, as one can scarce know one from th'other.

Wild. In your Chamber, perhaps; but abroad we find a thousand differences.

Oliv. As how, I pray? [170

Wild. Why, your true Lover leaves all Company when the Sport begins, the Table when the Bottles are call'd for, the Gaming-house when the Cards come up; is more afraid of an Engagement, than a Lawyer in Term-time; wou'd less miss the last Act of a [175 Play, the Park, or indeed any abominable old Ladies, where he may hope to see the party, then a young

Wench can *Grayes-Inn*-walks, the firſt Sunday of her new Gown.

Oliv. What, is this all ?   [180

Wild. Not half : ask him to sup, he has business ; or if he promise, 'tis ten to one he fails, and if he sees his Miſtress, is so transported, that he forgets to send his Excuse ; if he cannot find her, and so chance to keep his word, sits in such dismal [185 Dumps, that he spoils the whole Company.

Oliv. And will you be such an Animal for my sake ?

Wild. Faith I'm afraid so, but if not well us'd, I shall find the way home again.   [190

Oliv. Whatever you think, Sir, I shall contribute no more to the keeping you my Servant, then I did to the making you so.

Wild. Well, do but use as proper means to keep me your Servant, as you have done to make me [195 so, and I am satisfied.

Oliv. Why, what means ?

Wild. As your Beauty bred my Affeċtion, so let your kindness nourish it.

Oliv. Mr. *Wildish*, you have been so [200 pleasant upon this new Argument, that I had almoſt forgot my Visit to *Diana*.

Wild. I'm upon equal terms with you there ; for I have made *Ned Eſtridge* and *Harry Modish* ſtay this half hour for me at the French House : and so [205 your Servant.   [*Exeunt.*

SCENE II. ⟨*Althea's Chamber.*⟩

Enter Althea.

Alth. Under what Tyranny are Women born !
Here we are bid to love, and there to scorn ;
As if unfit to be allow'd a part
In choosing him, that muſt have all our heart ;

Or that our liking, like a head-strong beast,   5
Were made for nothing, but to be opprest;
And below them, in this regard we are,
We may not flye the cruelty we fear.
The Horse may shake the Rider from his back,
The Dog his hated Master may forsake;   10
Yet nothing of their native worth impair,
Nor any conscious sting about them bear.
But if a Virgin an Escape contrive,
She must for ever in dishonour live,
Condemn'd within her self, despis'd of all,   15
Into worse mischiefs then she fled from, fall.
Duty commands I shou'd *Horatio* wed,
Love does as strongly for *Eugenio* plead;
My mind, distracted thus, a storm abides
Like Seas, when winds blow full against their
    Tides.   20

Enter Horatio.

  Hora. Madam, methinks you look not pleas'd;
    I fear
My hapless passion did too late appear
For my content; and only now can prove
The wretched Triumph of some elder Love.
But, fair *Althea*, you were much to blame   25
With your own breath to blow a hopeless flame.
Ah! had you to its Childhood been severe,
As now to its full growth you cruel are,
'Thad dy'd with half that pain it now must bear:
Young Plants with ease up by the Roots we tear;   30
But when well grown, the Ax must be imploy'd,
And they with force and labour are destroy'd.
  Alth. Generous *Horatio*, forbear to blame
Me, as the cruel Author of your pain.
How cou'd I know that you my Lover were,   35
Until your self your passion did declare?
How had it look'd in me to have complain'd
Of thoughts, perhaps, you never entertain'd?

How could I check, alas, those hopes in you,
Your Heart did never harbour, that I knew?   40
   Hora. Not know, *Althea*! why shou'd the same
     eyes
So slowly see, so suddenly surprize?
The very minute I beheld your face,
You might in mine my growing passion trace.
Now trembling fear did her pale colour spred,   45
Then springing hope brought back the native red:
Joy may be seen, and grief it self unfold,
And so may love, though it be never told.
In every look my passion was confest,
And every action my high flame exprest.   50
As foolish Witnesses their Cause o'rethrow,
My Arts to hide it, did it clearer show.
   Alth. But as fond Parents will not seem to know
A fault they needs must punish when they do;
So I at first was loth to see a crime   55
In one, I otherwise did so esteem:
For know, *Horatio*, setting Love apart,
None then your self is deeper in my Heart;
Your worth and honour I can value, though
I no requital to your flame allow.   60
   Hora. You can give all things else above their due,
And yet wrong that which most belongs to you:
Madam, these words, sooth with a cruel art
Where I less feel, and wound a mortal part;
With friendship and esteem you strive in vain,   65
Kind Maid, to ease a Lover of his pain:
For where your Beauty once has rais'd a flame,
To offer less, and nothing, are the same.
Love and Ambition of their aim deny'd,
No other way can e're be satisfi'd.   70
   Alth. You that cou'd faithless to *Victoria* prove,
Methinks shou'd blush even at the name of Love.
Her numerous Charms your loud accusers are,
And call *Horatio* false, as she is fair.
   Hora. You shou'd with pity, not displeasure see 75

The change that your own self creates in me.
The Roman Senate had their greatness worn
Perhaps till now, had *Cæsar* n'er been born.
Darius self cou'd not his Persians blame,
Because that *Alexander* overcame.   80
In Love like War, some Victor still there grows,
Whose spreading Empire nothing can oppose.
　　Alth.　Countries are fix'd, and cannot flye, although
They apprehend a certain overthrow.
Lovers, the force they can't oppose, might shun,   85
And may with safety and with honour run.
Who then would pity him that stays to dye,
When Vertue and his Duty bid him flye?
　　Hora.　*Althea*, in Loves wars all Heroes are,
Death does less terrible than flight appear;   90
As Gamesters, when they lose, still deeper set,
Helping ill Fortune to encrease their debt:
So Lovers, when a Nymph gets half their heart,
Themselves, alas, betray the other part.
　　Alth.　*Victoria's* wrongs my gratitude deter;   95
Your gifts to me are robberies from her.
　　Hora.　I came at first, *Althea*, 'tis most true
With Love to her, and but Respect to you.
But, ah! how soon within my tortur'd brest
You of each others places are possest!   100
　　Alth.　Beauty, the wrongs of Beauty shou'd revenge,
And the fair punish, when the faithless change.
　　Hora.　I change *Althea*, but (as pious men
Become blest Saints) never to change agen.
If none your matchless Beauty must adore,   105
But such alone as never lov'd before,
You do unjustly, and too high advance
In Love th'already too great power of chance:
Since that you shou'd their first affection be,
Let's you their Fortune, not their passion see.   110
　　Alth.　It lets me see they falshood never knew.
And gives me leave to hope they will be true.
　　Hora.　Sure none can faithless to such Beauty prove;

He that's in Heaven, can no higher move.
 Alth. A Lovers Heaven in his Phansie lyes, 115
Which Beauty oft neglects, and oft supplies.
 Hora. 'Tis not, *Althea*, that you question mine,
But 'tis *Eugenio*'s faith does brighter shine;
'Tis he that makes *Victoria*'s wrong your pain,
My Love a Crime, a Vertue your disdain. 120
These tales of falshood, and of former Love,
Reproaches only, where we like not, prove.
 Alth. *Horatio*, I am glad your dis-respect
Has turn'd so soon to Justice my neglect:
You that reproach me with a former Love, 125
Your self unfit but for my anger prove. [*Exit Althea.*
 Hora. O stay a while! sure you must joy to see
The torture you're so pleas'd to work in me;
Not that I hope I shall your pity find,
But that the fight may glut your cruel mind. 130
Nature inconstant to her own designs,
To a fair form a cruel temper joyns;
She makes the heedless Lover kneel in vain,
And in Loves Temple, to adore Disdain. 134
        [*Exit Horatio.*

 ⟨SCENE III. *A Street near Widow Brightstone's*
      House.⟩

 Enter Sir Samuel Forecast *and* Jack Wildish.

 Fore. When am I to see your fair and wealthy
Cousin, Mr. *Wildish*?
 Wild. This minute if you please, Sir.
 Fore. I doubt you are not stirring in the business,
You do not lay the necessity of marrying home [5
enough to her: I might have got access ere now else,
and our Counsel have been drawing the Writings.
 Wild. It must be done by degrees: if I shou'd
have been too forward, it might have caus'd in her a
suspicion of my purpose, and so my worthy [10

Friend Sir *Samuel* have come to her upon some prejudice, which I wou'd not for half her Fortune.

Fore. Pray, Mr. *Wildish*, is she so concern'd for
her late Husband as the world talks ?

Wild. Ten times more; looks upon his [15
Picture all day long, as earnestly as if she were to
copy it; since he dy'd, has us'd no Pocket-Handker-
chers, but what was made of his old Shirts, and wets
two a day of 'um with her tears; Because he dy'd on
a Monday, fasts that day of the week; takes [20
none into her Service but *Thomases*, because 'twas his
Christian Name, and has now sent into *Wales* for a
Thomas ap *Thomas* to be her Gentleman-usher.

Fore. 'Tis strange she shou'd so affect his name!
What think you then: if you call'd me Sir [25
Thomas Forecast ?

Wild. Faith, Sir, what you please; but I think it
will be altogether needless, and if she shou'd come
to discover, it might spoil all, s'light, she might
mistrust your particular, if she shou'd find you [30
put a trick upon her in your name.

Fore. Well, I'le be rul'd by you, Mr. *Wildish*,
you know her humour best.

Wild. I can't but think how she'l look upon me
when I talk to her of another Husband; but [35
I'le venture, Sir *Samuel*, to serve you. Come let's
away, her House is here hard by.

> [*They enter the Widows house.*

⟨SCENE IV. *A Room in the Widow's House.*⟩

Wild. I show the way, Sir.
> [*They find her looking upon her Husbands
> Picture, and* ⟨*she*⟩ *does not see 'um.*

Fore. Excellent woman, she sees us not! O the
endless treasure of a virtuous Wife! It extends even
to our memories, and pictures.
> [*Wildish goes up, and speaks to her.*

Wild. Madam, here is Sir *Samuel Forecaſt* [5 come to wait on you.

Wid. Sir, I hope you'le pardon me, if I have let my grief employ any part of that time which was due to my acknowledgment for this favour; you were my Husbands friend, and as such will ever be [10 moſt welcome to me; and though his too scrupulous kindness allow'd me not the acquaintance, scarce the sight of any man; yet I did always place a value where he gave his eſteem, especially, so highly as he did to you. [15

Fore. Madam, I am much bound to you for your good opinion, and come to condole with you: your Husband was an honeſt, prudent, and a wealthy Gentleman, kept good hours, and even reckonings, lov'd me well, and we have drank many a Dish [20 of Coffee together.

Wid. Sir, whilſt you repeat his vertues, you do but count my loss, and telling me how good he was, make me but more sensibly want him.

Fore. He and I were juſt of an age, and when [25 we were Boys, of a ſtrength.

Wid. And what of that, Sir?

Wild. Why, Cousin it makes me think that Sir *Samuel* wou'd make as loving a Husband to you, as your laſt was, and I'le swear it troubles me [30 heartily to see my pretty Coz. here not yet out of danger of smooth-fac't younger Brothers, such as marry Wives only to keep Wenches, and never bring 'um to Town but to pass away some part of their Eſtates. [35

Fore. Some such there are; but Heaven bless the Eſtate, and Widow of my good Friend your Husband out of such hands.

Wi⟨l⟩d. Now I have brought you together, I'le leave you; Cousin, you are not afraid to be left [40 alone with Sir *Samuel*? [*Exit.*

Wid. I know his Vertue, and my own too well.

Fore. Don't you find, Madam, business very troublesome ?

Wid. I do indeed, and have the misfortune [45 to be involv'd in it.

Fore. Have you many Law-suits ?

Wid. But one considerable, which being with a man in power, in these corrupt times, a Woman unfriended and unknown as I am, muft expeft to [50 lose.

Fore. Of what value ?

Wid. Five thousand pounds : I shall have enough left however, to make me happy with a man that loves me. [55

Fore. Enough left ! such another word wou'd make me foreswear, not only thee but thy whole Sex; five thousand pounds well dispos'd, why I tell thee, 'tis able to procure us Judgments on half the young Prodigals of this Age; thou and I might live [60 comfortably on the forbearance money, and let the Intereft run on.

Wid. I did but put the worft, not that I doubt my title, if I have common Juftice.

Fore. No, thou shalt secure thy Title, I am a [65 near Kinsman to the Judge, and a by-way to his favour.

Wid. How do you mean ?

Fore. Why I have many times bought a thousand Pounds worth of other mens Lands of him for [70 a hundred.

Wid. I wou'd not corrupt Juftice for a world.

Fore. What agen Widow ? nay then I perceive thou do'ft it on purpose to lose my heart : but to say truth, it were unreasonable to expeft thy tender [75 years shou'd underftand the true worth of money, so far, that for its sake to trample on those unprofitable and foolish principles the honourable Beggars of former times Govern'd their lives by : But thou wilt one day know, that Age hath its beauties too, as well as [80 youth, and more universally ador'd.

Wid. Gravity and Wisdom, Sir, I know men may expect, but our Sex has no pretence to them.

Fore. No, wealth and power, Widow, which awe the grave and wise; Gold and Silver are the best [85 red and white; the other, every Milk-Maid may boast equal with a Countess.

Enter Sir John Everyoung, Modish, *and* Estridge, *with Fiddles playing.*

Wid. What rude fellow's that?

Ever. Hold, let's parlee first. [*To the Musick.*] Faith, Widow, one that loves you but too well. [90

Wid. Love me! upon what acquaintance? I n'ere saw your face before in my days.

Ever. And do'st thou like it now?

Wid. Not so well as your self, you may be confident. [95

Ever. All this shan't cross my honest purpose, I came in meer charity to prevent thy ruine; and if thou be'st not lost to all sence and reason, nay, even all natural appetite, I'le do't.

Wid. I know no ruine neer, this is the [100 worst accident has befaln me a good while.

Ever. Hear me but out, and thou shalt bless it; canst thou be such a Traytor to flesh and blood, as to count it nothing to be join'd to that old Trunk there? if he encrease or multiply, it must be [105 thy Bags; Interest, and Broakage are his best instruments.

Wid. You don't consider that all this might be as well apply'd to your sweet self.

Ever. Yes, most properly, why 'tis that [110 makes me hate Matrimony, and puts me at distance with, To have and to hold; I confess my Tick is not good, and I never desire to Game for more than I have about me. Now second me.

Mod. The minute you marry, Widow, you [115 are not worth a Groat, all is your Husbands; and if hereafter you shall come to a sence of your unequal choice, and endeavour to repair it in some young and worthy friend; the old Gentlemen takes pet, turns you over to a tedious sute for Alimony, which [120 your Friend furnishes you with money to follow, for a while, and in time grows weary of it himself.

Estr. Then like an old Gamester, that has lost all he has upon the square, your only way is to turn Rook and play upon advantage. [125

Wid. Why, do you know these Gentlemen?

Fore. I, to my shame, the Ring-leader of 'um is my Brother, there is no remedy but patience.

Wid. Gentlemen, you talk at a strange rate for the first time; but whom ever I marry my [130 vertue will secure him of my constancy.

Mod. Pray Madam, don't prophane that honourable Name; 'tis meer obstinacy to an old man, a fault methinks you have too ingenious a Countenance to be guilty of. [135

Ever. If thou should'st be so improvident, as to neglect the comfort of a Gallant, thou'lt never 'scape the scandal, having such a Husband.

Mod. If you are precise, Madam, they'le give you your Chaplain; if you love business, your [140 Lawyer; if you keep a Gentleman-Usher, you are undone.

Estr. If you take some honest Gentleman (which by my troth I think is your best Course) upon the first hard journey, as the world goes now, 'tis [145 ten to one he falls lame of an old bruise.

Wid. You are very tender of my credit, if you had been as careful, Gentlemen, of your own Sobriety, I fear I had mist all this good Counsel.

Ever. O! are you edified? it is good [150 counsel then: and for the warmth that ripen'd us to this care of thee, be thankful, and enquire no further. But Brother, methinks you are over-serious for a man that comes a Sutering.

Wid. He does not find your mirth take [155 so well.

Enter Wildish *apart.*

Wild. S'light here's Sir *John Everyoung*, he'le spoil all, if I don't take him off instantly.

[Wild. *goes out, and brings in three of the Widows Maids.*

Fore. Brother, Brother, these frolicks do you no right in the eye of the World. [160

Ever. Hang the world, give me the pretty black-eye of the Widdow. [*A Song.*

Wild. Gentlemen, here's work for you.

Ever. A muss, a muss! You see, *Wildish*, we found the House, though you wou'd not tell [165 us where it was, 'tis dangerous to give a hint to men of our parts. Brother, take your Widdow, show her that you are so far qualified towards a Bridegroom, as to lead a Country Dance.

Widd. I'le have no dancing in my House. [170

Fore. You see they are a little merry, humer 'um in this, they'le be gone the sooner.

Wid. Well, Sir *Samuel Forecast*, any thing to serve you. [*They Dance, and* Forecast *steals away.*

Mod. Sir *Samuel* gone? [175

Ever. Faith then the sport's at the best, let's all be gone: Farewel Widow, I have done my part, if thou fallest now, say thou hadst fair warning.

[*Ex. omnes.*

ACT III. SCENE I

⟨*The Lodgings of Eugenio and Philander.*⟩

Enter Eugenio, *and* Philander.

Eug. Dear friend, I am in doubt whether I shall This scape, a blessing, or misfortune, call;

Since now I live to hear, *Althea* muſt
Be to her Duty, or to me unjuſt.
Ye Powers that were so kind, my life to spare,   5
Oh why was not my Love as much your care ?
You sav'd my life, that I might live to feel
Despair can wound as mortally as Steel.
My cause till now my antidote has been,
'Gainſt all the mischief it cou'd plunge me in ;   10
The ſtricteſt Prison, I have freedom thought,
And been on Scaffolds without terrour brought.
But these few words (*Althea* is a Bride)
More wound my Soul, than can the world beside.

    Phil.   Why does *Eugenio* Fancies entertain,   15
That are *Althea*'s wrongs, and his own pain ?
Like Boys, who in the dark, ſtrange shapes create
In their own brain, themselves to tremble at :
Despair's the portion of the damn'd below,
And in a generous mind shou'd never grow ;   20
Truſt to *Althea*'s virtue, truſt her love,
And you will safe in either of 'um prove.

    Eug.   But sure no friend cou'd so my quiet hate,
As this Report, of nothing, to create.

    Phil.   Perhaps her Father does no less intend,   25
And she, a while, her Answer may suspend.
Not that her vertue doubts, what it shall do,
But that she may gain time to speak with you :
Every black Cloud does not with Thunder swell,
Nor every symptom a Disease foretell.   30
Some ſtorms blow over ; though thy Fate appear
Thus gloomy now, anon it may be clear.

    Eug.   It may, but who can unconcerned be,
A Tempeſt heard, and his whole wealth at Sea ?
I with more ease all other harms cou'd bear,   35
Than of *Althea*'s loss but simply hear.

    Phil.   All that we hear, we are not to believe.

    Eug.   Our hopes do oftner, than our fears deceive.

    Phil.   The advantage man o're Beaſts in Reason
      gets

He pays with interest in fond conceits ;   40
They cannot fear misfortune till it fall,
And when 'tis gone remember't not at all :
But man 'gainst his own Rest in Battel plac'd,
Feels mischiefs e're they come, and when they're past.
The smiles of Fortune you so false have found,   45
Methinks, you shou'd not mind her when she frown'd :
How wou'd *Althea*'s Vertues grieve to find
Themselves suspected in *Eugenio*'s mind !
Like Princes murder'd on the Royal Throne,
Where   'till   that   minute   they   had   brightest
   shone.   50
   Eug.   Sure my *Althea* cannot disapprove
These fears that spring but from excess of love.
Of love and courage none too much can share.
   Phil.   But 'tis their use, that does their worth
   declare :
Courage, when brutal, ceases to be brave,   55
And love, grown jealous, can no merit have.
   Eug.   A higher mark of love there cannot be,
We doubt no Lover, whom we jealous see.
   Phil.   So Fevers are of life sure proofs we know,
And yet our lives they often overthrow ;   60
Diseases, though well cur'd, our bodies mar,
And fears, although remov'd, our loves impair :
True love, like health, should no disorder know.
   Eug.   But who, alas ! such love, or health can show ?
Our passions, like our selves, are fram'd to dye,   65
And have still something they must perish by ;
We none (brave friend) for being hapless blame,
But all allow, 'tis baseness to be tame ;
He that has rais'd this Tempest in my mind,
Shall in the Billows his own ruine find ;   70
I'le fight him instantly, and make him know,
I am not more his Rival than his Foe.
   Phil.   Thy life, alas (dear friend) 's no longer thine,
Thou hast engag'd it in a brave design :
Thy bleeding Country, and thy Princes Right,   75

Are th' only Quarrels that thy Sword shou'd fight,
If you into the Tyrant's hands shou'd fall,
Twou'd pull a sudden ruine on us all.
Which, if you ftir, we may have cause to fear,
Since Tyrants Eyes and Hands are every where.   80
   Eug.   Now thou haft touch'd me in the tendreft
     part,
Though Love possess, Honour muft rule my heart;
My Nation's Fate's too great a Sacrifice
For me to make, though to *Althea*'s Eyes;
No, I am calm'd, and happy am to have   85
A friend so full of temper when I rave,
And hope the gods, whilft I my own negleft,
To fight their Quarrel, will my Love proteft.   88
                         [*Exeunt.*

SCENE II.   ⟨*A Room in Sir John Everyoung's
House.*⟩

Enter Viftoria *and* Olivia.

   Vift.   Sifter, I doubt we are a little too free with
our servants, this *Modish*, and his friend *Eftridge* : few
Plays gain Audience by being in Print, and fewer
women get Husbands by being too much known.
   Oliv.   But ours are moft accomplish'd Moun-   [5
sieurs, muft be assaulted on all parts e're they'le
yield; muft have their Ears charm'd as well as Eyes:
'Twere ill husbandry in a Mercer to be thrifty in his
Patterns, it often disparages a good ftuff; and too
great reserv'dness in one of us, especially at the   [10
firft, might give a discouragement to our further
Acquaintance.
   Vift.   Now might I have my wish, I wou'd come
all new, nay my voice and name shou'd not be known;
where I wou'd be lik'd, I wou'd have the few   [15
Charms I am Miftress of, make their Assault at an
inftant, all at one time:

For sure *Horatio* did their power subdue,
By conquering one, e're he another knew.

Oliv.   Fye Sister, think no more of him; but   [20
to the matter in hand, who ever caught any thing
with a naked hook? nothing venture, nothing win,
and for my part I am resolv'd to allow all innocent
liberty; this Matrimony is a Pill will scarce down
with a young man without guilding; let   [25
Estridge believe I am in love with him, and when he
leaves me, he'll find I am not.

Enter to them Wildish.

Wild.   So he will, when he marrys you, or I am
deceiv'd, Madam.

Vict.   What, turn'd Eaves-Dropper, Mr.   [30
Wildish?

Wild.   No Ladys, but your heads are so taken up
with these Heirs Apparent, that you can't see a
younger Brother when he comes into the Room.

Oliv.   Not when our backs are towards him,   [35
but otherwise as an elder, any where, but before a
Parson.

Wild.   You are in the right; Jointure, and allow-
ance for Cloaths, have clearly got the better ⟨of us⟩:
Dear Madam, I consider not your Portion, but   [40
your Person; give your Estate where you please,
so you will but settle your affection upon me, my
Fate depends upon your Answer; and the like
Artillery of unlanded Lovers: But I never repine
at that; for fine Women, like great Tables,   [45
though they are maintain'd by men of Fortunes, are
ever open to men of parts.

Oliv.   Why now, *Wildish*, you talk like your self
again; ever since I saw you last, I have been in most
terrible apprehension of a whining Copy of   [50
Verses.

Wild.   Expectation you mean, Madam, but 'tis
not come to that yet; though I talk a little Extrava-

gantly when I see you, I am not so Through pac't a
Lover, but I can express my self in Prose. [55

Vict. But you, being a new Convert, can't give
too many marks of your Devotion: and I shou'd
mistrust I were not as I ought to be in my Servants
heart, if I did not run sometimes in his head, and then
Verses follow infallibly. [60

Wild. Faith, Madam, that's much as the head
lyes, there are some you may search every cranny
over, and not find three Rimes; very good Lovers
too; and to say truth, 'tis unreasonable a man shou'd
be put to seek fresh words to express that to his [65
Mistress, which has been as well said already by some
body else; I think 'tis very fair if he set his hand
to't, and that I am ready to do to the most passionate
Copy of Verses you can find.

Oliv. How much Love and Constancy will [70
you engage for then?

Wild. As much as you can find in that Paper
there.

He gives a Paper to Olivia, *she gives it
to* Victoria.

Oliv. Sister, here read 'um, I shall put the Accent
in the wrong place, stop out of time, or one [75
mischief or other, and so put my poor Servant into an
Agony.

Vict. To a very young Lady. [*Reads the Title.*

Oliv. That's I, *Wildish*: come, you have been
dabling; proceed, Sister, I fear 'um not, I have [80
no more pity on a Rhyming Lover, than on a Beggar
that begs in a Tone.

Vict. Are not these Verses somewhat too weak
to ⟨stand⟩ allone?

Wild. Faith, Madam, I am of your mind, [85
put a Tune to 'um, 'tis an easie Stanza.

Victoria *sings.*

Ah Cloris ! *that I now could sit*
   As unconcern'd, as when
Your Infant Beauty cou'd beget
   No pleasure, nor no pain.   90

2.

When I the Dawn us'd to admire,
   And prais'd the coming day;
I little thought the growing fire
   Must take my Rest away.

3.

Your Charms in harmless Childhood lay,   95
   Like metals in the mine,
Age from no face took more away,
   Then Youth conceal'd in thine.

4.

But as your Charms insensibly
   To their perfection prest,   100
Fond Love as unperceiv'd did flye,
   And in my Bosom rest.

5.

My passion with your Beauty grew,
   And Cupid *at my heart,*
Still as his mother favour'd you,   105
   Threw a new flaming Dart.

6.

Each glori'd in their wanton part,
   To make a Lover he
Employ'd the utmost of his Art,
   To make a Beauty she.   110

7.

Though now I slowly bend to love
   Uncertain of my Fate,

If your fair self my Chains approve,
I shall my freedom hate.

8.

Lovers, like dying men, may well　　　　115
At first disorder'd be,
Since none alive can truly tell
What Fortune they must see.

Enter a Servant.

Serv. There's an old Gentleman below in a Chair enquires for Mr. *Wildish*, as fine as an Em-　[120 perour, my Master Sir *John* is no body to him; as he peep'd through the glass, I thought it was Sir *Samuel Forecast.*

Vict. It is impossible it shou'd be he.

Wild. Yes faith it is Ladies, I am privy to　[125 the plot.

Oliv. Good Mr. *Wildish* bring him up, I wou'd give any thing to see him.

Wild. Do you step into that Closet then; for I must swear the Coast is clear: set the door a　[130 little open, and you may see him perfectly, his Bravery on my word is not design'd for this place, and he is so politick, that he will think your seeing him may be a prejudice to his design.

Wildish *goes out, and brings in Sir*
Samuel Forecast.

Wild. Sir *Samuel*, now you shine indeed;　[135 my Cousin will be ravish'd to see you transform your self thus for her sake.

Fore. She is a tender piece, and though her discretion helps her to conceal it, in her heart cannot but love a little Bravery; I have two Laces in　[140 a Seam more than my Brother *Everyoung*, and a Yard more in my Cravat.

Wild. Nay, you are most exact, and in this dress methinks not unlike Sir *John*.

Fore. I came only to show my self to you,   [145
and am for my Widow presently; shall I have your
Company ?

Wild. I have a little business here, but I'le be
with you by that time you are there, I see you came
in a Chair.   [150

Fore. Do you think I had a mind to have the Boys
follow me in the ſtreets ? pray be secret, Mr. *Wildish*,
for I wou'd have no body know I am in this Dress,
but your self, and your fair Cousin, for a world : and
therefore I will make haſte from hence, do you   [155
follow me according to your promise.   [*Exit.*

Wild. I shall, Sir *Samuel.*

Oliv. I never saw a City-Bridegroom ſo friz'd,
so lac'd, so perfum'd, and so powder'd in my life.

Vict. I think verily he was painted too, I   [160
vow I shou'd not have known his Worship, if you had
not given us a hint of his Bravery before.

Wild. Well, I muſt recover my old Knight :
Farewel Ladies.

Oliv. Pray be here anon, and give us an   [165
account of this Adventure.

Vict. Certainly it muſt be very pleasant.

Wild. I shall obey you, Ladies.   [*Exit* Wildish.

Enter Everyoung, Victoria, *and* Olivia *laughing.*

Ever. Hey-day ! what, are the Girls mad ?

Vict. No, Sir, but I think my Uncle *Fore-*   [170
caſt's little better.

Ever. Why, what of him ?

Oliv. He is, Sir, at this time the greateſt Spark
in *London*, dreſt so like you, that if his condition
requir'd it, I shou'd think, Sir, he were going   [175
to a Scrivener to personate you for a good Sum.

Ever. Well, I'le handsel his new Cloaths, and put
him as much out of conceit with Bravery as ever he
was in his life.   Boy, call in the three Prentices were
brought before me for breaking Windows laſt   [180
night.

Enter three Prentices.

I suppose, young men, you wou'd not scruple at a small piece of service to the man that shou'd procure your Liberties.

Omn. Free us, and command us any thing. [185

Ever. Well then follow me, and when I show you a certain Chair, take the Gentleman out of it, and cudgel him; I'le be at a little Diſtance, and if you want help, be ready to assiſt you: be sure you call him Sir *John Everyoung*, and tell him of a [190 Lady he affronted.

1 *Pren.* We shall call him what you please, Sir, and beat him as much as you please.

Exit Victoria *and* Olivia.

⟨SCENE III. *A Street.*⟩

Forecaſt *coming by in his Chair.*

Ever. That's the Chair.

They take out Forecaſt, *and cudgel him.*

Fore. If you have humanity, if you had Women to your Mothers, be more merciful, Gentlemen, I never injur'd you, nor saw any of you in my life.

Pren. I perceive, Sir *John Everyoung*, you [5 have forgot the affront you did a Lady laſt night.

Fore. What affront, Sir, what Lady?

Pren. The affront, Sir, was a great affront, and the Lady, a great Lady, that thinks fit to have you beaten for't. [10

Fore. You miſtake, Gentlemen, you miſtake; for as I am a true Servant to the State, I never did kindness or injury to any Lady since I was in Commission.

2 *Pren.* A true Servant to the State, and a man in Authority! he shall have three kicks more for [15 that.

Enter Estridge *and* Modish.

Estr. What, three upon one! who e're he be, the Cause becomes a Gentleman: Let's rescue him at all adventures.

They draw, the Prentices run away.

Fore. Estridge *and* Modish! nay then I am [20 utterly undone, I have only scap'd a little more beating, to be laught at as long as I live.

Estr. Sir, we are very happy that our occasions led us this way, since it has given us an Opportunity of serving a Gentleman, especially oppress'd by [25 odds.

Fore. I shall take some other time, if you will let me know where to wait on you, to give you thanks for this your seasonable Assistance: now, Gentlemen, my hurts require a Chirurgion. [30

He offers to go away.

Mod. Nay, Sir, take your Hat and Sword along with you; there they be. [*He looks a little for 'um.*] I never heard any man speak so like Sir *Samuel Forecast* in my life.

Estr. But he is drest very like *Everyoung*, [35 a meer medly between the two Brothers; But we'l see who he is before we go.

Mod. Have you receiv'd any hurt in your Face, that you cover it with your Handkercher?

Fore. A slight one only. [40

Estr. I have Sympathy-powder about me, if you will give me your handkercher while the blood is warm, will cure it immediately.

Modish snatches it off, and discovers him.

Estr. Sir *Samuel Forecast*, why do you hide your self thus from your friends? we expected [45 nothing for our pains, neither is your hurt so dangerous, but it might endure the Air.

Mod. Methinks you shou'd rather have hid your self from your Enemies: but, Sir *Samuel*, whatever

the matter is, I never saw a man so fine in all my [50
life.

Fore. Now the Broakers take all fine Cloaths,
and the Gaol all that Love 'um; they have helpt me
to fine beating.

Estr. Why do you think the Rogues wou'd [55
have had more mercy on your high crown'd Hat,
Black Cap, and Boots.

Fore. No, but they took me for my Brother
Everyoung, who it seems, has lately affronted a Lady
and I suffer for it.   [60

Mod. The best advice we can give you, is to go
home and shift, for fear of more mishaps.

Estr. Farewel, Sir *Samuel.*   [*Exeunt omnes.*

ACT IV

SCENE I. *The Mulberry-Garden.*

Enter Jack Wildish.

Wild. I was to blame no earlier to use my self to
these Women of Honour, as they call 'um; for now
like one that never practis'd swimming, upon the
first occasion I am lost; there are men would have
fool'd with *Olivia*, and fool'd her too, perhaps [5
by this time, without ever ingaging in one serious
thought: your good Fencer always thrusts in Guard,
he's but a Novice that receives hit for hit: this *Modish*
and *Estridge*, I know not what to make of their continual Visits, Methinks Love and Jealousie [10
come too quick upon a man in one day. [*Enter*
Modish *and* Estridge.] Here come the men, they are
open enough to let me know all at large; but I wou'd
fain contrive it, that the Ladies might be witnesses
of their Servants most invincible secrecy: I'le [15
steal off e're I am seen, and think on't.

Enter Victoria *and* Olivia, *as he goes
out he meets 'um.*

Wild.   Slip into that Arbour, Ladies, and trust me
for once for a quarter of an hours diversion.

Oliv.   Pray, Sister, let us go, he has somewhat in
his head, I'm confident.   [20

> *He puts them into an Arbour, and meets*
> Modish *in a Walk.*

Wild.   Your Servant, *Modish.*

Mod.   O your Servant!

Estr.   Your Servant, Mr. *Wildish.*

Wild.   What, is there store of Game here, Gentlemen?   [25

Mod.   Troth little, or none, a few citizens that
have brought their Children out to air 'um, and eat
Cheese-cakes.

Wild.   I thought this place had been so full of
Beauties, that like a Pack of Hounds in a Hare-   [30
Warren, you cou'd not hunt one for another: what
think you of an Arbour and a Bottle of Rhenish.

> Wildish *brings 'um to the next Arbour to
> the Ladies.*

Estr.   I like the motion well.

Wild.   And how go the Ladies? will they go
abroad alone? are they come to kissing yet?   [35

Estr.   What Ladies?

Wild.   Why, Sir *Johns* Daughters, the Ladies.

Mod.   You are merry, Mr. *Wildish.*

Wild.   I should be so indeed, if it were with me as
it is with you, Gentlemen, that have two such   [40
fine Women in love with you, and every Night sitting
up together till morning.

Mod.   I go only to entertain *Victoria* in meer Friendship to *Ned Estridge*; 'tis he that is the happy man.

Estr.   'Tis a part of friendship that you dis-   [45
charge very willingly, and very effectually, for sometimes we see neither of you in an hour; and then

you return exclaiming againſt the Heat of the weather, and cruelty of your Miſtress.

Wild. What, that she kept him a little too [50 hard to't, or so ?

Mod. Fye, *Wildish*, they are women of honour.

Wild. Well, here's their health, to make 'um amends ; and, faith they lose none with me, in being Civil to an honeſt Gentleman, 'tis the only [55 Wealth is left poor women to exercise their good nature with : A friend at Court may get you a place, a General of an Army give you an Employment, a Bishop a Church-Living, and a fair Lady a good turn ; every one in their way, and I hold him [60 ungrateful that burys an obligation of any sort in silence : besides 'twere meer robbery to your friends, not to let um rejoice in your good fortune.

Mod. But say I have made a vow to the contrary ; not that there is, or ever was, any such good [65 Fortune ; and womens favours, like the gifts of Fairies, if once spoke of, vanish.

Wild. O your Servant, what say you *Eſtridge* ? are you under a vow too, or are the favours you have receiv'd, yet, only such as the hope of further [70 obliges you to secrecy for a while ? but you are so serious, I doubt you intend to commit matrimony.

Eſtr. Not as long as I can have simple forni- cation for love or money : I am not for those Ladies that deal by whole-sail, a bit off the Spit serves [75 my turn as well as the whole Joint, and methinks has a prettier relish.

Wild. That is, metaphorically saying, you have sped with your Mrs.—my service [*Drinks to him*] to you, remembring the Bit off the Spit ; and [80 how, is she buxam ? does she think happiness con- siſts in motion, or in reſt ? what Seƈt of Philosophers is she of ?

Eſtr. A *Pythagorean* ; I, Sir, in all these cases say nothing. [85

Wild. Nay, you had as good speak out now, and make me your confident.

Modish *takes* Estridge *aside.*

Mod. *Jack Wildish* is an honest fellow, 'tis not a Pins matter what we say to him; and they are two of the prettiest women in Town : it sounds [90 handsomly, to boast some familiarity, you understand me : he knows 'um not, and will never find us out; I'le begin with him——I wonder, *Wildish,* we could never get you along with us ; the Ladies have not vow'd virginity, they are no such Bugbears [95 as you take 'um for.

Wild. I take 'um for honest women, or which is e'ne as bad, pretenders to it.

Estr. There is no harm in pretending to it, that like a high price, only serves to keep off ill [100 Company.

Wild. Yes, yes, I know what kind of cattel they are, well enough, there's no having a simple Kiss amongst 'um without a journey into the Country ; nor getting 'um abroad without a Sister, or a [105 Cousin at least, and then they must beat Home too by ten a Clock, have the Syllabubs, and Tarts, brought into the Coach to 'um ; drink more Sugar than wine, and so foul all the Glasses, put you to four or five pound charge, and let you see nothing but [110 themselves, that's man's meat for't ; I have been once or twice plagu'd with such Animals as these.

Mod. Can'st thou imagine, *Wildish,* we wou'd fool away our time with such shadows of women as thou describ'st ? we have solid and substantial [115 Pleasures.

Wild. What ? a Riband, or a lock of hair, I warrant.

Mod. No, two young juicy Girls, that stick as close to us, as the Bark to the tree, and part as [120 unwillingly from us, as green fruit does from the stone ; and all this through the reputation of sober and discreet Servants to their pleasure: If such a scandalous fellow as thou come into the House without our introduction, the Ladies wou'd cry out, [125 O my Honour! as far as they cou'd see thee.

Wild. Methinks, Sir *John Everyoung* (an old smellsmock as he is) shou'd take the alarm, and so remove these so juicy Girls.

Eff. I hope you don't think we mean his [130 Daughters all this while? (that were a trick indeed.) We speak of two Ladies that shall be nameless.

Wild. Faith, Gentlemen, I can speak of none such, for all my acquaintance have two or three Names apiece, I assure you. [135

Mod. Well *Jack*, to return your civility in the laſt health you began, here's to all those incomparable Ladies, that like Roman Conquerors have two or three names apiece: But if thou wou'dſt leave this Rambling, thou wou'dſt lose nothing by it; [140 There's as hard drinking in Gentlemens Houses nowadays, as at Taverns, and as hot service in many a Ladys Chamber, as at *Giffords*.

Wild. But how shou'd a man do to get into Reputation? there are your men of fashion, [145 as well as Stuffs, and they go out again no body knows how.

Mod. 'Tis true, in the firſt place you muſt shake Hands with your old friends, *Hoquemore* and *Burgundy* for a while; leave your *Chaſte Ling*, and *La-* [150 *Fronds*, dine with my Lord such a One one day, my Lady what d'you call 'um another; and be sure to talk on't in the next Company you come into, drink Wine and Water at Table, a Dish of Tea after Dinner, like nothing but what is French, before the [155 Ladies; lose your money very much like a Gentleman to 'um in the Afternoon, and the work's done.

Wild. This is a hard Chapter.

Eff. If thou knew'ſt once the pleasure of such a sprightly Girl as *Olivia*, the kind quarrels, the [160

fondness, the pretty sullenness after a little absence,
which must be charm'd out of it with Kisses, and those
thousand other Devises that make a Lovers happiness;
thou wou'dst think all this as easie, as lying a bed in
the Country in a wet morning.   [165

Mod.   Or, if he cou'd but see *Victoria*'s reserv'dness
a little mollifi'd, and brought to hand with a good
Supper and the Fidles.

Estr.   Or *Olivia* in her morning dress, with her
Guittar, singing to it most enticingly, and then   [170
as kind in her discourse, her little breasts swelling
and pouting out, as if they came half way to be Kist.

Mod.   Or the others haughty look melted into
smiles, the pretty combat of pride and pleasure in
her Face, at some certain times.   [175

Estr.   My Mistress is in the very spring of beauty.

Mod.   And mine in the Midsommer of perfection.

Estr.   Mine is——

Wild.   Nay Gentlemen, one at once, and no quarrelling I beseech you; you are happy men both,   [180
and have Reason to be in love with your sweet lives,
but I thought *Victoria* had so obstinately doted on
her old Servant *Horatio*, that there had been more
hope of winning a Widow at her Husbands Funeral,
then of any favour for her now.   [185

Mod.   People will be talking, but on my word
she'l n'er break her heart for *Horatio*; I and my
Fellow-labourer, Time, have done his business.

Wild.   You are the great Masters of your Art,
these are the two Beauties, that the whole Town   [190
runs mad after.

Estr.   We know it, we know it, and it is no small
part of our felicity, to have that Lord send his Coach
and six to carry 'um to the Park; this Gentleman
offering to play at Angel-beast with 'um, though   [195
he scarce know the Cards, and has no more visible
Estate then what he may lose at a sitting: a third
begging to give 'um the four and twenty Violins,

which his Father in the County hears of and dis-
inherits for, whilst the Ladies put 'um off with [200
some slight Excuses, and send the whole Town over
after us.

Wild. You have 'um it seems in most excellent
order.

Mod. O there's no true pleasure but in [205
your person of quality, the others love all men so well,
they can love none best: they are indeed (like your
more generous Creatures) somewhat hard to tame,
but I have seen a Lyon as Gentle as an Ox: time and
industry will do any thing. [210

Estr. Come, drink a Glass round.

Mod. I can't get down a drop of this Wine more
without a Frolick.

Wild. Every man name the woman that has
oblig'd him last, and drink all their Healths in [215
a Brimmer.

Mod. Content, begin *Estridge.*

Estr. *Olivia*: now, *Modish*, name yours.

Mod. *Victoria, Victoria*: we must have your person
too, *Wildish*. [220

Wild. Mrs. *Betty.*

Mod. *Betty* what?

Wild. Nay faith, I can go no further, and may
very well be mistaken in that too.

Estr. Here's a Lock of Hair, shall I dip it [225
for one Glass more?

Wild. Whose is it first?

Estr. *Olivia's*, whose shou'd it be? black as Jet,
and shining as her Eyes: here's her Picture too in
little. [230

(Wildish *steps a little aside, and looks upon it.*)

Wild. O Impudence! his Sisters Picture, he
forgot he show'd me a month ago; this lock of hair,
produc't so confidently, frighted me a little, till I
saw the colour.

Enter to them Snappum.

Snap. Gentlemen, I beg your pardon for [235
pressing thus rudely into your Company; but the
business concerns no less then all my Fortunes: I
have been long a Suitor to a rich Widow, and have
at laſt prevail'd with her to marry me suddenly.

Eſtr. What is that to us, Sir? [240

Snap. *Wildish,* you'l I hope make my Excuse to
your friends: coming into the Garden about half an
hour ago, I loſt a Bracelet of her Hair, wrought with
her own hands, so that there is no deceiving her with
a counterfeit: a Waiter here tells me, he saw [245
one of you take up such a thing.

Wild. Is this it?

Eſtr. That's mine, and compos'd of hair so dear
to me, that I would fight with *Hector,* the top of your
order for leaſt of 'um. [250

Snap. And I with *Hercules* for mine: but pray
Mr. *Wildish,* let me see it; if it be that I look for,
no body will quarrel for 't, for 'tis full of gray hairs,
I assure you.

Wild. Shall he see it? [255

Eſtr. No.

Wild. I'le make bold for once though.

Snap. 'Tis my old Woman's. [*Shows it him.*

Wild. By the mark I'le swear, for 'tis as grizl'd
as a Silver-hair'd Rabbet; I may venture to [260
let him have it, *Eſtridge,* I suppose, mayn't I?

Eſtr. Yes, yes, now I remember me, I sent mine
to have a new ſtring put to it.

Snappum *goes off,* Wildish *follows him
a little way.*

Wild. Adieu, *Snappum.*

Snap. Are any of these Gentlemen good [265
Bubbles, Mr. *Wildish?*

Wild. What do I know, you had beſt ask 'um.

Snap. No, I thank you, Sir, I can be satisfied

on easier terms; but you were always a Lover of ingenuity, pray tell me.   [270

Wild. Away, away. [*Exit* Snap. Wild. *returns.*] I'm sorry your Miſtress has gray hairs so young, I doubt you are not kind to her, *Eſtridge.*

Mod. Nay, *Wildish,* don't insult upon a miſtake.

> *Eſtridge is out of Countenance, and looking up and down, sees the women in the next Arbour.*

Eſtr. I think we have neighbours in the   [275 next Arbour, and fine women they seem to be in their Masks.

Mod. Let's entertain 'um—what Ladies, come a padding for Hearts here in your Vizards? A pretty device to make a man in Love with he can't   [280 tell who.

Eſtr. What, rob us of our Liberties without one word? not so much as ſtand and deliver?

Oliv. If we shou'd rob you of your Hearts, Gentlemen, 'twere but petty Larceny; *Victoria*   [285 and *Olivia* wou'd never send Hue and Cry after us.

Mod. You know us, Madam.

Oliv. Yes, Gentlemen, somewhat better then we did this morning, though I always suppos'd no less.   [290

Eſtr. Then what?

Oliv. Then that you were the vaineſt Coxcombs in the whole Town, Fellows that wou'd hate a woman that were kind to you, because she takes from you the pleasure of belying her.   [295

Eſtr. *Olivia?*

Oliv. The very same, Sir, whose Picture you have in your Pocket, and about whose Hair you had like to have quarrell'd so manfully but now; who sends all the Town after you, and puts others   [300 off with slight Excuses; the obliging Lady, whose health you drank by that name.

Eſtr. 'Twas another *Olivia* I meant, one I knew abroad.

Vict. And another *Victoria* that you meant, [305 *Modish*?

Mod. Right, right, my Landladies Daughter at the *Cheval d'Or*, since gone into a Monaſtery.

Oliv. The Daughters of a French *Everyoung*, I warrant too. [310

Eſtr. La *Jeunesse* was their Father, which is all one with *Everyoung* in English.

Mod. On our Honours, Ladies, we were ever moſt tender of your dear Credits, and are heartily sorry our Miſtresses light to be of your names. [315

Oliv. Pray will you do me favour to let me see my Picture, I'm confident 'tis very like me.

Eſtr. Your French Name-sakes you mean, Madam; that *mal adroit Wildish* let it fall and broke the Cryſtal, and I sent it juſt now away to have [320 a new one put to it, as I hope to be sav'd, Madam.

Mod. But, Madam, cou'd you think me so sense-less, as discourse of you at that rate? here's *Jack Wildish* has heard us speak of these Wenches a hundred times. [325

Wild. 'Slight, these fellows. [*Wildish apart.*] Will lye themselves into credit again, if I han't a care of 'um inſtantly: Gentlemen I underſtand no winks, the few lyes I'le venture upon I am resolv'd to keep for my own use. [330

Eſtr. Prithee *Wildish* help us but this once.

Wild. No, no, go on, methinks you are in a very fair way; I am a ſtranger, the Ladies won't mind what I say.

Oliv. Yes, yes, we'll take your word. [335

Wild. Why then, Ladys, I assure you upon the Honour of a Gentleman, and by my friendship to those worthy persons I dare answer, they are too much Servants, to discourse so long of any thing but your selves: and for the French women [340 you know as much of 'um as I, having never heard tittle of 'um till this minute.

Vict. You have brought a very sufficient Witness with you Gentlemen, we do believe him.

Mod. Ours is not the first good cause has [345 been lost by ill Witnesses: but I perceive, Ladys, you don't know *Jack Wildish*, he is the verryest Droll in the whole Town; has a hundred of these fetches.   [*To* Wildish *apart.*

Estr. Pox on't, thou mayst bring all off yet. [350

Wild. [*alowd.*] Faith my conscience won't give me leave to deceive a Lady in a friends behalf. ⟨[*aside.*]⟩   To do it now, and in my own is all I can obtain of it.

                    [*Estridge comes up to* Wildish.

Estr. 'S death, Sir——

Wild. Nay *Estridge*, no huffing, you know   [355 I mind it not, and 'tis uncivil to fright your Mistresses.

Mod. But that we are two to one, and scorn Advantages, you shou'd not carry it off thus.

Wild. I shou'd be more afraid if you were three to one: but some other time for these matters. [360

Oliv. Never blame *Wildish*, we were all the while in the next Arbour, so that if he had taken your Cue never so readily, 't had done you little service.

Vict. Gentlemen this matter will bear no more Raillery; we are sensible of our Honours, and   [365 the injury your extravagant discourse might have done us, with any but so worthy a Person as Mr. *Wildish*; but he we are confident understands himself too well to have any ill thought of us from your Vanity: we can do no less than forbid you our   [370 House, and pray forbear it without further Ceremony.

          Wildish *takes* Victoria; Estridge *offers to take*
                    Olivia, *she refuses.*

Oliv. No, Sir, you'le say I come to pick you up in the Garden one time or other.   [*Exeunt omnes.*

⟨SCENE II. *Outside Sir Samuel Forecast's House.*⟩

Enter Eugenio *like an Officer, and three more.*

Sir Samuel Forecast *above.*

Enter a Servant.

Serv. Sir, there are some Souldiers below, say they muſt search your House for some suspitious person.

Fore. I warrant they mean *Eugenio* and *Philander*, I am utterly undone, suspeɕted for a Traytor, [5 and all long of those ungracious Girls! I am very glad I have got my Chriſtian Cloth on again: go and let 'um in.

Euge. Sir, I hope you will excuse us, we do but follow our Orders, and having search'd your [10 House for some dangerous persons will leave it you again in peace: *Eugenio* and *Philander* were your Sons, and therefore moſt probably judg'd to have made your House their Sanɕtuary.

Fore. My House their Sanɕtuary! I had [15 rather it shou'd be their Grave: since they made the State their Enemy, I have been so too.

Euge. Then you have no thoughts of 'um for your Daughters?

Fore. No, Sir, I assure you: and to remove [20 all doubt, *Althea*'s shortly to be marry'd to *Horatio* (one that will bid you welcome, Sir, if you please to come to the wedding) and I hope to dispose of *Diana* e're long to some honeſt Gentleman of our party. [25

Enter Althea.

Fore. I command you, on my blessing, to answer all things this Gentleman queſtions you about, precisely, as it were my self.

Euge. Sir, you do well, but you muſt retire a

little, whilst we examine your Daughters; a [30
man, though never so well meaning himself, can't
answer for others.

[Exit Forecast.

Euge. Lady, your Father here has shew'd himself
a faithful Subject to the Common-Wealth; it now
remains to know what Correspondence you [35
entertain with *Eugenio* and *Philander*, your former
Servants.

Alth. Upon my honour not the least, we are too
strictly watch'd to have a correspondence with any
man, and are too careful of our selves to hold [40
one with persons so obnoxious.

Euge. Are you resolv'd you never will?

Alth. As things are now they never shall.

Euge. Must you then marry *Horatio*?

Alth. My Father tells me so, and I have [45
hitherto been Dutiful.

Euge. *Horatio*'s an accomplish'd Gentleman.

Alth. He is Sir, and worthy of more happiness
than I can bring him to.

Euge. By Heaven, she loves him. *[Aside.]* [50
You lov'd *Eugenio* once, and gave vow for vow.

Alth. I did perhaps.

Euge. A Stranger and an Enemy as he is I pity
him.

Alth. 'Tis noble in you, Sir, but we must all [55
obey our Fortunes.

[Eugenio *lets fall his Disguise.*

Euge. And curse 'um too, if they be all like mine,
That love where beauty, and not virtue, shine.
O that the Tyrants knew that I were here!
Death does more lovely now than life appear.   60
Since thou art false, 'tis she alone has charms;
Neglected love rests only in your arms:
When I am dead you may your choice avow
Without reproach, which sure you cannot now:
And I shall want the sence of all my wrongs,   65

My death both to my reſt, and thine belongs.
   Alth. Can this *Eugenio* be, and so unkind,
What ſtrange Diſtemper rages in thy mind ?
Cou'd once my Soul of a base thought allow,
He that believes me false shou'd find me so.   70
   Euge. Muſt you not, Madam, with *Horatio* wed ?
'Tis a belief that your own words have bred.
   Alth. Forgive my fear, if any word of mine
Unto that hateful sound seem'd to encline :
Your rude appearance, of a Souldier, made   75
My tender heart, and very love afraid :
I durſt not speak, what moſt I did believe,
But us'd such words as you wou'd beſt receive.
   Euge. Alas, *Althea* ! what you told me here,
Did not create, although encrease, my fear :   80
That you muſt make him happy, is not new,
Nor did I learn the killing sounds from you ;
The Streets are full of it, and every where
I can of nothing but this *Hymen* hear.
   Alth. 'Tis true, my Father does a match
     design   85
'Twixt me and this *Horatio*, and does joyn
'Threats to Commands, urges th' uncertain ſtate
Of your affairs, your Party, and the Fate
Of such as do a well form'd Power invade ;
How they are always conquer'd or betray'd.   90
My Beauty fatal to it self the while
Inflames *Horatio*, and discourse (like Oyl)
Foments the fire : of such a Love he tells,
As would prevail but where your Image dwells ;
But ſtill in vain the Heart I gave to you,   95
The one does threaten, and the other woo.
   Euge. An absent Lover ill maintains the field :
Does not my Image to his presence yield ?
   Alth. I'm sure it ought ; reproaches so severe,
They that deserve 'um not will never bear.   100
'Twere juſt that Faith which you so ill deserve,
For one of nobler thoughts I shou'd reserve.

 Euge. We oft are made by a too great concern
(Like too much light) unable to discern.
The leave I gave to your surprise so late,   105
Now for my own distraction I intreat.
Where there is much of Love, there will appear
Mixt with our boldest hope some little fear.
 Alth. That fear in a true Lover soon wou'd dye,
Which to my Virtue is an Enemy.   110
 Euge. Hope is the passion of a calmer brest,
But high concernments are with doubt opprest.
To few, alas, is such assurance given
Not to fear Hell, although they hope for Heaven.
I not your Virtue, but my Fate accuse,   115
Which still does me with highest rigour use.
 Alth. Though Fate, *Eugenio*, for Misfortune meant,
I wou'd refuse to be the Instrument.
That dire necessity it seldom gave
Of harming them, whom we wou'd only save. 120
 Euge. But hark, I think I hear a noise of Swords.
 Alth. The sound, alas, no room for doubt affords.
You might perhaps be safe in your disguise.
 Spoke within by Souldiers. Where are the rest of
'um ? Down with the doors there.   125
 Euge. Their sudden coming all such hope denies,
'Tis me they seek, I am betray'd ; but yet
Since I can't shun, I'le try to break the net.
This Paper will inform your Sister where
She may of her unhappy Servant hear,   130
Make him remove, help him to shun that Fate
Which does for the unblest *Eugenio* wait.
My Rival in their head ! by all the Gods,
Horatio, this is an unmanly odds ;
Yet if on thee I can but fall reveng'd,   135
I life for death most happily have chang'd.
 Hora. *Eugenio* here ! I thought of nothing less,
But my clear meaning this will best express.
       He fights on Eugenio's *side.*

Officer.   Down with 'um both.
                         The Souldiers prevail, they are taken.
Euge.   Sir, let my life the cruel forfeit pay,   140
And bear not rashly so much worth away.
Horatio was too far by Vertue led,
And sav'd that blood he nobly should have shed :
He being my Rival fear'd the world might say,
He for my hated life this train did lay.   145
Honour ingag'd his Sword in my defence,
And Honour is a kind of Innocence.
   Hora.   *Eugenio* leave to intercede for me,
I only grieve I cou'd not rescue thee,
That so thou might'ſt thy preservation owe   150
To the same Vertue thou so ill didſt know :
And I some fitter time might make thee owne
The injuſtice of thy mean aspersion,
To think I came thus rudely to invade
The place where all that I adore is laid ;   155
And then to take my Rival in a snare,
Where if I wou'd I knew I cou'd not spare,
Was an affront thou with that life hadſt paid,
Which I defended : but revenge shows base,
Which on our Honour more dependence has.   160
   Euge.   Some other time for this dispute we'll take,
Revenge by threatening we the harder make.
   Officer.   Come, Gentlemen, you muſt away, my
Orders press ; you will have time enough to talk of
these things in the Tower.   [165

         Enter two Souldiers bringing in Sir
                     Samuel.
Officer.   Sir, you muſt along.
Fore.   Who I ! for what ?
Offic.   For harbouring *Eugenio* here, a known
Enemy to the State.
Fore.   You brought him with you for ought   [170
I know, I n'er saw his face, I answer'd an Officer, and
two Souldiers that came to search for him even now,

and as I thought, gave 'um satisfaction. But when I heard the clashing of Swords, because I wou'd not be made accessory to any thing that might [175 happen, I confess I retir'd into a corner of my Garret.

Offic. Sir, this won't satisfie, the Receiver is as bad as the Thief; I have found a Traytor in your house, and you shall answer it.

Fore. *Eugenio*, you are an honest Gentleman, [180 pray, speak, did I know any thing of your being here?

Euge. Not in the least, Sir: but my word I fear will do you little service.

Enter Wildish.

Wild. What, Sir *Samuel*, agen under perse- [185 cution? Nay, faith, I can do you no service now, these are a sort of Gamesters I dare not meddle withal.

Fore. I am undone! here's *Eugenio* found in my House, and they are carrying him to the Tower.

Wild. Come, bear up, Sir, if there come a [190 turn, you'l be a great man.

Fore. I shall be hang'd on that side, and to speak my own Conscience, I have deserv'd it.

Wild. No, to lye in Prison for concealing Cavaliers, will be great merit; and let me tell you as a [195 friend, there's like to be a turn suddenly, 'tis thought the General will declare like an honest man, I say no more; therefore carry your self moderately, this accident may chance to do you good service, if you have the grace to make the right use on't: but [200 how came *Eugenio* and *Horatio* of a side?

Fore. I came but just now among 'um, and know nothing; but 'tis a strange thing a man can't be believ'd in his own defence: carry me to Prison? I'le see what Justices hand they have for it. [205

Offic. We shall find hands enough, ne're fear it.

Exeunt omnes.

ACT V. SCENE I

⟨*Philander's Lodgings*⟩

Enter Philander *solus.*

Phil. 'Tis strange I nothing of *Eugenio* hear,
So long an absence may be worth a fear:
His friendship was not wont to hide from me
Of his most secret thoughts the new Decree.
I doubt his Love impatient of delay,   5
Has to *Althea* found some desperate way,
His passion cou'd not my slow cure attend,
On which, alas, he did in vain depend.
I was to blame, no sooner to provide
Against deluded hope's unruly tide;   10
Which now I fear has born him on a shelf,
Where he'll unkindly perish by himself.

Enter Diana *in Man's Cloathes.*

Ha! a strange face! wou'd I had not been seen;
But 'tis too good for Treason to lurk in.
Sure Gentle youth the place you have mistook,   15
I cannot be the man for whom you look.
    Dian. *Philander* in your troubled face I read
Some apprehensions that you are betray'd:
But when you shall my woful story hear,
A Juster sorrow will remove your fear.   20
    Phil. Thou hast my name, and yet I know thee not,
Quickly unty sweet youth this painful knot.
    Dian. Know you this hand?
    Phil. Alas it is my own,
This from *Eugenio* cou'd be had or none: 25
Speak, is he dead? is this his Legacy?
And has he sent it, gentle youth, by thee?
Has he *Horatio* fought? killing, or slain,
He almost equally wou'd breed my pain.
    Dian. He and *Horatio* fought, but on a side.   30

Phil.　What wonder beyond this can Fate provide.
I knew, *Eugenio*, thou wert always brave,
And that thy Love was ſtill thy Honour's slave.
　　Dian.　On your friends part you have the vertue
　　　brought,
But 'twas *Horatio* for *Eugenio* fought.　　　　　35
　　Phil.　Such a prodigious union cou'd not fail.
　　Dian.　A Band of Souldiers did o're both prevail.
　　Phil.　Is my unhappy friend a Prisoner made?
　　Dian.　He is, and close in the White Tower laid:
He bad me tell you so, that you might shun　　　40
The desperate hazard that his life muſt run.
　　Phil.　How came he, gentle youth, thus to expose
My life to one whom he so little knows?
　　Dian.　I am his near Relation, and have been
Privy to all Designs he has been in.　　　　　45
He bids you to remove without delay,
For y'are endanger'd hourly by your ſtay:
The Souldiers about him a Paper took,
Which, though obscurely, of your Lodging spoke.
　　Phil.　In vain we to that wretch good counsel
　　　give,　　　　　　　　　　　　　　　　50
Resolv'd to perish, and unfit to live:
When he is gone, what business have I here?
What can again be worth a hope or fear?
The hour he dyes this shall be my relief,
　　　　　　　　　　[*Pointing to his sword.*
If I cou'd need another wound than grief.　　　55
　　Dian.　How can you hope to please *Eugenio's*
　　　Ghoſt,
In killing him whom he eſteems the moſt?
In life our friends we chuse, but those we hate
We rather wish Companions of our Fate:
If I a present to his shade wou'd send,　　　　60
It shou'd be of his Foe, and not his Friend.
But yet I hope *Eugenio* may escape;
Safety has come in an unlookt for shape.
　　Phil.　That hope alone makes me consent to live.

Dian.   Can you for life no other reason give ?   65
Phil.   None that, alas ! is fit for thee to hear.
Dian.   Does then *Diana*'s heart so vile appear ?
Phil.   I hope thou wilt my better Genius prove,
Since thus thou know'st my business and my love.
    Dian.   She tells me you have often fill'd her
    Ears   70
With gentle words, and wet her arms with tears ;
Vow'd that your hope and fear, grief, and delight,
Her frowns or favours only cou'd excite.
    Phil.   Why so I did, sweet youth, and told her true,
But I'm amaz'd it shou'd be known by you.   75
    Dian.   Of late she has worn a face of discontent,
That seem'd neglected friendship to lament :
Eugenio to her Sister found a way,
Though various hazards in his passage lay.
    Phil.   Unwisely   he   the   short-liv'd   pleasure
    sought,   80
Too soon 'twas paid for, and too dearly bought ;
Like *Orpheus* for one poor untimely look,
He has the hope of all he lov'd forsook.
    Dian.   That haste exprest a passion, though to
    blame :
Impatience is of love the best extream.   85
    Phil.   That Heir's accurs'd, that for a present sum
Resigns the hope of all he has to come.
I would *Diana* to the world prefer,
And for her venture any thing but her.
But, gentle youth, methinks thou speak'st as though 90
Thou mad'st a doubt, whether I lov'd or no.
    Dian.   Pray Heaven *Diana* mayn't : your fault was
    great,
To think of Honour when the day was set
For *Hymens* Rites ; when nought else could destroy
Your hopes, which then were ripening into joy,   95
You were a Traytor to the State declar'd,
And in the glittering toyls of Fate ensnar'd.
    Phil.   Be witness Heaven, and all ye Powers above,

That see our infant passions weakly move,
E're they have force into the face to climb,   100
Or to one action can our wills encline,
If ever, for one moment, in my breast
I gave to any (she inspir'd not) rest.
    Dian. Why did you then such daring projects
      frame,
And danger court that not concern'd your flame ?   105
    Phil. 'Tis true, before I knew *Diana*'s charms,
I courted Fame in danger and in Arms,
And thought no Cause cou'd lasting glory bring,
Like the just quarrel of our injur'd King.
Eugenio's friendship too that Fire improv'd,   110
And made me wed that Cause I ever lov'd :
What since I did was on a former score,
My Fate she can't condemn, but must deplore.
I was in honour pre-engag'd too far,
E're to retire, and yet to merit her.   115
But whence could'st thou this hated knowledge gain ?
He worse than kills, who makes me live in pain :
Thy Beauty, Youth, and Words do all perswade,
Thou happy in her neerest trust art made.
              Diana *here drops a Ring, pulling out*
              a Handkerchief.
Ye Gods ! the Ring I to *Diana* sent !   120
Do not frail man beyond his Nature tempt.
The good thou hast done, I thus forget it all,
And let my vengeance on my Rival fall.   [*He draws.*
Draw, or I'le leave thee dead upon the ground.
                   She pulls off her Perriwig.
    Dian. I dare not draw—and sure you dare not
      wound.   125
    Phil. With sudden light I for a while am blind,
I sought a Rival, and a Mistress find ;
Where I thought all my rage, my love is due,
So high a pitch my wishes never flew ;
I am not by degrees to pleasure led,   130
Nor slowly made the doubtful steps to tread,

But in an inſtant, my exalted mind
Feels all her hopes set free, and fears confin'd:
So Kings in Battels that they gave for gone,
Redeem their own and win another Crown.   135
　　Dian.　That Faith, which nothing shou'd in ques-
　　　　tion bring,
From a few words you doubt, and from a Ring:
How can I hope a laſting friendship, where
So light appearance brings so mean a fear?
　　Phil.　Such　a　surprize　a　jealous　pang　might
　　　　give   140
To any breaſt where so much love does live.
But why, *Diana*, in this ſtrange disguise?
Was it to make me happier by surprise?
　　Dian.　Cou'd I my fear, as well as love o'recome,
You'd been preserv'd, and never known by whom; 145
Such a concern I wou'd not have betray'd,
Till I were surer of your passion made.
　　Phil.　What accident ill underſtood, cou'd prove
Of that dire force to make you doubt my love?
You needs muſt know how we were all betray'd,   150
And the hard scape I and *Eugenio* made;
And since it had been fatal to be seen,
So that this Chamber my whole world has been.
　　Dian.　What made me doubt, it matters not to know,
Let it suffice I do no longer so.   155
The dreadful Sword, which at my breaſt you held,
Though with much fear, I with more joy beheld:
For he that truly does his Rival hate,
Declares he loves his Miſtress at that rate.
　　Phil.　Look on thy self, and measure thence my
　　　　love,   160
Think what a flame so bright a form muſt move:
That Knot be confident will ever laſt,
Which Passion ty'd, and Reason has made faſt.
　　Dian.　Farewel, *Philander*, think on what I've said,
And kindly judge the weakness of a Maid.   165
　　Phil.　Thou art too cruel in so short a ſtay;

Thus would I gaze my very sight away.

   Dian. Though for your safety nothing was too dear,

Now give me leave for my own self to fear. [*Ex. Diana.*

   Phil. She has appear'd like Lightning to my sight,   170

Which when 'tis vanisht, leaves a darker night.

                          [*Exit* Philander.

⟨SCENE II. *Outside the Entrance to the Mulberry Garden*⟩

Enter Eſtridge *and* Modish.

   Eſtr. 'Twas certainly that Rogue *Wildish* that betray'd us; the Arbour and Bottle of Wine, were his motions.

   Mod. Without all peradventure, you saw the Ladies, when they threw us off, took him home   [5 with 'um, nothing could be plainer—what think you if one of us fought him?

   Eſtr. Why, faith I think we had e'en as good let that alone; hang him, he'll fight; 'twas only a trick he put upon us, and let's rall it off, and serve [10 him in his own kind.

   Mod. As how?

   Eſtr. Do you remember a certain Cousin of his that *Everyoung* carry'd us to, the Widow of a rich Alderman, who dy'd suddenly, and left her all [15 he had? this Widow he intends for Sir *Samuel Forecaſt*, and I make no queſtion but he is to have a round Sum for his good word. What think you now, if I order it, that one of us marry this Widow, then I hope we are sufficiently reveng'd?   [20

   Mod. But how is't possible?

   Eſtr. Nothing so easie: her Maid has promis'd me to perswade her to take a walk in the Mulberry-

Garden; this is a time there is little or no Company
there, 'tis but waiting at the door with a trusty   [25
Servant or two, and we may force her whither we
please, and then of her own accord she'll marry either
of us.

Mod. Why so ?

Estr. If for no other, for the same reason   [30
that men eat Horse-flesh in a Siege; because she can
come at nothing else.

Mod. If it were a foolish Girl, we might do somewhat with her indeed; but these Widows are like
old Birds, not to be tam'd; she'll fight and   [35
scratch, and fly about, there will be no enduring her.

Estr. Fear nothing : when she considers she has
no other way to save her Reputation, she'll hear reason.

Mod. Well; but being equal Adventurers, how
shall we agree about the Prize ?   [40

Estr. He that marries her, shall give the other a
Statute upon his Estate, for two thousand Pounds,
a pretty good Sum, and will serve to stop a gap.

Mod. Content, and I wish thee joy of her with
all my heart.   [45

Estr. You shall find me as good a Pay-master
as her Husband the old Alderman wou'd have been :
but stand close, here she comes.

Enter the Widow and her Maid, they seize 'um.

Wid. Thieves, Murderers, Villains ! what do you
mean ?   [50

Estr. Nothing, nothing, but I'le make bold to
stop that pretty mouth of thine, Widow, for once.

They carry 'um off.

Mod. Whither shall we carry 'um ?

Estr. To a little house I have taken a quarter of
a mile off for that purpose, where no body   [55
could hear 'um, though they had Falconers or Hunts-
mens voices.   *[Exeunt.*

⟨SCENE III. *Inside the Tower*⟩

Enter Sir John Everyoung, *and Sir* Samuel Forecaſt.

Ever.   Give you joy, Brother, give you joy.

Fore.   Of what ?

Ever.   Why, of your Lieutenancy of the Tower:
I know you can be here upon no other account, and
indeed your fidelity to the Publick claims no   [5
less.

Fore.   Sir, give you joy of your new Suit, and
Fair Perriwig there.

Ever.   Faith, Brother, it sits with no Fortune
to day, what ere's the matter, I was never worse   [10
put together in all my life, and but to congratulate
your advancement, wou'd not have left the Company
I din'd with.

Fore.   I hope to return your kind Visit in the *Fleet,*
and see your Daughters sell Ale and Cakes there,   [15
and your Worship with fewer Trappings on; for
thither your extravagant Courses point.

Ever.   May my Perriwig never know a good day,
nor be taken for my own hair again, but come off
always with my Hat, if it coſt me above twelve   [20
pounds.

Fore.   Pox on your Hat, and your Perriwig, can
you tell how I shall get out ?

Ever.   No more then how you got in; but you
are wise, and know business: alas, I know   [25
nothing but how to sort Ribands, make Horse-
matches, throw away my money at Dice, and keep
my self out of the Tower.

Fore.   O my ungracious Girls !

Ever.   What of them ? have they broke   [30
prison, and taken Sanctuary in the Arms of some
ſturdy Prentice, Fencing-maſter, Brother of the Blade,
or any other inferior Rascal ? you were so ſtrict to
'um, I never look'd for other.

Fore. Not so faſt; but if you can be serious   [35
for a minute, do: they are vertuous, but *Eugenio* a
former Servant to *Althea*, since declar'd a Traytor
to the State, was taken in my house; I suspeſted to
have been privy to his being there, and so carried
along with him hither: I proteſted my Innocence   [40
to the Officers, urg'd my former Service, but all would
not do.

Ever. S'light⟨! I⟩ hope you had more wit, this is
the happieſt accident that ever befel mortal, for an
old notorious Round-head to be taken for a   [45
Cavalier at this time; why I never thought it had
been in you; this was a Stratagem might have become
Machevile himself.

Fore. Why, what's the matter? all's well I hope.

Ever. Yes, never better, the General has   [50
this day to some persons of quality declar'd for the
King; All Cavaliers are immediately to have their
Liberty; therefore make haſte to reconcile with
Eugenio and *Philander*: I have an order for the
delivery of all such Prisoners as are here upon the   [55
account of Loyalty to their Prince.

Fore. *Philander* and *Eugenio*, on my Daughters
Account, will do me all the service they can, and I
hope to make some advantage of this imprisonment.

Ever. I'le go and release *Eugenio*, and bring   [60
him to you; *Horatio* is discharg'd already: though
we fall out now and then about trifles, we are Brothers,
and ought to serve one another in matters of concern.

[*Exeunt.*

⟨SCENE IV. *A Room in Sir John Everyoung's
House*⟩

Enter Victoria, Olivia, *and* Wildish.

Wild. You see now, Ladies, what Fellows you
caſt your good opinions on: if I said any thing that

was disrespeĉtful to either of you, it ought to go for
nothing, I was meerly your decoy in the business.

  Oliv.   We are very well satisfi'd on all hands.   [5

  Viĉt.   Sure they'l never have the impudence to
trouble us agen.

  Oliv.   Now wou'd I were married to *Estridge*, that
I might plague him soundly.

  Wild.   How can you make that a Plague,   [10
Madam?

  Oliv.   A hundred ways: I wou'd never come
home till three a clock in the morning; tumble my
own Handkercher my self, to make him jealous;
break his soundest sleeps in Commendation of   [15
his bosom-friend, and never leave till I have made 'um
quarrel; fold up all manner of Papers, like Love-
Letters, and burn 'um just as he comes into th' Room.

  Wild.   I can tell you how to be reveng'd on him
beyond all this.   [20

  Oliv.   Prithee how, *Wildish*?

  Wild.   Why, marry me, make a good Wife to me,
and let him hang himself for rage.

  Oliv.   I am not so inveterate an Enemy, I'le
forgive him rather: if I were your Wife, I must   [25
board half a year with a Friend in the Country, tumble
about the other half in most villainous Hackneys, lye
two pair of Stairs high, and wear black farrendine the
whole year about; see you when you had no money to
play, and then be kist out of a Ring or a Bracelet.   [30

  Wild.   I wou'd not use a City Widow of five and
fifty so, with seven small Children: and am I to
suffer nothing all this while?

  Oliv.   What can you suffer?

  Wild.   Why, the loss of that which is dearer   [35
than life, my liberty; be known for a marry'd man,
and so put my self out of all capacity, of breaking
Gold, promising marriage, or any other way of ensuring
my self to scrupulous young Virgins I shall like
hereafter.   [40

Oliv. That is to be taken from the occasion of playing the Rascal : is that all ?

Wild. Not half ; if I make but love to a Chamber-maid, I shall be answer'd, you have a sweet Lady of your own, and why will you wrong her ? if [45 I get acquainted with any young woman, after the fourth or fifth visit, be look'd upon by her Father and Mother, worse than the Tax-Gatherers in a Country Village ; all this you count nothing.

Oliv. Not to a Lover, *Wildish*. [50

Wild. Well, there is no service so desperate, that a gallant man will shrink at, if he like his reward ; and to give his hand thus to a woman, in him that rightly underſtands what he does, is as bold an aɛtion as *Mutius Scævola*'s : yet that I may use it hereafter [55 where and when I please, upon my dear *Olivia* I'le venture it.

Oliv. Softly, when you please, and where I please.

Wild. Content Madam : will you do us the favour to be a Witness ? [60

Viɛt. Well Mr. *Wildish*, I'le dance bare-foot to serve you. [Wildish *leads off* Olivia.

Oliv. Hold, hold *Wildish*, my heart fails me.

Wild. 'Slight, I had a qualm too, there's certainly a more than ordinary providence attends me ; I [65 shall scape yet, I am now in a twitter, like a Gameſter upon a great by, that is heartily afraid he shall lose it, and yet his love to the money won't suffer him to draw Stakes. I muſt have her.

Viɛt. Nay, now you are come thus far, e'ne [70 go on.

Oliv. Well, *Wildish*, give me thy hand ; the firſt Time thou anger'ſt me, I'le have a Gallant ; And the next, make thee a Cuckold. [*Exeunt.*

SCENE V. ⟨*A Room in Samuel Forecaſt's House.*⟩

Enter Horatio *and* Althea.

Hora.   Madam, you know your Father does com-
mand,
That you shou'd shortly give me your fair hand
Before a Prieſt; but since I find no part
Goes along with it of your generous heart,
My mind the charming present can refuse,   5
Fearing t'indulge a passion you accuse;
My joy with your leaſt trouble weigh'd muſt ſtill
Appear, to my own self the greater ill.
    Alth.   Such words as these, *Horatio*, but heap more
Upon a debt that was too great before;   10
I'm cover'd with confusion when I weigh
How much I owe, how little I can pay:
You may with ease a fairer Miſtress find,
And with more ease such worth will make her kind;
And if I e're that happy Virgin know,   15
I'le sue to make her pay you what I owe.
    Hora.   To change your thoughts, I will no longer
try,
But with the ſtream I cannot turn, comply:
I to *Victoria* will my suit renew,
And hope to find an Advocate in you.   20
    Alth.   You may command me, and *Victoria's* mind
Is of it self to you too well inclin'd.
    Hora.   All this methinks shou'd your belief per-
swade,
I no contrivance with those Villains had,
To take my Rival in so mean a way,   25
But only came their sudden rage to ſtay
All that confusion, and surprize cou'd do,
My passion made me apprehend for you.
    Alth.   *Horatio's* Honour does too brightly shine,
To be accused of such a low design;   30
Had you within the bounds of friendship ſtaid,

V. v. 32.

Your self and me you had both happy made.
   Hora. With ease from friendship we to love are
    led,
That slipery path who can securely tread ?

   Enter Sir Samuel Forecaſt, *Sir* John Everyoung,
       and Eugenio.

   Alth. I see my Father, and *Eugenio* here,   35
And in all faces sudden joys appear.
        Forecaſt, Everyoung, *and* Horatio *seem*
          to discourse.
   Euge. Fortune, I pardon thee thy short-liv'd spite,
I for thy conſtant temper took a fit,
Th'art kind, and gentle, and 'tis we are blind,
Who do miſtruſt the ways thou haſt design'd   40
To make us bleſt, though better than our own.
   Alth. Can you have joy, and yet *Althea* none ?
   Euge. May I all misery firſt undergo,
E're joy divided from *Althea* know.
   Alth. What is this wonder hangs upon thy
    tongue ?   45
Delay does only to ill news belong.
   Euge. Madam, your Father licenses my flame,
And you alone can now oppose my claim ;
That Cause which Armys did in vain support,
And nobleſt spirits did, successless, court,   50
We in a bloodless triumph shining see,
Without the dire effects of Victory.
For in the Generals breaſt (the nobleſt Scene)
The Fate of *England* has transacted been :
On *Albion*'s Throne he will our Monarch place,   55
Our Neighbours terrour, and our Nations grace,
Whilſt at his bleſt approach, all factious minds
Vanish, like leaves before Autumnal Winds.
   Alth. Such truth in love and loyalty y'ave shown,
What less for both cou'd by juſt Heaven be done ? 60
   Euge. This happiness, though great, yet is not all,
My deareſt friend I soon shall Brother call ;

Diana mu&t his deathless Flame repay.

    Alth.   Fate, to be pardon'd, had no other way.

    Euge. See how your Father kindly &trives to evade   65

His former promise to *Horatio* made.

    Alth.   That work's so nobly in his brea&t begun,

That a few words will finish what's undone :

Horatio does all happiness despise,

From my obedience, which my love denies.   70

    Fore. ⟨*to Eugenio*)⟩ *Horatio* has releas'd me of my promise to him, and seeing your changeless love to one another, was resolv'd to have mov'd it to me, if I had not prevented him.

    Euge. Such honour, noble youth, I mu&t confess,   75

Gives wonder equal to my happiness.

    Hora. *Althea* I resign, my guilty flame

Was too unju&t to reach so fair an aim :

Vi&toria's wrongs did my success oppose,

And my lo&t passion its own penance grows.   80

So some Offenders are their duty taught

By th' ill effe&t and nature of their fault.

    Eug. My apprehensions by these words are clear'd,

And I dare love that Virtue which I fear'd.

In love alone this my&tery we find,   85

Men be&t agree when of a different mind.

    Hor. There now remains but one thing more to do,

'Tis that *Philander* may be sent for too.

But see he comes.

Enter Philander.

    Fore. Brother, if your Daughter were here, [90
we might have a Dance. Sir, you are heartily welcome, I kept my Girl safe for you, she has not been so much as blown upon since you saw her ; I knew hone&t men wou'd not be always kept from their own, there wou'd come a time.   [95

Phil.   Sir, I was ever moſt oblig'd to you——
Eugenio here! then I am doubly bleſt,
And only fear to be with joy oppreſt.
   Euge.   The joys of Friendship well prepare our
      mind
For the high raptures we in love shall find: 100
The name of Brothers we shall soon obtain.
   Phil.   Friendship so perfeᶜt by no name can gain.
                              [*Enter* Diana.
Fate is at length asham'd, or weary grown
Upon a Flame ⟨that⟩ smil'd so long, to frown;
As Vessels toſt upon the raging Main,   105
With greater joy the wisht-for Port obtain;
Our love this short, fierce tempeſt having paſt,
Will joys more high, since less expeᶜted, taſt.
   Dian.   But in the Storm did you throw nothing
      out?
   Phil.   Wrong not my love with so unkind a
      doubt.   110

             Enter Ever. Viᶜt. Oliv. Wild.

   Ever.   *Wildish*, thou'rt an honeſt fellow, I'm glad
I found thee.
   Wild.   Sir, the honeſt fellow desires to be known
to you by another name, having newly marry'd your
Daughter *Olivia*.   [115
   Ever.   When, pray Mr. *Wildish*?
   Wild.   Juſt now, Sir, the words are scarce out of
our Mouths.
   Ever.   Well, this is a day I could not have been
angry if thou hadſt got her with Child upon a   [120
Contraᶜt; But you might have ask'd my leave, e're
you went about to make me a Grandfather.
   Wild.   If I had had a good Jointure to offer, so I
wou'd, but if I do make you a Grandfather, 'tis not
done maliciously, I'le swear.   [125
   Hora.   My guilty Cause my self I dare not plead,
But beg your innocence will intercede:

Since all my fault your matchless beauty made,
Your goodness now shou'd my excuse perswade.

Alth. I in *Victoria* will my int'rest try, 130
You, and me both, she hardly shall deny.

Hora. *Victoria's* mind I cannot hope to move,
Unless a Parents power assist my love;
Her duty will not your commands withstand,
She'll take a worthless Servant from your hand. 135

Ever. I'm sure she can have no exception to so
deserving a person as *Horatio*; Lovers, like Spaniels,
do but show their mettal in a little ranging: though
you had a twittering to *Althea*, you'le make ne're the
worse Husband to *Victoria*. *Victoria*! [140

Vict. Sir, what's your pleasure?

Ever. That which will prove yours in the end: I
charge you upon my blessing, give *Horatio* your
Hand, go and be marry'd with your Cousins, and
make but one work of it. [145

Vict. Sir, I am all obedience: who e're strove
At once against her duty, and her love?

Wild. But *Estridge*, what fine Lady have you got
there?

Estr. A certain Widow which I have cast [150
my self away upon: a Kinswoman of yours, *Wildish*,
that you formerly design'd for the Right Worshipful
Sir *Formal* there: do you know her now?—Sir we
made bold with her without your consent.

Wild. Old acquaintance, i'faith, how is't? [155
I have made as bold, and been as welcome too, as e're
you'le be Sir: but why did you steal a marriage thus?

Wid. You know I always lov'd stoln pleasures,
but this marriage stole me; your old Knight [160
was uncertain, came on by inches, this Gentleman
leapt into the matter, forc'd me into a Coach, and
marry'd me in an instant: I cou'd have been content
to have been a Lady, that I might have taken place
of my Mistress when she comes to Town. [165
But a Bird in the hand——

Estr. Why, have you a Mistress ?

Wid. As sure as you have had a hundred, and now have a Wife.

Mod. I doubt as things go, I shall scarce [170 find you as good a Pay-master as the old Alderman.

Estridge *pulls his hand from her, and looks angry.*

Wild. Nay, never use her ill now, 'twas none of her Fault, she is a very good Creature, and one that I plac't to personate my Cousin, on purpose to catch Sir *Samuel Forecast*; you know he took the [175 forfeiture of a Mortgage that concern'd a very good Friend of mine, and I was resolv'd to be reveng'd of him ; if you will needs run your Head into the Noose that's prepar'd for another, who can help it ? my Cousin is married in *Ireland*, whither she went [180 last Summer to look after some money, due to her last Husband.

Wid. I am her House-keeper though, and can bid you welcome till she returns.

Oliv. A pretty pert thing, I like her [185 humour, she carries it off well : but *Wildish*, you shall visit her no more now we are married.

Wild. Fear not, *Estridge* will take order for that.

Hora. ⟨(*to Victoria*)⟩ How I do hate my self ! that could so long
At once such Beauty and such Goodness wrong. [190

Vict. My kindness has forgot you were to blame,
You⟨r⟩ guilt consum'd in your reviving flame.

Ever. Now you are all pair'd, let's have a Dance.
                    After the Dance, a great shout within.

Euge. I hear the peoples voice in joyful crys,
Like conquering Troops o're flying Enemies ;   [195
They seem to teach us in a ruder way
The Honour due to this all-healing day.

Phil. Let's part a while, and vye who shall express
The highest sense of this great happiness.   [199
                    ⟨[*Exeunt omnes.*⟩

EPILOGUE

Poets of all men have the hardest Game,
Their best Endeavours can no Favours claim.
The Lawyer, if o'rethrown, though by the Laws,
He quits himself, and lays it on your Cause.
The Souldier is esteem'd a Man of War,   5
And Honour gains, if he but bravely dare.
The grave Physitian, if his Patient dye,
He shakes his head, and blames Mortality.
Only poor Poets their own faults must bear
Therefore grave Judges be not too severe: 10
Our Author humbly hopes to scape your Rage,
Being no known Offender on the Stage,
He came by chance, is a meer Traveller;
All Countries Civil unto Strangers are:
Yet faith he's arm'd how e're your Censures go   15
And can prevent the harm, though not the blow.
No Poet can from this one Comfort fall,
The best ne're pleas'd, nor worst displeas'd you all.   18

FINIS

ANTONY

AND

CLEOPATRA:

A

TRAGEDY.

As it is Acted at the DUKES
THEATRE.

Written by the Honourable
Sir *CHARLES SEDLEY*, Baronct.

Licensed *Apr.* 24. 1677. *Roger L'Estrange.*

LONDON,

Printed for *Richard Tonson* at his Shop under
Grayes-Inne-gate next *Grayes-Inne-lane.*
MDCLXXVII

EDITOR'S PREFACE

Sources, etc. Sedley's " Antony and Cleopatra " belongs to a long line of English plays on the subject, which began in the reign of Elizabeth. Shakespeare's great tragedy (*c.* 1608) had been preceded by the Countess of Pembroke's " Trajedie of Antonie," translated from the French of Garnier (published 1595 but written 1590), and Samuel Daniel's graceful " Cleopatra " (1594). It was followed by Fletcher's " The False One " (*c.* 1620), dealing with the earlier part of Cleopatra's life, and Thomas May's " Cleopatra " (acted 1626), a blank verse tragedy of some merit. Cleopatra appears in " La Mort de Pompée," the drama of Corneille which Sedley and his friends translated and published in 1664 under the title of " Pompey the Great " (see " Sir Charles Sedley," pp. 80, 81), and it was probably this play that suggested to him the idea of a tragedy on Cleopatra's death. The chief source of Sedley's play is Plutarch's Life of Marcus Antonius. The Sale Catalogue of his Library includes a copy of the Greek text of the Parallel Lives with a Latin translation published in 1650, and an Italian translation published at Venice in 1620. There is no English translation in the Sale Catalogue, but it is almost certain that Sedley knew North's great version, which had been reprinted in 1657, and in the year of the play, 1676. The version known as Dryden's did not appear until 1683.

In accordance with the new classical fashion, Sedley, unlike Shakespeare and May, only treats the latter part of the story, and begins the action after the battle of Actium. He has to telescope the events that followed the battle in order to approximate as nearly as possible to the unities of time and place. According to Plutarch a considerable period elapsed between Actium and Antony's final overthrow at Alexandria, during which Antony went to live in Athens, where he was joined by Cleopatra after her unsuccessful attempt to escape towards the Persian Gulf. Sedley makes Octavian (" Cæsar ") proceed to Alexandria immediately after Actium and transfers the desertion of Antony's legions from Greece to Egypt. He also introduces certain events which have no historical basis. The most notable are the plot of " Photinus " and his love for Iras, Cleopatra's maid. The idea of the plot was apparently suggested by events in Cleopatra's early life, as related by Plutarch in his Life of Julius Cæsar, and used by Corneille in " La Mort de Pompée." According to Plutarch, Potheinos (in Latin versions " Pothinus " : in Corneille it becomes

" Photin ") was a villainous eunuch who advised the young king Ptolemy, Cleopatra's brother, to order the murder of Pompey when he sought refuge in Egypt. Afterwards Potheinos conspired against Julius Cæsar, who discovered his plot and put him to death : Sedley, who knew of these incidents from Corneille's tragedy, transfers the plot of Potheinos or Photinus to the period following Actium. Photinus's love for Iras, Iras's love for Antillus and Mæcenas's passion for Octavia are all pure invention.

Genest's statement that Sedley " borrowed nothing from Shakespeare " is too sweeping. Although his debt to Shakespeare's " Antony and Cleopatra " is very slight, there are certainly echoes both of that play and of " Othello " and " Julius Cæsar " (see notes to Act III. sc. ii. ll. 103, 308, IV. ii. l. 27, vi. 96, 101).

Stage History. Sedley's " Antony and Cleopatra " was first acted at the Duke's Theatre in Dorset Gardens in February 1677. The Marquess of Worcester, in a letter to the Marchioness, writes on March 17 that it has been " acted often." It had a musical setting by Jeremiah Clarke, and the cast, which is recorded in the quarto editions, is a very strong one, including such brilliant actors and actresses as Thomas Betterton and his wife, Harris, Medburn and Mary Lee. Genest states that the part of Photinus was specially written for Sandford.

There is no record of a revival of Sedley's tragedy. It was probably completely superseded by Dryden's " All For Love," which was staged at the King's House in 1677. Dryden apparently refers to Sedley in his Preface, where he writes that " the Subject . . . has been treated by the greatest Wits of our Nation after Shakespeare." He is said by the eighteenth-century poet Eusden to have been fired by his friend's example.

> " So Dryden sweetest sang by envy fir'd,
> Thirst of Revenge, when Phœbus fail'd inspir'd,
> His Anthony did Sedley's muse o'ertake,
> And Absolom was writ for Zimri's sake."

There is nothing in common between Sedley's tragedy and " All For Love " except the fact that Dryden seems to have taken Sedley's hint in adding fictitious events to those recorded by Plutarch. It must be admitted, however, that Dryden's fictions, such as the quarrel of Antony and Ventidius and the encounter of Octavia and Cleopatra, are much happier than Sedley's.

Beauty the Conquerour. Sedley recast " Antony and Cleopatra " as a classical tragedy with choruses between the acts under this name. This version, which seems to have been unfinished at the time of the poet's death, was included in a fragmentary form in Ayloffe's edition of 1702. In " Beauty the Conquerour " the character of Photinus is eliminated and the villain is an Egyptian officer called Achillas (see " Sir Charles Sedley," pp. 279, 280).

PROLOGUE

As a brisk Gallant dancing to his Glass,
Does here and there in nimble fleurets pass ;
Likes every step, and wishes for a Ball,
Where he at once may shew his Parts to all :
So Poets (with the like conceit) undone, 5
Think that dull Verse which pleas'd 'em when alone,
Must have the like effect on the whole Town.
Our Poet all such hopes of Praise disclaimes,
Like a true Lover of the Sport, he Games,
And to come off a Saver only aimes. 10
Did he affect to be esteem'd a Wit,
Like you, he'd take an easier way to it :
Write Songs and Prologues, shew 'em up and down,
And tear applause from every Fool in Town ;
Make Love to Vizards in a Wit-like Noise, 15
Dull in his Sense, yet aiery in his Voice,
Catch at each Line that grates, and keep ten good,
With his damn'd Noise, from being understood.
'Tis well most Wits have something of the Mad,
Or where shou'd Poets for the Stage be had ? 20
Cripples may judge of Vaulting he well knows,
Cowards of Courage ; and of Verse and Prose
They that know neither ; yet if too severe
Damning those gifts of which they have no share,
Their Envy more than Judgement will appear. 25
He none excepts, no, not his Enemies ;
For those he hopes his Friends will counterpoise :
And spight of Faction on both sides he knows,
There is an honest Party in this House. 29

Persons	represented by
Cæsar.	M⟨r.⟩ *Smith.*
Agrippa.	Mr. *Jevon.*
Mecænas.	Mr. *Harris.*
Lucilius a Roman.	Mr. *Norris.*
Thyreus.	Mr. *Crosby.*
Antony.	Mr. *Betterton.*
Canidius, his General.	Mr. *Medburn.*
Photinus.	Mr. *Sandford.*
Memnon. ⎱ Two Egyptian Lords.	Mr. *Percivall.*
Chilax. ⎰	Mr. *Gillow.*
Cleopatra.	Mrs. *Mary Lee.*
Octavia.	Mrs. *Betterton.*
Iras.	Mrs. *Gibbs.*
Charmion.	Mrs. *Hughes.*

Guards, Messengers, Villains, Souldiers and Attendants, Men and Women.

ANTONY AND CLEOPATRA

ACT I

Scene the First. *Cæsar*'s Tents.

Enter *Cæsar*, *Agrippa*, *Mecænas*.

Cæsar.   Our Arms an easie Victory have found
Over a Foe, in love and pleasure drown'd.
  Agrip.   I am pleas'd we have *Antonius* subdu'd,
Yet rage to think a *Roman* was pursu'd:
Our souls did once our conquer'd Bodies loath,   5
And seldome did one World contain 'em both.
Yet now by hopes we're flatter'd to live on,   ⎫
And with the Common Herd of Mankind run,   ⎬
Crouching to Fate, which we by death might shun.   ⎭
  Cæs.   His Army's yet entire, and on the Shore ;10
No Troops so far the *Roman* Eagle bore:
Armenian Kings they have in Triumph led,
And *Parthian* blood in ten set Battles shed:
Their General to the last they will defend.
  Mecæn.   None can defend those, who them- ⎫
    selves betray: ⎪
He with his Queen again will run away,   ⎬   15
And leave 'em fighting, as he did at Sea.   ⎭
  Agrip.   Remember, Sir, the joy the World exprest,
When threatning Wars and Mischiefs you redrest⟨,⟩
With a late Peace, which an Alliance ty'd,   20
And your fair Sister made *Antonius* Bride.
The like again you to the World may give,
If you content with half of it can live.
  Cæs.   Against all strokes of Fate who can prepare?
That Match is half th' occasion of this War.   25

To him I did my dear *Octavia* give,
That *Rome* in peace, she might in Empire live;
That to one Emperor by blood ally'd,
And to the other by her Marriage ty'd,
She might all growing jealousie remove,   30
And be her self the Bond of lasting love.
But see th' unblest event; *Antonius* slights
That Tye, which even enemies unites;
And more than drunk with *Cleopatra*'s charms,
He scorns both *Roman*-Love and *Roman*-Arms.   35
    Agrip.   Love of our Country and our Interest
Is the true passion of a *Roman* Breast.
All other are Usurpers——
    Cæs.   'Tis most true:
Yet this vile Flame he never will subdue,
Which spight of time and of enjoyment lives,   40
And of it's bane miraculously thrives.
He thinks his life depends upon her eye,
As that of Plants does on the Sun relye.
The ignorant are learn'd, if she think so,
And Cowards even *Hercules* out-do.   45
At her request he Provinces bestows,
And no mans worth but by her stamp he knows.
Whilst my *Octavia* leads a Stepdames life,
And tends the Children of his former Wife,
Ungrac'd without authority or sway.   50
    Mecæn.   The wrongs of that fair Princess, Sir, are
      great,
And rage in all, but in her self create.
What Hers forgives, our virtue shou'd chastise:
Mortals revenge the blasphem'd Deities.
And strait the Impious wretch in pieces tear,   55
Whom Heaven in clemency wou'd long forbear.
From equal pow'r how can you be secure?
And less *Antonius* never will endure.
    Agrip.   *Antonius* worsted will no league refuse,
And give in peace what battle could not lose.   60
He may *Octavia* receive again,

And in his Bed and Empirie make her reign.

   Mecæn.   Men leagues and peace in their diſtress
    embrace,
But keep 'em only till affairs change face.
Ambition's never safe till pow'r be paſt,   65
As men till Impotent are seldom Chaſte.
Follow the blow, and doubt not the success ;
But Fortune for her utmoſt favours press.
On petty Kings you trifling Conqueſts make,
Antonius brings you here an equal ſtake ;   70
The World to be divided at one blow,
And Fate already has declar'd for you.

   Agrip.   Men that have once an equal pow'r enjoy'd,
May see the Ballance chang'd, but not deſtroy'd.
He that is lessen'd to a Slaves degree,   75
Still conscious of the firſt equality,
Muſt hate the other, and himself much more.
Who ever saw a Captive Emperor ?
With honour treat and yield perhaps he may,
But he can never like a Slave obey.   80

   Cæs.   Peace we will offer, that he may refuse,
And the whole World his bloody mind accuse.
Thyreus knows the Queen : Him I will send,
Charge him that ſtrait he in my Tent attend.   84
                       [*Ex. omnes.*

Scene the Second.   The Palace.

Enter Memnon *and* Chilax, *two Egyptian Lords.*

   Memn.   Was ever Queen like *Cleopatra* curſt ?
Of *Egypts* Monſters sure her love's the worſt.
Where is that falshood does the Sex pursue,
Or are they only to their ruine true ?
I said *Antonius* might have laid the Scene   5
Of War and Rapine further from the Queen,
That our weake State shou'd to the Victor bow,

And humbly the Decrees of Fate allow.
She tells it him, and I muſt be displac't.
    Chil. 'Tis hard men for their love shou'd be dis-
      grac't,   10
    Memn. No man may now his bleeding Country
      mourn,
Romans our Lords, and we their Slaves were born.
    Chil. The Times our honeſt Councels cannot bear,
And men their Thoughts muſt in disguises wear.
    Memn. Let Women, and Her Parasites seek to
      please.   15
Physitians should not flatter the disease.
Her dang'rous ſtate 'tis Treason to conceal,
Which nothing but *Antonius* death can heal.
    Chil. 'Tis a rough Medicine she will never use,
And fatal were th' advice should she refuse.   20
We know his intereſt does her Councel sway.
    Memn. We this advice muſt privately convey,
Make her believe *Octavius* loves her too : ⎫
On that she will an easie faith beſtow,   ⎬
And in that hope what is't she may not do ?⎭   25
    Chil. 'Twere all in vain, and we our lives should
      lose,
Tamely and vilely laught at by our Foes :
Be Thieves and Rogues to execution led,
Let us die warm, and at an Army's head.
The *Romans* will not ever be thus ſtrong ;   30
Thousands as well as we for changes long.
    Memn. Let's silent wait the opportunity,
And by main force expel their tyranny.
    Chil. I love my Queen, and to rebel am loth. 34
    Mem. I would but free her from *Antonius* pow'r,
And that once done, lay down my arms next hour.
    Chil. Let us some plot againſt his life devise :⎫
He's not our Prince ; for publick good he dies, ⎬
And for our Country falls a Sacrifice.   ⎭
But see He comes, and for his late disgrace,   40
His conscious vertue raging in his face.

Enter *Antonius, Canidius, Photinus.*

Ant.　　How slippery is the Top of humane ſtate,
And on exalted Heads what tempeſts beat?
Whom *Jove* will ruine he makes deaf and blind,
So that they hugg th' ill fate he has deſign'd;　　45
I else could never have bold *Roman* Swords
Crowded and throng'd within these floating Boards⟨,⟩
Ships, whom the winds more than their Pilots sway,
Where eager courage for a wave muſt ſtay.
The Valiant cannot board, nor Coward fly,　　50
But at the luſt of the unconſtant sky.
At land my *Romans*——
　　Can.　　　　　　　Sir they bravely fought;
Tho rude in Ships and Sea affairs untaught.
Six hours they did a doubtful fight maintain, ⎫
Deserted by your base *Egyptian* Train; 　　⎬　55
And by your self, if I may be so plain. 　　⎭
　　Ant.　　The juſt reproach has rows'd my Lyon heart,
Nor am I angry at the friendly smart.
I fled, *Canidius*, basely run away, 　　　　⎫
And fought for Empire below those for pay. 　⎬　60
Of my new shame too much thou canſt not say.⎭
　　Can.　　They, who by Ships would such a Cause
　　　　decide,
Did not for conqueſt, but for flight provide.
Pardon me, Sir, my bluntness muſt go on;
By barbarous fears and councels you 're undone.　65
　　Photi.　　We in Neutrality secure might wait,
And calmly expeꞔ an Emp'ror from Fate;
But in your quarrel half our Fleet we loſt,
Led by that *Roman* courage which you boaſt.
　　Memn.　　Our Ships with a promiscuous crowd were
　　　　fill'd,　　　　　　　　　　　　　　　　70
Neither in Battle, nor in Sailing skill'd.
Reapers and Ploughmen half ne'r tug'd an Oar,
Nor saw the foaming Sea but from the Shoar.
Muſt we be ruin'd and despis'd at laſt?
　　Canid.　　Did we by land a viꞔory forego,　　75

That a vain Queen might a rich Galley show ?
My Legions——
    Anto.   *Canidius* no more.
I know they ſtood impatient on the Shoar :
Nineteen such Legions as might fate controul,
And fortunes wheel at their own pleasure roul.   80
    Can.   A loss at Sea let trading Nations mourn ;
Victorious *Romans* to land Conqueſt born,
Trophies at Sea as much as gain despise,
Of which an Island is the higheſt prize.
The trembling world did to the Victor yield,   85
Crown'd with the Laurels of *Pharsalia*'s field.
    Chil. Since we have loſt 'tis well the gain was small,
One lucky blow at Land recovers all.
    Phot. Th' Enemy is already at our Walls,
And our diſtress for sudden Counsel calls.   90
Our Queen amazed at the Siege appears.
    Ant. But yet her love is ſtronger than her fears,
Her Country she has made the Seat of War,
'Tis juſt her safety be our early'ſt care :
I will her Guard within these Walls remain ;   95
And 'gainſt the angry Gods her Cause maintain.
Whil'ſt you *Canidius* to your Legions haſt,
Slight our defeat, their loyal hearts make faſt
To our juſt Cause : our Enemies despise,
And for my absence some excuse devise.   100
    Can. Sir, I am blunt, unknowing to deceive,
I'le say you cannot *Cleopatra* Leave :
That you in her defence alone can fight,
And bleſt in love, the Roman Empire slight.
    Ant. What shall I do, shall I my Queen for-
    sake,   105
And not her danger, I create, partake ?
Cæsar, this night, may *Alexandria* ſtorm,
And all that luſt or rage inſtruct, perform.
Her beauty may the Conqueror disarm,
And his success and love that beauty charm.   110
Her Subjects weary of the Wars, may rise

And make her blood their common sacrifice.

Memn.   They say, their Queen in policy of State,
Should buy her Country's peace at any rate.

   Ant.   They say! who says?   *Memnon* you fain
     would vent,   115
In others names, your private discontent.
I see a sullen fierceness in your brow
Which you wou'd put in act, if you knew how.

   Mem.   Sir, I am known to love my Country well.

   Ant.   So they say all that purpose to rebel.   120

   Chil.   Some with your head would young *Octavius*
     greet,
And on those bloody terms a Peace compleat:
Under such Polititians *Pompey* fell
With tumults backt what may they not compel.

   Ant.   How shall they foes, who cannot tumults
     quell?   125
The giddy multitude, we must not fear,
But what we once resolve on, make 'em bear.

   Mem.   'Tis ill to discontent whom we must use,
And men fight best when they their party choose.

   Ant.   'Tis chosen for 'em by their Soveraign;   130
And 'tis sedition in them to complain:
Maxims too popular you still maintain.

   Mem.   Sir, my plain speech does no design contain;
'Tis the meer issue of my heart and brain:
If it offend——

   Ant.   It does, be gone.   135
Nor will I learn of you what's to be done.   [*Exit.*
When things go ill, each Fool presumes t' advise,
And if more happy, thinks himself more wise.
All wretchedly deplore the present state
And that advice seems best which comes too late.   140

   Phot.   You loose your self in rage and have forgot:
Amintas, *Deotorus*—and the rout
Of vulgar Kings have meanly turn'd about.

   Canid.   *Pelusium* by *Seleucus* is betray'd.
Some say the Queen did his revolt perswade.   145

Ant.   Monſter, such horrid blasphemy forbear,
Both were his own, the falshood and the fear.
   Can.   Sir, I but speak the language of the World.
   Ant.   Henceforth be ever dumb that World and
     thou :
It cannot, muſt not, nor it sha'nt be so.   150
   Can.   Nay if it sha'nt, I have no more to say.
   Ant.   Aside all passion and all heat Ile lay,
And cooly argue : what can be her end
There to betray, whom she does here defend.

     Enter Cleopatra, Charmion, Iras *with* Seleucus's
          young Son, Egyptians.

But see the Queen : Heart! but this once ſtand
     faſt—   [*aside.*
And I'le forgive thee all thy weakness paſt.   156
How can your goodness to a wretch extend ?
Who all he lov'd so poorly did defend :
   Cleop.   'Twas not your life, but me, you cou'd not
     loose,
Love turn'd your back, not Fear upon your Foes. 160
   Ant.   The timerous Deer, their female ſtanding by,
Each other will to wounds and death defie.
Love gives short courage to the meaneſt soul,
The creeping things he arms, and winged fowl.
Yet overcharg'd with love, I loſt the day,   165
And in my Miſtress presence ran away.
Cover'd with shame, I fear to meet those eyes.
   Cleop.   To them you never were more dear than
     now :
A manly look over your sorrows throw.
The Captain of my Gallies I have try'd,   170
And for his cowardice the Villain di'd.
With him die all remembrance of what's paſt,
I my *Cæsarion* have toward *India* sent :
This day *Antillus* to *Armenia* went.
What Merchant in one Ship wou'd venture all ? 175
They may survive and so revenge our fall,

Ant.   'Tis well they're gone, their youth was useless
  here,
And we for them more than our selves shou'd fear.
  Cleop.   See here the false *Seleucus* only Son,
                                        [*He spies* Seleucus's *Son.*
On whom I beg quick juſtice may be done.   180
His fathers Treason might on me reflect
Shou'd I the Son from your reveng⟨e⟩ protect:
My love and honour, let his death secure,
The shorteſt doubt they neither can endure.
  Ant.   None dares be impious to that degree,   185
To lay on you the Villains treachery.
Now my revenge I cannot execute,
Leſt I shou'd seem your virtue to dispute.
  Cleop.   You doubt me not I know, but others may,
Let his death take their jealousie away.   190
  Can.   She safely may the cruel offer make, [*apart.*
Which she well knows *Antonius* will not take.
  Ant.   He muſt not die, nor is it true revenge,
When the offenders suffer by exchange.
The youth it seems is not *Seleucus* care,   195
Or our resentment thus he wou'd not dare.
  Cleop.   Let him at leaſt for an example die,
Princes invite, who pardon treachery.
  Ant.   'Twere cruelty to kill the Innocent
For Crimes they neither knew, not cou'd prevent: 200
I beg his life my Queen—
  Cleop.   You may command
Or Life, or Death, at *Cleopatra*'s hand.
We who but now might halfe the World command,
Are overthrown at Sea, besieg'd at Land:
Each hour the news of some fresh Treason brings   205
From Faithless States or from revolted Kings.
  Ant.   Let those Crown'd Slaves from out our
    Party go:
A Treach'rous Friend, will be a Tim'rous Foe.
  Cleop.   The Plains about are cover'd with our Foes,
Hiding the Earth, as when our *Nile* o're-flows. 210

Yet ⟨find⟩ I in *Antonius* Courage reſt,
As if that Heart he gave me fill'd my Breaſt.
    Ant.   When *Brutus* this *Octavius* over-threw,
In a pitch'd Field I *Cassius* did subdue.
And turn'd the Fortune of that fatal day,   215
Which thus ungrateful *Rome* and He repay;
But here remaining I those Legions loose,
Which all commands but from my Mouth refuse.
    Cleop.   They ever us'd *Canidius* to obey;
May he not go, and my *Antonius* ſtay?   220
For you my Peoples love and more I loſt,
Muſt I not keep what has so dearly coſt?
    Ant.   Ah Madam, you shou'd take the weakeſt part,
And help a Lover to defend his Heart.
Thô swounding Men with ease resign their Breath, 225
Their careful Friends ſtill pull 'm back from Death.
You should my Lethargy of Honour chide,
And drive me thô unwilling, from your side.
Die at your Feet the meaneſt Lover might,
But in your quarrel the whole World shall fight. 230
    Cleop.   If I am Captive to the *Romans* made;
Surpriz'd in this weak place, or else betray'd;
Think not I'le live to be redeem'd again,
And like a Slave of my proud Lords complain.
At the firſt Dawn of my ill Fate I'le die.   235
    Ant.   O name not Death we'l meet in Triumph
      here:
I'le raise the Siege e're you have time to fear.
    Cleop.   But then your Love, in absence, will it last?
Men think of joys to come, and slight the paſt.
    Ant.   My Heart shall like those Trees the Eaſt
      does show,   240
Where Blossomes and ripe Fruit hang on one Bough.
With new desires, soft hopes, at once be preſt;
And all those Riper Joys, Love gives the bleſt.
Courage and Love shall sway each in their turn,
I'le fight to conquer, conquer to return.   245
Seeming Ambitious to the publick view,

I'le make my private end and dearer, You.
This Storm once paſt; in Peace and Love we'l Raign,
Like the Immortal Gods, the Giants slain.
   Cleop.   Moments to absent Lovers tedious⎫
      grow;   ⎪   250
'Tis not how time, but how the mind does go.⎪
And once *Antonius* wou'd have thought so too.⎭
   Ant.   Dearer than ever think not that I part,
Without the utmoſt Torment of my Heart.
Whil'ſt you perswade, your danger chides my ſtay, 255
Make me not caſt me and your Self away.
How well I lov'd, you did at *Aĉtium* see,
When to be near you I left Viĉtory.
And chose to be companion of your flight,
Rather than conquer in a diſtant Fight.   260
Press not that heart you know so well, too far,
Our Fortune will no second frailty bear.
   Cleop.   The trueſt Misers choose to sit about,
And tell their wealth: but dare not truſt it out.
I know as well as you, 'tis fit you go,   265
Yet what is beſt I cannot let you do.
   Ant.   For my attendance I some few will take;
All other *Romans* of your Guard I make.
   Cleop.   If you muſt go, it quickly shall appear,
My love sought this delay, and not my fear.   270
When you attaque, we'l sally from the Town,
And blood inſtead of *Nile* our Plain shall drown.
We'l in the midſt of *Cæsar*'s Army meet,
And like *Bellona* I my *Mars* will greet.
   Ant.   Wou'd Goddesses themselves to me en-
      dear,   275
In *Cleopatra*'s shape they muſt appear.
   Cleop.   My heart can danger though not absence
      bear,
To Love, 'tis Wax, but Adamant to Fear.
   Ant.   Mine has such Courage from your Firmness
      took,
That I can almoſt bear a parting look.   280

Cleop.   Take it ; and each unto their charge make
haſte.

Ant.   Our hardeſt victory I hope is paſt.

[*Exeunt omnes.*

ACT II

Scene the Firſt.   The Town.

Enter Antonius, Canidius.

Ant.   Empire and Glory both farewell : Come
shame,
And shed thy Venom on *Antonius* Name :
Wither the Lawrels on his Brows and teach
The World to scorn its moſt inglorious Wretch.
Forsaken in the choiceſt hour of time,   5
My hopes and resolutions in their prime.
Honor, my Queen and I Dictator made,
And all his rough Commands cou'd have obey'd.
Love for a while, we purpose to dethrone,
As Mariners in Storms their Sails take down.   10
Can *Romans* thus their General forsake ?
    Can.   They urg'd want of Provision and of Pay.
    Ant.   Both which had been redreſt without delay :
Th'obliging Queen——
    Can.   Whom you may thank for this—
Their general Discontent at her was lowd :   15
But Souldiers are a rude uncivil Crowd.
Play'rs and Minſtrels, Singers and Buffoons,
Are the great Inſtruments and Props of Thrones.
I my old Legions to your Aid have brought,
Firm to your Side, not tainted in a Thought—   20
They say *Photinus* in the Camp was seen,
And that he was imploy'd there by the Queen.
    Ant.   At a revolt so ſtrange I am surpriz'd.

Can. Pray Heaven it were not in the Town
    devis'd.
Your upright Nature stoops not to Descry   25
The low and subtil ways of Treachery.
Thô you may fail, She can't; Beauty will find,
Victorious and young Monarchs ever kind.
    Ant. Your honest meaning does your life protect:
Presume no more her vertue to suspect.   30
    Can. May I not say *Photinus* is a Knave?
    Ant. Tax not the man, unless good proof you have.

        Enter Photinus *pursued by six Villains.*

    Phot. Those two you must destroy, and me disarm.
Ah, Sir, from Murtherers defend your Life:
See with my blood, they have begun the Strife.   35
            *They draw, two of the Villains fall, the
                    other run.*
The Gods a Guard for Vertue still provide:
Courage with Treason seldome doth reside.
Th'are fled and you unhurt——
    Ant.   I am:
But say, *Photinus*, whence these Villains came.
    Phot. Just as I left the Throng   40
They set upon me Crying this is He,
That with *Octavius* lets us not agree,
Antonius Friend, and his own Countreys Foe;
And strait that word was followed with this blow.
Some of the popular faction set 'm on,   45
Who think to govern all if I were gone.
    Ant. 'Tis most unlucky these were Kill'd out
    right,
Of their whole Plot we else might gain some light.
            Phot. *stabs one lying on the ground, he
                    mutters out.*
1. *Villain.* *Photinus* is a Villain . . .
Phot.   See their spight . . .
Even at their Death, which I will thus requite—— 50
                        [*Can. interposes.*

Why wou'd you save from my juſt rage so ımpudent
   a Slave ?
   1. *Villain.*   *Photinus* set us on :
   Phot.   Unheard of villany . . .
My self to Kill, they did conspire with Me !
But great *Antonius* is himself too juſt
Me on a Murd'rers malice to diſtruſt.   55
   Canid.   Slight not too much the words of dying
   men,
They who hate truth before will speak it then.
   Phot. My conſtant zeal and firmness to your side,⎫
So oft in Council and in Aċtion try'd,   ⎬
This accusation cannot but deride.   ⎭60
What is't a Murth'rer missing of his blow,
In his laſt rage would not both say and do ?
   Can.   Who dares die,
And the juſt Gods provoke with such a lie ?
   Phot.   He that dares basely Kill, what dares he
   not,   65
No Crime a Murtherer cou'd deeper blot.
   Can.   Yet to that crime ingratitude may add.
   Phot.   You speak as of my guilt you wou'd be glad.
   Ant.   My friends, let this untimely discord fall.
   Phot.   Although much wrong'd, at your Command
   it shall.   70
   Can.   I wish, Sir, to my Souldiers you wou'd speak,
and let 'm know how well their loves you take.
   Ant.   I go : their Faith shall so rewarded be—
The reſt shall soon repent their treachery.
                                  [*Ex.* Ant. Can.
   Phot.   Had they fought well their danger had been
   small,   75
Cou'd they not fear at firſt or not at all ?
Curse on all middle ways : Courage enough
When once engag'd, can only bring us off.
But the next blow by fate shall be my own,
And I'le ſtrike home for *Iras* and a Throne.   80
My person is ungraceful, I well know

It was contriv'd for use and not for show.
Besides I 'm old, that too when I am great,
She may have the Ambition to forget.
This gentle Maid all other ways have try'd,   85
Hopeless of Love, I'le now attempt her pride.

Enter Iras.

But see she comes, and charming as new light,
Appear'd to the firſt Mans amazed sight.

[*A noise of Drums.*

You hear how Drums and Trumpets fill the Air,
And for a Scene of Blood our Minds prepare.   90
    Iras. 'Tis Love, vile Love whence this Disorder
        springs.
    Phot. The tender Parent of the frightful'ſt Things.
Yet blame not Love, when to it's objeƈt fixt;
It only harms when with Ambition mixt.
When raging Winds raise Tempeſts on the Main, 95
The gentle Brooks creep mildly through the Plain.
'Tis only to the Great these Storms are known,
Photinus passion fears your scorn alone.
    Iras. What is this Love, we never can exclude ?
But whatsoe're we talk of, 'twill intrude.   100
    Phot. Of Storms the Seaman tells, of ploughs the
        Hind ;
Lovers in such discourses ease their mind.
'Tis the glad business of young Hearts, the pain,
The old, for their presumption muſt suſtain.
    Iras. Is't a disease beauties infeƈtion spreads ? 105
Pray does it seize you in your hearts or heads ?
    Phot. Sweet Innocence ! it enters at the eyes,
And to the heart like subtle lightning flies.
When Lovers meet it is all extasie,
And when they part again they more than die.   110
    Iras. How chance that I have scap't this mighty
        ill ?
I gaze and ſtare at every thing my fill.
The Wise, the Handsome, and the Brave, I love,

Yet feel no pain at all when they remove.

    Phot. Passions lye yet within your tender
      breaſt,   115

Harmless and weak as Eagles in the Neſt:

But Love hereafter on your heart will prey.

    Iras. If ever any one escap't, I may.

    Phot. 'Twere moſt unfit you shou'd, Nature does
      ſtill

Provide some soveraign thing for every ill.   120

For Beauties wounds their kindness is the cure:

Scorpions who cou'd without their oyl endure?

    Iras. If I have hurt you 'twas againſt my will.

    Phot. Your Charms not like a Foe, but weapon, kill.

    Iras. Their farther ill effects I will prevent,   125

And of what's paſt, though innocent, repent:

I'll go where you shall never see me more.

    Phot. That muſt not be, from you whom I adore.

Absence is raging pain, presence a joy;

Which will at leaſt voluptuously deſtroy.   130

    Iras. Wou'd you not have me go nor ſtay! what
      then?

This Love I see makes errant Fools of men.

    Phot. Stay gentle *Iras*; learn to love of me,

How easie were it, cou'd I charm like thee.

    Iras. Does no man else adore me as you do?   135

    Phot. None ever did; I'l place you on a Throne,

A Scepter may for pers'nal wants attone.

Beauty and Youth, your Sexes glories are,

In men they soon decay, or not appear.

    Iras. I did not know you were a Prince dis-
      guis'd: 140

At your new Majeſty I'm much surpriz'd.

    Phot. I am no King.

    Iras.   How then shall I be Queen?

O I could ſtrut with *Cleopatra*'s Mein.

    Phot. The *Roman Empire* can a Crown beſtow.

    Iras. Such gifts may be *Antonius* overthrow.   145

    Phot. So let 'em be.

Iras.   But what he gives you, *Rome*
Will take away, if *Cæsar* overcome.

Phot.   My hopes, sweet Innocence, in *Cæsar* lye,
And e're I reign *Antonius* muſt dye.

Iras.   You have but the Reverſion of a Crown, 150
And e're he dies how old you will be grown.

Phot.   Your youth a while may for such glories
   wait,
But you may truſt my Love to urge his Fate.

Iras.   Muſt I then marry you, or be no Queen ?

Phot.   I'm not so wither'd, nor are you so
   green :   155
Nay *Charmion* will accept what you refuse,
And when she reigns your peevishness accuse—
It works——

Iras.   No no ! my self I'll have you firſt—
To see her Queen I should with envy burſt.

Phot.   Will she then promise to love me alone, 160
When I have plac'd my *Iras* on a Throne ?

Iras.   I will do any thing, to be a Queen ;
I could love one whom I had never seen.

                              [*Enter Messenger.*
Mess.   Madam, the Queen much wonders at your
   ſtay.   [*Ex. Iras.*

Phot.   She's gone, she's gone, and I me-⎤
   thinks have more   ⎟ 165
A thousand times to utter than before,   ⎬
So inexhauſtible's a Lovers ſtore.   ⎦
To her Ambition I her Love muſt own ;
But Fate⟨,⟩ her youth, my age will have it so.
How false a Joy in that fair Scx he takes,   170
Whom once the hope of equal love forsakes.

Scene the Second. *Cæsars* Tents.

Enter *Cæsar, Mecænas, with Atendants.*

Cæs. *Mecænas* see ſtrict discipline they keep
Through the whole Camp, that neither wine nor sleep
Betray us to surprize : thô peace seem near,
Wise Pilots at the Port a tempeſt fear.
 Mecæn. Great Sir, your Souldiers find they have
  to do   5
Not with a rude unarm'd and barb'rous Crew,
But Romans like themselves, in Conqueſt bred,
And next your self, by the beſt Captain led.
Their jealousie of Fame and Love for you,
Will make 'em any thing forbear or do.   10
           [*A shout of joy.*

Enter Agrippa.

 Agrip. *Antonius* Legions newly are arriv'd,
And through the Camp are with loud joy receiv'd.
Tir'd with his impotent and diſtant sway,
They now, Great Sir, will you alone obey.
 Cæs. Then vanish all his hopes, and all my fears, 15
In my whole sky of Fate, no Cloud appears :
That one black corner did a tempeſt threat.
 Agrip. You much are to *Photinus* care in debt :
Him in the Camp, when I arriv'd I found.
 Cæs. Yee Gods ! why am I to a Villain bound ? 20
Tell my new friends, I their arrears will pay ;
A *Roman* Emperor they ſtill obey.
 Mecæn. *Antonius* now will any Laws receive,
What from weak Foes we do not take, we give.
Demand the *Roman* Legions yet behind,   25
And that his pow'r to *Asia* be confin'd.
 Cæs. The man was once my Friend, my Brother⎫
  ſtill :   ⎪
What are these thoughts that wou'd ambition chill ? ⎬
 Mecæn. Forget that name he has deserv'd so ill. ⎭
The spoil of *Egypt* will the War defray ;   30
For a meer peace *Rome* will repine to pay.

Enter Octavia.

Him brother, let Ægyptian Princes call,
He has no Interest in your blood at all.
Since the best Ty he slights, and in her place
Does a less fair Ægyptian Queen embrace.   35
  Oct.   Pernicious Counceller that does foment
A War, all but the *Parthians* wou'd prevent.
My Wrongs shall never thy Ambition hide,
I'le tear the Masque of pity from thy pride.
I thought thee once deserving thy great place,   40
Of *Tuscan* Kings sprung from the glorious race.
But thou art false, cruel, and bloody now,
That open hatred thou durst never show.
To my dear Lord, does still in malice lurk,
And on this dire Occasion seeks to work.   45
  Cæs.   Sister, your Husband I would but reclaim,
And make him worthy of your virtuous flame.
His present life does his past glory stain,
He makes a Queen the Partner of his raign.
The Roman Empire he does much deface,   50
And with the Spoil adorns her foraign race.
Arabia where the *Nabatheans* live.
And part of *Syria* he did lately give.
To their new issue one he stiles the Moon :
To name the other, he profanes the Sun.   55
  Oct.   If he has given much, he conquer'd more :⎫
His valour, for his bounty, found the store ;   ⎬
And pardon somewhat on a Sisters score.   ⎭
  Cæs.   The names of Emperor and Queen they
      scorn,
And like immortal Gods themselves adorn.   60
He does for *Bacchus*, she for *Isis* pass,
And in their shapes, the wond'ring Crowd amaze.
  Oct.   To Gods of their own honour leave the Care,
Since they both Jealous and Almighty are.
I fear so high you'l my concernments press ;   65
You'l break on that you never can redress.
  Cæs.   I understand no Riddles, but he shall

Do my *Octavia* sudden right or fall.
The rest I cou'd with small excuse forgive :
But under this affront I cannot live.   }70
    Oct.   You say his other faults you cou'd forgive.
    Cæs.   Empire's our real quarrel, but I must *[Aside.*
Her virtuous Mind with no such secret trust.
I could——   74
    Oct.   Then that pretence I'le thus remove and dy :
                [Stabs her self. Mec. *interposes.*
Still more inhumane must I then remain,
The cover of your Pride and Lust to reign.
Tho I were dead you might your ends pursue,
But let me vanish from the painful view.
    Mec.   Not for the World such virtue shou'd not
    dy,   80
But be intire translated to the Sky.
    Cæs.   I Sister your late rashness can forgive,
So you henceforth will promise me to live.
Mecænas see remov'd all means of Death,
Let Nature and not rage conclude her breath.   85
            [Ex. Cæsar, Agrippa, &c.
    Oct.   Peace to the World and my unhappy Lord,
My Brother but for you wou'd soon afford.
    Mec.   Condemn not actions till you know their end,
But mine perhaps will then but more offend.
    Oct.   I know you'l say 'tis brave to rule alone,   90
That my great Brother wou'd become that Throne.
And raising him you in proportion rise,   ⎫
But still remember there are Deities   ⎬
Above you both, just, pow'rful, and wise. ⎭
    Mec.   Ambition never overturn'd my mind,   95
I am already more then I design'd.
    Oct.   Why do you then the general peace oppose ;
'Tis Avarice or Ambition makes Men foes.
    Mec.   I Madam wou'd some marks of courage
    show,
And what I durst for my great Master do.   100
    Oct.   Romans of courage need no other proof,

Since to be born a Roman is enough.

    Mec. 'Tis truth, but yet——

    Oct.   Some unjust pique you bear,⎫
My dearest Lord, you cannot well declare,   ⎪
But good *Mecænas*; for such once you were; ⎬ 105
T'obstruct this Treaty for my sake forbear.   ⎭

    Mec. 'Tis for your sake alone, it must not be.

    Oct. If it be good for *Rome*, regard not Me.

    Mec. Y'are Sister to my Emperor and Friend,
My utmost care, must your concerns attend :   110
I do not as you think confusion seek,
Nor keep I to your Lord a secret pique :
But if this Treaty be confirm'd to day,
I must at *Rome*, and you in *Asia* stay.

    Oct. It is the part of the whole World I'd
      chuse,   115
And gaining Him, what is't I care to loose.

    Mec. Ah Madam, seem less virtuous or less fair,
Who can behold you and not vengeance sware.
Such suffering goodness will mankind ingage,
And on *Antonius* pull their publick rage.   120

    Oct. This to the Sister of your Emperor ;

    Mec. This to the only Beauty I adore :
Beyond my patience you have rackt my Breast,
And my deep guilt at last must be confest.
I love you, Madam——   125

    Oct. My next request you'l then not disallow,

    Mec. Speak it, and I a blind Obedience vow.

    Oct. Let me then die for I have liv'd too long,
And heard of Love in my *Antonius* wrong.

    Mec. Not in his wrong ! I'le the reversion wait, 130
And live like Heirs in hope of an Estate.

    Oct. Your word is past recall. My Death I claim.

    Mec. From me who both your Guard and Lover
      am.

    Oct. I not the stroak, but means of Death
      require :
By my own hand I noblest shall expire.   135

Will you then promise to promote the peace.
   Mec.   You offer poison, to my known Disease :
But from those hands I nothing can refuse.
I'le ruine all my hopes, so you will live :
   Oct.   Yes, I will live, but not an hour survive.   140
My dear *Antonius* him you muſt preserve,
If ought you from *Octavia* would deserve——   [*Ex.*
   Mec.   Whom, whilſt he lives I never can enjoy,
And if he dies she will her self deſtroy.
" I am undone ; obey or disobey !   145
" I needs muſt perish, but may chose my way.
                                        [*Ex. omnes.*

ACT III

Scene the Firſt.   *Cæsars* Tents.

Enter *Cæsar, Mecænas, Agrippa.*

   Cæsar.   The *Asians* now with double Taxes preſt,
His slothful Days and drunken Nights deteſt ;
Buffoons and Players chiefly have his ear :
He dares not the free tongues of *Romans* hear.
To marry Whores to Fencers is his sport,   5
And with their Issue throng his loathed Court.
" Now lewd *Cytheris* has a greater Train,
Than his own Mother or his Wife maintain.
From such a Foe as this what can we fear !
In whom all symptoms of loſt pow'r appear.   10
   Mecæn.   The flatt'ring *Greeks* his easie nature
      praise ;
But on the reſt he heavy burthens lays.
In drunken Bounty, for a riotous treat,
He gave his Fav'rite Cook a spacious Street :
Men say no hour dares move without its Feaſt,   15
Which is for their fantaſtick pallats dreſt.
Now muſt the rising Sun their Riot view,

Which the next day prevents the Evening dew.
" In every draught they some rich Gem consume,
" And spend a private Fortune in one Room.   20
  Cæs.   Empire, of pains and virtue, the slow fruit,
How ill doſt thou with vice and riot suit ?
Cinna was bloody, *Marius* unjuſt,
Tarquin and *Appius* raging in their Luſt :
Lucullus was luxurious, loud his ease,   25
Thus on each man his single vice did seize !
But all these faults are in *Antonius* met.
  Mecæn.   His Court with *Asian* Flatt'rers is fill'd,
And Lying *Greeks* the only Servants held.
These serve the turns of riotous delight,   30
Whilſt *Romans* only are thought fit to fight.
  Agrip.   Example is a living Law, whose sway,
Men more than all the written Laws obey.
Princes of all men therefore shou'd take care,
How in their manners they the Crowd ensnare.   35
But above all his dotage on the Queen
Employs my wonder : was it ever seen
A Woman rul'd an Emperor till now ?
What Horse the Mare, what Bull obeys the Cow ?
Nature that Monſter Love does disavow :   40
In all her kinds only fantaſtick Man
Finds ways of folly which no other can.
  Mecæn.   He that will vilify the pow'r of Love,
In the firſt place let him our Gods reprove,
Who oft their heavenly Mansions have forsook,   45
And the mean shapes of Birds and Beaſts have took,
To pursue Mortals in an amorous way,
And form their glorious Image in our clay.
  Agrip.   The God that lov'd, what Nymph yet ever
      rul'd ?
He was again a God, his Luſt once cool'd :   50
Had womens will our good or ill procur'd,
The World had never half so long endur'd.
The high embrace fill'd all their spacious thought,
And proofs of kindness were no farther sought.

   Cæs.   Th'unable sure, the ugly, or the old,   55
First in affairs of Love, made use of gold.
Then Princes to out-bid 'em threw in pow'r,
Now heart for heart's the Traffick of the Poor.
   Agrip.   Women should sit like idle Passengers,
While the tall Ship some able Seam⟨a⟩n ſteers.   60
Wisdom, high Courage, Piety are vain,   ⎫
If o're the Wise and brave a Woman reign.   ⎬
And this *Antonius* conduct has made plain. ⎭
   Cæs.   'Tis time the in⟨j⟩ur'd World we should
      redeem
From a mans sway so loſt in her eſteem.   65
   Agrip.   What is success in Arms if Conqu'ring
      Rome
By Troops of *Asian* Vices be o'recome.
   Cæs.   To set all right I muſt be absolute;
My leaſt commands None daring to dispute:
Rome's desp'rate ſtate can never find redress,   70
But from a pow'r as able to oppress;
Whilſt for the publick good my pow'r I use,
Seeing my end Men will the means excuse.
Th'Omnipotence of Gods, who thinks too great,
Since men below they with compassion treat.   75
   Agrip.   But envy does all mortal pow'r attend:
Men fear the Means, and ſtill suspect the end.
He that can hurt, who answers but he will:
Men pass in fear by sleeping Lyons ſtill.
Empire is safeſt moderately great,   80
And death unseen does on Ambition wait.
   Cæs.   He that can do no ill, can do no good,
And if in one, in both may be withſtood.
The actions of a Tyrant I abhor,
But as things ſtand I cannot want the pow'r.   85
   Agrip.   Our Laws the art of ruling beſt contain;
   Mecæn.   Fools find it there, wise Princes in their
      Brain.
   Agrip.   Pow'r long posseſt few Princes care to use,
But give it up for others to abuse:

From *Phœbus* self the World no hazard run,   90
But cou'd not bear one day his Vent'rous Son :
He through new wayes the flaming Chariot drove,
And all was fear below, and fire above.
    Cæs.   I to no *Phaeton* will the reins commit,
Nor in inglorious ease a moment sit :   95
Ile see the Common-wealth no mischief take,
And do and suffer all things for her sake.
    Mecæn.   *Rome* on your vertue leans her aged head,
As old *Anchises* on *Æneas* did,
And thinks she may with ease when propt by you   100
Factions at Home, and Foes abroad subdue.
You, whom the general voice of *Rome* does hold,
Bolder than Youth, and wiser than the Old.
    Agrip.   The name of Common-wealth is popular,
And every *Cæsar* may his *Brutus* fear.   105
    Mecæn.   *Romans* that barb'rous Murder so re-
      veng'd,
It shews the thoughts of a Republick chang'd.
    Cæs.   Men die of Agues, too much heat or cold,
And others grow ridiculous⟨ly⟩ old.
The thoughts of humane chance should make us
    bold.   110
Ile seize the Empire, which Ile die or hold.
             ⟨[*Ex.* Cæs. Oct. Mec. *manet* Agrip.⟩
    Agrip.   Born under Kings our Father⟨s⟩ freedom
    sought,
And with their blood the Godlike treasure bought,
We their vile issue in our chains delight,
And born to freedom for our Tyrants fight.   115
                  [*Exit.* Agrip.

      Scene the Second.   The Palace.

     Enter *Antonius, Canidius, Photinus.*
    Can.   For what Sir, must we then prepare ?
Thyreus ! does he bring us Peace or War ?

Anto. He offers Peace, but upon terms so high,
At the great rate I'd not an Empire buy :
My former gifts I meanly muſt resume, 5
And give accounts of all my aȼt⟨s⟩ to *Rome.*
My faithful friends from their Commands remove,
And place such as the Senate shall approve.
    Canid. True friends displac't will pardon your diſtress,
And thô your pow'r—— 10
    Anto. A Pageant pow'r and Empire but in show—
True Empire only those great Souls enjoy,
Who can in what, and whom they please employ,
And without leave from *Rome* a Crown beſtow,
Exalt a Friend, and trample on a Foe : 15
This by your Love and Arms I once attchiev'd,
Nor will be of it but by Arms depriv'd.
    Can. Ambition is the Dropsey of the Soul,
Whose thirſt we muſt not yield to but controul.
    Anto. Some Drudg of State may a less pow'r eſteem, 20
And ruling many, let a few rule him ;
Mean Slave to them, high Tyrant to the reſt,
With fear and pride at once defile his breaſt :
By *Hercules* I won't ⟨!⟩ if any here
Think that a Course too desp'rate I ſteer, 25
Let him retire, and his own fears obey.
    Canid. The Gods well know my fears are all for you,
And your moſt daring thoughts shall find me true :
It is not *Cæsar,* nor our blow at Sea,
That to these terms incline me to agree ; 30
But 'tis the love of *Rome* which you have loſt,
And that your Ryots here and Loves have coſt.
    Ant. *Cæsar* and I you know were never friends,
And only hung together for our ends :
Yet in his Cause this Tongue an Army rais'd, 35
And made *Rome* hate that deed she late had prais'd.
Brutus and *Cassius* felt the deadly ſting ;

And all to make *Octavius* more than King.
So blindly did I act, so little see,
Into the dark Decrees of Destiny.   40
The Common-wealth for him I overthrew,
Now in effect he claims my Empire too.
   Phot.   The Shell he leaves, the Kernell takes away,
You, Sir, must him, as others, you obey.
   Ant.   He wou'd a sway pretend over my Love, 45
And teach my free affections where to move.
To my embrace his Sister I must take,
And my best Queen ingratefully forsake.
   Can.   That Sister is your Wife.
   Ane.   So let her be
From past engagements, present Love, set free.   50
Hymen is but the Vulgars Deity . . .

    Enter Cleopatra, Charmion, Iras, *Egyptians.*

   Cleop.   O my *Antonius*! how I fear this Peace!
And must I to *Octavia* yield my place?
I love you so, that very sound wou'd kill,
And leave you free the promise to fulfil.   55
   Ant.   Were I to gain the Empire of mankind,
And for that pow'r, Eternity assign'd:
I cou'd not to the hateful change submit,
Nor my best Queen so barbarously quit.
   Cleop.   But your *Octavi⟨a'⟩s* loving, young, and
    fair,   60
And such a Rival! how can I but fear?
   Ant.   Her Hymen never did a Moment please,
The hard Condition of a needful Peace:
From every part I saw the growing storm,
A sudden shelter in her arms I took,   65
Which when 'twas over I again forsook.
   Cleop.   And can you for My sake a War sustain?
Her Brothers friendship and Her Love disdain?
   Ant.   All hearts a like, all faces do not move,
There is a secret Sympathy in Love: 70
The pow'rful Loadstone, cannot move a Straw,

No more than Jet, the trembling Needle draw :
Your Beauty only on my Heart can act :
All other ways, it is in vain attaqu'd.
    Cleop. Sure of this War I am the meer pretence, 75
How can our Love, to *Rome* give such offence ?
She shou'd revenge the Ghost of *Crassus* slain,
And haughty *Babel* level with the Plain,
But let in *Egypt*, Love and pleasure reign.
    Ant. *Rome* like her Eagles, did on Rapine thrive, 80
I am the first that taught her how to Give.
    Cleop. What y' have presented me or plac'd on
      Mine,
I to that griping Senate here resign.
I never did the gifts but Giver prize :
Some new pretence of War let 'm devise :   85
All but your self I for your sake can quit :
For you I did my Crown and Fame forget ;
And can you now weigh coldly what it is fit ?
    Can. Turn my best Master, from her charming
      Tongue,
'Tis hard to think such Beauty in the wrong :   90
Yet if you don't, we are for ever lost.
    Ant. I have resolv'd : to *Cæsar* I will send :
If he his Grace will to the Queen extend,
And let the Crown upon her Sons descend.
I'le kill my self, and rid him of his Foe,   95
If not, the last extreams I'le undergo.
    Can. What *Roman* will the hateful Message bear ?
    Cleop. Let us intreat, we may at *Athens* live,
And tast what joys a private Life can give :
Leaving our greatness and our pomp behind,   100
We shall in Love sincerer pleasures find :
But whether am I wrapt ? fond thoughts be gone,
And melt some tender Virgin of low race,
You are below a heart that wears a Crown,
Where Life, Love, all must to renown give place. 105
    Ant. Souldiers, when old we from the Wars dis-
      charge,

But Fate her Drudges never sets at large :
The higher place they fill, the greater Slaves,
Princes have no retirement but their Graves,
My equal pow'r this *Cæsar* cannot bear,   110
His Souldiers want my Provinces to share :
Unactive *Lepidus* he laid aside,
And will no longer now the World divide ;
Whose doubtful Title must by Arms be try'd.

               Enter Thyreus.

But see *Thyreus* here. . . .   115
He has some Message for your private Ear,
Which I without a jealous pang can bear.

    Can.   She is a woman, Sir, and when y'are gone,
By *Cæsars* Offers may be wrought upon.

    Ant.   Jealous ! yet truly honest.   'Tis strange
     how   120
In thy plain mind such wild suspition's grow,
I will return before their Conf'rence end,
But on her Love entirely I depend.   [*Ex.* Ant. Canid.

    Thyr.   Madam ! my Master's gracious as he's great
See's how y'are forc't t' allow this short Retreat, 125
To his proud Foe, and does himself excuse,
That Ayd perhaps you cou'd not well refuse :
The Ruines of a Roman Emperor,
In her own Kingdom may a Queen o're pow'r.

    Cleop.   I first was summon'd in *Romes* haughty
     Name,   130
E're I into *Antonius* presence came.
Brutus and his I was accus'd to Aid,
But soon acquitted and her Ally made ;
Since in *Antonius* I have *Rome* obey'd.

    Thyr.   If an Ally of *Rome* you shou'd disclaim, 135
The Man, whom she does Foe and Traytor name.

    Cleop.   Those very Titles She Great *Julius* gave,
And yet anon, obeys him like a Slave.
On the Success of War, her Voice depends,
The distant Foes she stiles the present Friends.   140

Let others from *Antonius* fortune fly,
I will support or in their ruine lye.
    Thyr. His Souldiers have another fence declar'd,
And are to ſtorm this ſtubborn Town prepar'd.
    Cleop. Base Mercenary Souls that fight for Pay
To morrow Kill, whom they defend to day :   146
But Princes Minds on Springs of Honour move,
And what can they not do, wound up by Love ?
    Phot. If not your Self, your harmless Subjeᶜts save,
They neither love so well, nor are so brave.   150
    Cleop. Despair shall make those heartless Villains
      bold,
While by worse fears, the fear of Death's controul'd.
I'le *Rome* provoke beyond all hope of grace,
Then in their Arms, they muſt their safety place.
    Phot. They'l sooner take those Arms up and
      Rebel . . .   155
    Cleop. *Antonius* Souldiers will such Tumults quel.
The People ever discontented are ;
Their Crouds were made to be the food of War :
                          [*Ex. Phot.*

    Thyr. *Cæsar* is pleas'd——
You shou'd keep all the Realms of which you are
      seiz'd ;   160
Some little to deserve this you muſt do.
    Cleop. Desert propos'd me from a mortal Foe ?
    Thyr. Give us but entrance in the dead of night,
We all will spare who are not kill'd in Fight ;
Like *Cæsar*, *Cleopatra* shall command,   165
Antonius falls into a Brothers hand.
    Cleop. Who will revenge the scorn his Siſter finds ;
Are these your deep, your generous Designs ?
    Thyr. You but precipitate the event of War,
And by that aᶜt a Sea of Blood might spare.   170
I have a ſtep beyond my Orders made,
Which were but to propose not to perswade.
But who can see such Beauty in diſtress,
And not the utmoſt of his thoughts express.

Cleop.   In Fates whole scope I fear but one
    event,   175
And that your self with honour may prevent.
  Thyr.   What is it, Madam? will you hear me
    swear,
You truſt your secret to a Lovers ear,
One that has long, and privately been so.
  Cleop.   Sir to make Peace, you were from *Cæsar*
    sent,   180
But make not Love, thô but in Complement.
If *Cæsar* take this Town by Fates decree,
Swear to inform, what he will do with me——
  Thyr.   'Tis not resolv'd, soon as I know I will . . .
  Cleop.   Then sound him dayly with your utmoſt
    skill.   185
  Thyr.   But is this all? I was in hope to serve,
In some design that might your Love deserve.
This for your meaneſt Slave I had perform'd.
  Cleop.   'Tis all of which I care to be inform'd——
  Thyr.   My Offers, Madam . . .
  Cleop.   They are such as show,
Romans but ill of th' hearts of Monarchs know.   191
But on your promise may a Queen rely?

   Enter Antonius, Canidius *unseen, and Souldiers.*

  Thyr.   You may: but doubt not *Cæsars* Clemency;
Your Crown and Person, thô provokt he 'l spare,   195
Conqueſt and Ruin will respeſt the Fair,
What mayn't such Beauty hope, nor is it new,
That he who rules the World should bow to you.
  Ant.   By Heaven, at Complements; I'le pause a
    while,
And see this subtle Scene of Womans guile.   200
  Cleop.   My Fates worse Face you will not then
    disguise,
I can behold it with undaunted Eyes.
  Thyr.   And may it prove as charming as your own;
  Cleop.   I fear you will forget me, when y'are gone.

   Thyr.   I swear upon my Knees and by that
       Hand :   205
Whose every touch, my Soul leaps up to meet :
Let me once more th' inflaming Bliss repeat.
Like the firſt drop which Men in Feavours taſt,
It to a deeper draught but makes me haſt.
Thus ſtarving Men, think every thing a Feaſt,   210
Whil'ſt some with taſtless plenty, ly oppreſt :
O that I were *Antonius* but one day !——
   Ant.   Slave from that poſture thou shalt never rise,
But be my Wraths immediate sacrifice.
   Can.   Hold, Sir, your Sword you shall not rashly
       ſtain ;   215
What hopes of Peace Embassadors once slain ?
   Ant.   Ambassador of Love the Villain came ;
And 'mongſt affairs of State he vents his Flame,
He Kiſt her Hand, some charming Message sure,
At leaſt of half my Empire, She's secure.   220
Which she perhaps muſt with my Life repay,
These are the Bargains made when I am away :
'Tis more than Madness to believe that you,
False to my Love, are to my Empire true.
   Cleop.   I false to you !   225
   Ant.   By *Hercules* you are : and had I ſtay'd,
None knows the faithless answer you had made.
   Cleop.   What is it that so ſtrange *Antonius* finds ?
He kiſt my Hand in taking of his leave,
'Tis a respeƈt that Queens from all receive.   230
   Ant.   The eager Kiss, no Lover can miſtake,
It extacy and sudden rapture spake,
Those of respeƈt are of a colder make :
Ye Gods ! he swore by't perhaps endless Love,
Or that he wou'd your Mediator prove.   235
   Cleop.   Ask him : His offers I have all refus'd,
And yet of falshood live to be accus'd
By you, for whom I suffer, is this juſt ?
One minute, brings long faith into Diſtruſt.
   Ant.   Minutes may ruine what in Ages rose,   240

Like Thunder, Love in instants overthrows.
He has disturb'd me.   And he shall be whipt.
Canidius see he instantly be stript.
    Can.   If thus you trample on all *Roman* Laws,
What *Roman* is there that will own your Cause ?   245
The Law of Nations too does this withstand,
To any thing that's brave I'le lend my hand,
But stir to no such infamous command :
    Ant.   Seize the bold Traytor.
    Sould.   Will you have him flead.
Say but the word, this minute he is dead.   250
    Ant.   There's a true Servant to his Masters will,
Whom I condemn, he questions not to kill,
    Thyr.   With this affront if thou dar'st glut thy hate,
No pow'r on earth can save thy falling state :
Cæsar will take revenge——
    Ant.   Away, away 255
And my command see strictly you obey.   [*Ex.*
    Cleop.   I do not know that I a smile misplac't.
Frown'd where you frown'd, and where you lik't I
    grac't
Not Wealth to Misers, Honour to the Brave,
Health to the Sick, or Freedom to the Slave   260
Cou'd be more welcome than you⟨r⟩ Love to Me,
Then think how felt, the cruel change must be :
    Ant.   What Change ?
    Cleop.   How can you ask ? while this distrust
    appears ?
Distrust, the first decay of Love in years.   265
What we desire we easily believe,
Love on the smoother side does still deceive.
    Ant.   Your Lover shall be whipt, and as you bear
That, I shall think you criminal or clear.
    Cleop.   Not to the Man, but to his Character,   270
Such an affront I wish you wou'd forbear.
It is a deed that might amaze the Sun,
And by the rudest People yet undone :
In all the Travels of his fruitful light,

He has not met so barbarous a sight;   275
Ambassadors are sacred next the Gods,
Above your Axes plac't as well as Rods.
  Ant.   Observe how, least I change his punishment,
All ways of my revenge she wou'd prevent,
He may not die . . .
  Cleop.   Nor shan't, unless your hate, 280
All human Laws resolve to violate.
Then kill me first.

Enter Photinus *in hast.*

  Phot.   The Cities up, the Souldiers Mutiny,
And all—long live the good *Thyreus* cry.
  Anto.   My *Romans* take and charge 'm instantly.285
  Phot.   What they demand, perhaps you'll not refuse
  Anto.   How'er their Insolence I'll not excuse.
  Canid.   Good Sir, abroad you know we want no foes,
This inward strife methinks we might compose:
Octavius work our selves, let us not do.   290
  Cleo.   My People Sir, I hope you'll not destroy,
Whose lives I for your service, wou'd imploy.
Photinus say their Queen bids 'm begon,
And trust our Love, what's fitting shall be done.

Enter Messengers.

  Mess.   Your *Romans*, Sir, joyn with th' unruly
      crow'd,   295
And to defend th' Embassador, have vow'd:
They say a *Roman* never shall be whipt,
While Sword or Spear a *Roman* arm can lift.
      1. *Mess.*   They have by this the Castle Walls broke
          down,
      2. *Mess.*   And set *Thyreus* safe without the
          Town.   300
  Ant.   Draw up my Guards, if I have yet a Friend;
This Tumult shall in death of Thousands end.
What must *Octavius* conclude of me?
If whom I once imprison, they set free.

Cleo.   They have done right by chance, excuse 'em
     for⟨'⟩t ;   305
Tempeſts sometimes drives Ships into the Port.
Ant.   The Rable is a thing below my hate,
But my own *Romans* I will decimate.

         Enter Lucilius *Captain of the Rout.*

Luc.   For what is done, I singly am to blame :
The reſt but on my call and credit came.   310
Anto.   What mov'd thee too't : Old *Ruffian*, thou
     shalt dye ;
In thee I'll punish the whole Mutiny.
Luc.   I saw my General about to blaſt,
By one rash act, his life and Glories paſt.
Th' unconſtant Rabble to my side I gain'd,   315
And spight of him, his Honor have I maintain'd.
Anto.   What art thou ?
Luc.   A *Roman.*
Anto.   No more ?
Luc.   In *Brutus* Camp some small Command I
     bore :
Subdu'd by Arms, since by your kindness won,
I am resolv'd your utmoſt fate to run.   320
If my late service grieve you, take my head ;
The common path of Love I never tread.
Brutus to save⟨,⟩ my self like him I shap't ;
So fell I in your hands, and he escap't.
Anto.   *Lucilius* ?
Lucilius⟨.⟩   The same⟨,⟩ my Intreſt com-
     mand,   325
Antonius shall both rule my heart and hand.
Anto.   Discharge the Rabble you have us'd in
     this.   [*They shout.*
Luc.   They humbly sue you'll pardon what's amiss.
They are return'd, and now with shouts of joy ;
They beg you woud their Swords and Lives imploy. 330
Anto.   Moſt willingly, juſt Heaven, what am I,
Whom the rude People, teach Humanity ?   [*Ex.*

ACT IIII

Scene the firſt. *Cæsars* Tents.

Enter *Cæsar, Agrippa, Mecænas.*

Cæsar⟨.⟩ My Offers scornd! Ambassadors abus'd!
Yet he of Pride unjuſtly is accus'd.
   Mec. *Thyreus* was ill chose, he long has been
A secret Servant to th⟨'⟩*Ægyptian* Queen.
What if I went with terms more moderate;   5
   I, who am less Obnoxius to his hate.
   Cæs. This Offer now the danger grows so near,
⟨I⟩ in a man less known, shou'd take for fear.
   Agrip. His Insolence no longer I defend.
   Cæs. See here the Challenge he thinks fit to
      send.   [*Agrip. reads.* 10
   Agrip. In single Combat let our Fencers fight:
With Armies, Emperors dispute their right.
   Cæs. Like him, I *Roman* blood would gladly spare,
And to a Combat would contraƈt the War.
My youth, and un⟨s⟩oil'd ſtrength, may Conqueſt
      claim   15
Over this Shadow of a mighty Name:
Now preſt with Age, and with Debauches worn,
Th' unequal Combat I not fear, but scorn.
   Agrip. He like an aged Oak in *Autumn* shows,
From whose dry Arms some Leaves each minute
      blows;   20
One King or Ally, ſtill forsake his side,
His Empire ebbs like a declining Tide.
Have patience, Sir, he of himself must fall,
Who in despair does for the Combat call.
   Cæs. To a brave Death I'll open him the way; 25
See an Assault be made without delay.
I at my Armies head shall soon appear,
And if he dares, he may engage me there.

Enter *Octavia*.

Octav. O Brother! if that name have yet a Pow'r,
And be not loſt in that of Emperor :   30
Pity my sad eſtate, since I alone
On both sides mourning, can rejoyce on none.
The World divided in their wishes ſtand ;
My self alone ſtab'd through on every hand.
A Brother here! These muſt a Husband fall ;   35
On the juſt Gods I know not how to call!
No chance of War can with my mind comply ;
But I muſt weep at eithers Victory.
     Cæs. If I o'rcome, your Husband I will spare.
     Octav. He will not spare himself, I more than
          fear,   40
Shou'd he prevail, th' *Egyptian* Queen will sway ;
Whom you, and I, and he, muſt all obey.
His am'rous heart muſt execute her will,
And whom she frowns on, in Obedience kill.
You to Ambition muſt a *Victim* bleed, ⎫   45
And from my hated Title to his bed,   ⎬
Muſt *Cleopatra* in my Death be freed ; ⎭
And haughty *Rome* acknowledg a vain Queen,
Or be of Civil Arms th' endless Scene.
     Cæs. He doth all terms of Reconcilement slight : 50
There nothing now remains but that we fight.
He's now a meer soft Purple *Asian* Prince ;
And *Rome* his Empire has disown'd long since.
     Octav. Ingrateful *Rome !* but moſt ingrateful you!
Can you forget whom *Cassius* overthrew ?   55
Who firſt to *Rome* a *Parthian* triumph show'd,
And the long Pride of that great Empire bow'd ?
Who the firſt *Cæsar* made, revenged his death,
And fixt that Empire, which he did bequeath,
On you almoſt unknown : Where they receive,   60
Base Natures hate ; and Love, but where they give.
     Cæs. Go serve th' *Ægyptian*, learn to dress her
          head ;

Your slighted Love, and your neglected Bed
Can you forget; and fulsomely pursue
The Man with kindness, who despises you ?   65
I shou'd my self scorn fawning Beauty too :
'Tis as absurd, as if the Gods shou'd sue.

    Oct. Wives (like good Subjects, who to Tyrants
      bow)
To Husbands though unjust, long patience owe :
They were for Freedom made, Obedience We,   70
Courage their vertue, ours is Chastity.
Reason it self in us must not be bold,
Nor decent Custom be by Wit controul'd.
On our own heads we desperately stray,
And are still happiest, the vulgar way.   75

    Cæs. Who ever did such Moral Nonsense hear ?
My Sister sure is turn'd Philosopher.
But we *Antonius* Pride will soon pull down ;
This hour shall give me his whole lifes renown.
I the long trade of Fame disdain to drive ;   80
But to the Top will at one step arrive.

    Octav. Since then my pray'rs and tears can nothing
      gain,
In the Foes Camp no longer I'll remain.
The Arms I hate, my presence shall not grace ;
Antonius Cause I'll openly embrace.   85
To *Rome* I'll go, and all thy acts disown ;
Make thy Ambition, and thy Falshood known
To every *Roman* of the Sword and Gown,
Till th'art more hated far than *Cateline*,
Then S⟨u⟩lla, *Marius*, or the *Tarquins* Line.   90
Some will for Freedom, some *Antonius* fight,
And against Thee both parties I'll unite ;
Amongst thy Foes I like a Spark will fall,
And to a sudden Flame convert 'em all.

    Cæs. You wou'd not sure my Love so ill repay. 95
    Octa. Your Love ! your Pride and endless Thirst
      of sway.
To gain my friends, my Quarrel you pretend,

But universal Empire is your end.
Rome's once great *Senate* now is but a name;
While some with fear, and some with Bribes you
tame.   100
Men learn at Court what they muſt there repeat,
And for Concurrence, not for Council meet.
At leaſt all such as think of being great, ⎫
They blindly labour at their own ill fate, ⎬
And dig up by the roots the tottering State. ⎭   105
    Cæs.   Againſt *Antonius* Riots they declare,
And I at their Command but wage this War.
    Octa.   Dull Long-gown Statesmen you may feel
    that Sword
Which thus you whet againſt my injur'd Lord.
When *Cæsar* wills a Law, for all your rules,   110
It will be better taught in Camps, than Schools.
    Cæs.   Your fears diſtract you, or you needs muſt see
Your hopes of happiness depend on me.
'Tis my success muſt make *Antonius* find
The dire effect of an unbridled mind.   115
    Oct.   Who ever did an Emperor reform?
Scarce Heav'n it self can that great Task perform.
    Cæs.   Heaven chooses me the fitteſt inſtrumcnt,
And on that glorious *Task* I'm wholly bent.
    Oct.   Is't thus *Mecænas*, you promote the Peace?
But you ne'r meant, and promise but to please.   121
    Mec.   All that I durſt, I have already said:
I urg'd him till he thought I was afraid.
But where such Beauty, and such Goodness fail;
What other Intercession can prevail;   125
    Oct.   *Mecænas*, I no Complements expect
From one, who does my firſt Commands neglect.
    Mec.   Men that like me have giv'n their Passions
    vent,
Are never after held indifferent.
Hatred, or Love, pursues the bold attempt;   130
It meets with a return, or with contempt.
I fear the latter is *Mecænas* lot.

Oct. I charge you, never entertain me more
With that false Love which hath so little pow'r.
Your breach of Word, I easily forgive,   135
I'm free, and am not now oblig'd to live : [*She weeps.*
Nor will I long, the first attacq survive.
    Mec. A sound like that, what Lover can indure ?
I'll move once more, shou'd I his hate procure.
Ah Sir, your weeping Beautious Sister view ;   140
Then if you can, her Husbands life pursue :
Such softness might an angry God disarm,
And from his hand, the brandisht Thunder charm.
    Cæs. What means *Mecænas* softened in her tears ?
Another Man he to my eyes appears.   145
Where is that Soul bids me be Absolute,
And the dissenting World with Swords confute.
Move forwards still, and spread my Conqu'ring Arms,
As far as *Cinthia* lights, or *Phœbus* warms.
    Mec. I can no more, you your own Cause must
      plead ;   150
I wou'd, but can't against my self perswade ;
Tho unsuccessful my endeavours were,
It was some Merit to obey so far.

Enter Messenger.

    Mess. The Enemy preventing our attacq,
Does a fierce Sally on our Forces make.   155
Our formost Troops the warm ingagement shun,
And to *Canidius* his Old Souldiers run.
    Cæs. Then be your Tent your Prison for a while.
                    [*To Octavia.*
Now let us seize the Lyon in our Toil.——
                    [*Ex. omnes.*

Scene the Second.   A Wood.

Enter *Antonius, Canidius, Photinus,* at one door, *Agrippa,*
Thyreus, at the other, Fighting.

    Antony. Turn back *Thyreus* ; 'tis *Antonius* calls ;
The Queen now sees thee flying from our Walls.

Think on that shame, and it muſt warm thy heart,
And do not from a single Rival ſtart.
  Thyr. A Thought like that, were all Mankind my Foes,   5
Wou'd send me headlong amongſt all their Blows.
  Ant. He dies of Mine that dares to interpose.
  Thyr. Of Mine he is my baseſt Foe that does.
                        [They fight. Thyr. *falls.*
Love, thou at laſt art juſt, and having made
My Life a Burthen, help'ſt me to unlade :   10
If he o'recome, Let *Cleopatra* know,
She muſt to *Rome* in *Cæsars* triumph go.
So now my promise to the Queen is paid,
The firſt and laſt Command I ever had.
  Ant. Then all my Fears were false.
  Thyr.   False as my hopes,
Or the short vigor which my Being props.   16
The Queen was Cruel and thy Sword was Kind.
  Ant. Thou didſt attempt her Villain :
  Thyr.   Yes, I did,
And with my dying Breath I boaſt the Deed. *[Dies.*
  Ant. What words fit to appease her shall I find ? 20
Jealousie for ever from my Soul remove,
Thou magnifying Glass to erring Love ;
Thou Viper like, doſt thy young Teeth employ,
And wou'dſt that Love, which gave the⟨e⟩ Birth,
    deſtroy.

       Enter Cæsar *and* Mecœnas.

  Cæs. Charge you *Canidius* with your Troops,
    whilſt I   25
Againſt *Antonius* self my Fortune try.
Here is the utmoſt bound of thy success,
The Ocean may as soon his limits pass,
As thou this spot of Earth whereon we ſtand.
  Ant. You speak as you had Thunder in your hand,
The Gods ! Heaven ! Hell and Fate at your command ;   30

Which if you hadst I'd not one step retire :
But one by one, their Prodigies wou'd tire.

> [*Cæsar is beaten back.*

Enter Messenger.

Mess.   You must not stay your fortune to pursue,
Agrippa's got between the Town and you ;   35
Which Stratagem when *Cleopatra* found,
She Sally'd out, and is incompast round.
Photinus stays behind to awe the Town,
And keeps those of the pop'lar Faction down.

Ant.   My Queen ingag'd ! To her relief lets fly, 40
Death has more Charms near her, than Victory.
Me in her Cause, the Legions that withstand,
Must fall like Corn, before the Reapers Hand.

Can.   Must we again a Victory forgo ;
This Queen was born to be our Overthrow.   45

Ant.   What is't you mutter ?   Follow me or dy.

Can.   My Life you'd sooner want ⟨by half⟩ than I :
Take it, of 'tis to me an hourly pain,
Follies of Friends are nothing to the slain.
But whil'st I live, methinks you shou'd pursue,   50
Retiring Foes and Victory in view.

Ant.   I cannot stoop to argue, but Obey ;
And till my Queen be safe, let Conquest stay.   53

Scene the Third.   A Wood.

He discovers Agrippa's *Army, and the Queen taken.*

Ant.   By *Hercules* she's tane !   So have I seen the
    Dove,
Under the Pounce of eager Falcons move :
O ! that I were my self the Dart I throw,
For now, all other Motion seems too slow.

> [Ant. *rescues the Queen, Charges through*
>   Agrippa's *Army.*   Agrip. *Re-*
> *treats to the Town.*

Augures and Entrails, Boys and Quails you ly!   5
And I henceforth your Omens will defy.
Call'd by his Name, may such ſtill prosp'rous be,
While thus the Gods give Victory to Me.   [*Exeunt.*

⟨Scene the Fourth.   In the Town.⟩

Enter Photinus *as within the Town.*

Phot.   They are ingag'd by this :   now is the Time,
And all things seem propitious to my Crime.
Let Fools the Fame of Loyalty divide ;
Wise men and Gods are on the ſtrongeſt side.
The Town is wholly left to my Command,   5
To make 'em rise I need but slack my hand :
They'r prone to Mutiny.   Their Queen they hate,
And shew all signs of a diſtemper'd State. [*They shout.*
But hark already they are up and roar,
Like an high Sea that scorns its wonted Shoar.   10

Enter Iras.

But see fair Iras whose bright form in Tears,
Like Sun-shine mixt with sudden Rain appears.
   Iras.   *Photinus*!   Oh the Queen!   The Queen is
      gone,
And we that ſtay behind are all undone.
The Pallace flames ; *Memnon* and *Chilax* rage,   15
And all the *Egyptians* on their side engage.
   Phot.   Fear nothing Madam, never was a time,
When Innocence and Beauty were a Crime :
Each shout you hear, your Greatness does advance :
Nor is this Mutiny, th' effect of Chance.   20
But my design——
Through Craggy ways we for a while muſt tread :
But gentle *Iras* to a Throne they lead :
Ah!   Cou'd I make you Kind as well as great,
Photinus happiness were then compleat.   25
   Iras.   All other Forms I'le ſtudy to forget :

And think how much I'm to your Love in Debt:
Antillus is a young gay handsome Man,
Yet to please you, I'le hate him if I can.
He still like you lies squeezing of my hand, 30
Hangs o're my Neck, and from me will not stand.
    Phot. Ye Gods! She loves and knows not yet
      disguise
The happy Name, flasht at her youthful Eyes.
    Iras. The Manly Gown when he did first put on,
He was more gaz'd at than *Cæsarion*: 35
But for all that I will not love him tho,
'Tis so long since I have forgot him now . . . .
    Phot. Our Serpents though new born are poyson-
      ous still,
And Women ne'r so young have Craft and Guile.
She has forgot him! Oh that I cou'd Her! 40
Too plain, but yet too strong I see the snare.
I got my Rival to *Armenia* sent,
His Name returns and ruins my content.
    Iras. You seem disturb'd——
    Phot.   False and inhumane . . .
    Iras. What are you mad? 45
What is it I have done! What have I said?
    Phot. Thou hast for ever rob'd me of my rest.
    Iras. By all my hopes to reign I love you best.
    Phot. Ay there's your love to me.
But that for him how ill you do contain? 50
    Iras. For whom? I understand you not, be
    plain.
    Phot. Why for *Antillus*? Your young Gay De-
    light.
    Iras. May I not name, but I must love him
    straight?
    Phot. The Works soon done ⟨,⟩ with Wind and
    Tide they move;
Whom equal Years and Thoughts dispose to love. 55
And to say truth I stand condemn'd within,
That I did ever an Address begin

To you, whom Beauty and such Youth adorn :⎞
I preſt with Age, for Toil, not Pleasure born :⎬
And every way the Objeᶜt of your Scorn.   ⎠   60
Go to *Antillus* ! Fly into his Arms,
And meet with equal heat and equal Charms.
Whilſt my ambition I henceforth pursue,
And recompence those Joys I lose in you.

   Iras. He wou'd not have me if I wou'd, I fear, 65
He's great and may expeᶜt a Kingdoms Heir.

   Phot. She fears he wou'd not have her . . . Oh
    juſt Heaven !
I to the laſt extremity am driven.
She'l ask me sure anon to joyn their hands.

   Iras. All thoughts of me your self you have
    resign'd,   70
And I may now to whom I please be kind.

   Phot. All thoughts of you ! I cou'd resign my
    breath
With half the pain . . . .

   Iras. Some other Maid you purpose to make
    Queen,
And I but flatter'd, and abus'd, have been.   75

   Phot. My Love, a fierce Convulsion did endure,
And in the pain I talkt I know not what ;
But reſt for ever of that heart secure,
Where too much Love did the short ſtorm create.

Enter a Servant.

   Serv. The Caſtle is beset, and all have vow'd, 80
To ſtain their Weapons in your treacherous blood.

   Phot. Step in a while : They that will rise muſt wait,
And at each Throw assiſt their lab'ring fate. [*Ex.* Iras.
Let 'em all enter, no resiſtance make,
I can die gladly for my Country's sake.   85

Enter Memnon *and* Chilax *with the Rabble.*

What is't my honeſt Countrymen demand ?
You need not ask with weapons in your hand.

Memn. Thou haſt thy Country to a laſting War
    betray'd——
Chil. And therefore for thy death prepare.
Phot. Who! I! alas I but my Queen obey'd, 90
And both were of *Antonius* pow'r afraid.
Like you I wisht an opportunity
When *Egypt* was from *Roman* Forces free:
That we might then with *Cæsar* make our peace.
    Chil. Now Fate presents it, this occasion seize, 95
In our Queens absence you the Town command;
Egypt requires her Freedom at your hand.
    Memn. The City Gates againſt *Antonius* shut,
So thou wilt put thy meaning out of doubt. 99
    Phot. But then our Queen——
    Memn.   She is *Antonius* Slave,
And merits amongſt us nor Throne nor Grave;
This once perform'd, be thou our General,
If not, like a faint Slave unpitied fall——
                  [*Offers to run at him.*
    Phot. I'l do unforc't what ever you require,
But now you bind me to my own desire; 105
I ever thought *Antonius* Cause unbleſt,
I did his Riot loath and Loves deteſt:
So we did all I think: and 'twere unjuſt,
We shou'd defend, who ſtill abhorr'd his luſt.
Let Pimps and Parasites his Battels fight, 110
Buffoons, and loose Companions of the night,
Male-Bawds, and let that goatish drunken Herd
Which made him odious, die, to make him fear'd.
    Memn. *Antonius* now (at *Rome*) despairs of all,
And seeks to crush our *Egypt* with his fall; 115
But he shall find that some of us ſtill wake,
Who nothing fear, and all dare undertake.
    Chil. Let's man the Town with all the Force we
    have,
Keep out *Antonius*, and our Country save:
Cæsar will hold us Enemies no more, 120
But call ⟨us⟩ Friends and Allyes as before.

Memn.   For us the people do in throngs declare,
Tir'd with the danger and the charge of War.
   Phot.   I'm brav'd here by *Canidius* at each turn,
And with revenge and rage like you I burn :   125
The mighty Charge I greedily accept ;
Your Town shall be with Faith and Courage kept.
In your disgrace, believe I had no part,
But honour'd your free Tongue and honeſt Heart.
   Memn.   How   we   were   all   miſtaken   in   this
      man ?   130
                                       [*Exeunt.*

Scene the ⟨Fifth.   Outside the Town.⟩   The
                Gates being shut.

Enter Antonius, Cleopatra, Canidius, *and Attendants.*
   Anto.   How well⟨,⟩ my Queen⟨,⟩ doth this one aɛt
      reprove
My needless Jealousie, and shew your Love ?
   Cleop.   Her ! whom you not eſteem, why wou'd
      you save ?
But thô unjuſt, *Antonius* ſtill is brave.
   Ant.   I not eſteem you ! by the Gods I do   5
As much as Love——
   Cleop.   No my *Antonius* ! No !
You think me all that can a Queen disgrace,
Lighter than Woman, and than Man more base.
How cou'd I else forsake you in diſtress ?
Or could *Thyreus* in a moment please.   10
   Anto.   It was the raging Feaver of my Love,
And ſtrongeſt Natures, ſtrong Diſtempers prove :
Forgive it Madam, as my Loves excess.
   Cleop.   Had *Cæsar* su'd, I had his flame disdain'd ;
And cou'd you think another entertain'd ?   15
When the whole World shall to his Fortune yield,
My Heart againſt your Foe shall keep the Field.

Anto.   On me so thick your obligations fall,
I muſt subdue that World to pay 'em all,
And make proud *Rome* acknowledge you her Queen ; 20
Your Glory does demand no less a Scene.
　Canid.   'Tis very fine, here's all the Sense he has !
His Legions, Empire, all are in that face !
I do not think he knows he is besieg'd,
But quite undone, talks how he is oblig'd !　　　25
Pray, Sir, do you consider where we are,
If we ſtay long we shall have *Cæsar* here.
　Ant.   Were he in sight I'd not one word forbear
Till I did guiltless to my Queen appear.
Thyreus dying——
　Cleop.　　　　Have you kill'd him then——　30
I shall be hateful to the Race of men.
To *Cleopatra* it is death to speak :
On him she loves, she a swift War does call,
And those she looks on, by *Antonius* fall.
　Anto.   He clear'd your Vertue with his dying
　　Breath.　　　　　　　　　　　　　　35
　Cleop.   You ſtain'd it in the manner of his death.
　Anto.   Lovers like Misers cannot bear the ſtealth
Of the leaſt trifle from their endless wealth.
I saw him kiss your hand, for that he dy'd :
And shou'd had he Ten Thousand lives beside,　40
You seem not pleas'd with my revenge enough.
　Cleop.   It was too rash, and for his crime too rough.
　Anto.   T' attempt the spotless Honor of my Queen,
Is such a Crime, as it is death to mean.
　Cleop.   He shou'd have liv'd, if that he lov'd
　　indeed,　　　　　　　　　　　　　　45
My Scorn all other Torments might exceed :
His life had been but one continued pain,
And mine but one long A� of my disdain :
But now all means to clear my self are loſt ;
You can but think me innocent at moſt.　　　50
　Anto.   I from that Viper such an Oyl have wrung,
As heals that Love which he before had ſtung :

Since from a dying Rival's mouth I hear,
His hope was as ill grounded as my fear:
He call'd you moſt Ingrateful as he dy'd;   55
Confess'd his Passion, and accus'd your Pride:
What ſtronger demonſtration can be thought?
    Cleop.   Could nothing I might say, the like have
      wrought?
Then vain is all I've suffer'd, and have done:
My slighted Fame, and my endanger'd Throne,   60
Can nothing weigh; and 'twas *Thyreus* grace,
That I was clear'd!   *Antonius* held me baſe.
    Anto.   O say not so!   My Love of its own ſtrength
Had overcome that jealousie at length:
To him indeed I owe my speedy Cure.   65
    Cleop.   Are you for ever from relapse secure?
    Anto.   I rather will believe all that is ſtrange,
The whole Sex true, than that my Queen can change.

       Enter Souldier from the Town.

    Sould.   The Town is loſt, your *Romans* kill'd or fled,
And false *Photinus* does the Traytor⟨s⟩ head: 70
Memnon and *Chilax* in bright Arms appear,
And for *Octavius Cæsar* all declare.
             Anto. Canid. *appear with their Army*
                 under the Walls and find opposi-
                 tion, some that go near are kill'd.
    Anto.   Treason before, and Enemies behind;
In such a choice 'twere equal to be blind.
I know not which I shou'd attacque the firſt;   75
I'm only sure of all;   Delay's the worſt.
Storm then the Town with all that we can make
E're *Cæsar* see, and this advantage take.
Safe at a diſtance here my Queen muſt ſtay,
                         [*Charge without.*
While we with blood and slaughter force our way. 80
                          [*They are beat off.*
    Canid.   It is in vain, these Barb'rous Villains dare
Not hope for the fair Quarter of a War;

And are turn'd desperate.
   Anto.   We are like,
Desperate with them,
When for the whole both Parties ſtrike,   85
Courage muſt carry't, Charge them once again.
                     [*Charge.*
                     [*Shout.*

Scene the ⟨Sixth.   Outside the Town.⟩   The
Gates drawn open.

A shout from the Town.   Photinus *is attacqued from
behind.*

Antonius *Enters.*

   Anto.   Spare on your Lives th' unarm'd and meaner
       sort,
And all who to Our Clemency resort.
This easie entrance to some Friend we owe:
We from within came pouring on the Foe.
   Canid.   They are no Traytors till they kill our
       men,   5
And then as vanquish't muſt be spar'd agen.
   Anto.   They're *Cleopatra*'s Subjeᷓs: let that be
A full *Proteᷓion* in our Viᷓory.

Enter Lucilius *with* Photinus, Memnon, *and*
Chilax *Prisoners.*

   Lucil.   Health to *Antonius*, in whose Cause to fight
Is less *Lucilius* duty than delight.   10
Take from my hand your treacherous Enemies,
And use 'em as your Safety shall advise.
   Memn.   Traitor's a name my Vertue cannot brook;
How cou'd I break a Truſt I never took?
   Anto.   Armes 'gainſt your Lawful Queen are ſtill
       unjuſt,   15
A Subjeᷓ born betrays a Native truſt.

But thou *Photinus* beyond Villains base,
Whom with her Trust and Friendship she did grace,
Whom Birth and Fortune both had laid so low,
To raise thee up again she scarce knew how ;   20
Only rash Favour, whose extravagance
Seems yet a blinder Power than that of Chance,
Remain'd thy Friend——
    Phot.   I do confess, my Queen
From nothing made me all that I have been ;
And much I to *Antonius* favour owe,   25
Whom then should I depend on but you two ?
    Anto.   We two ! whom thou didst shut the Town
       against,
And to whom now thou but repentance feign'st.
    Phot.   From this seditious Rout what cou'd I gain ?
I might not hope in *Cleopatra*'s reign :   30
Weigh then my Int'rest, by that Scale you'l find
My Crime, though great, lay never in my mind :
I shou'd have dy'd, I know, I wish I had,
Rather than seem'd to have my Trust betray'd :
I shou'd have chose their Dagger, scorn'd their side ; 35
It had been past, and I had nobly dy'd.
    Chil.   O that thou hadst !   I would have driv'n it
       home,
Till forth with the broad-point thy Soul had come.
    Phot.   Death I have often met in open field,
With my Sword sent, repell'd him with my Shield : 40
Surpriz'd, defenceless ! I confess I shook,
And cou'd not in cold blood his visage brook
'Twas all my Crime ! you *Romans* only can
Serenely and unshaken, put off man.
    ⟨*Chil.*⟩   We might have known that Party needs
       must fall,   45
Who to his own fear, owe their General.
    Phot.   Kill me ! alas ! I do not ask to live !
Shou'd you, I never cou'd my self forgive.
Death to my fear is due, why shou'd I plead ?
I was no Traytor, I was worse, afraid :   50

Love, Faith, and Zeal, if Resolution fail,
No more than the faint Glow-worm's Fire avail.
All that I now repent, is that with shame
I lose that Life, I might have loſt with Fame.
    Anto.   How cam'ſt thou to appear in open Arms, 55
For thy black Soul has Treachery such Charms?
    Phot.   Had I not been their General I had dy'd,
Death turn'd the Scale, and so I took their side.
Besides, I for your Service thought it beſt,
I shou'd with them maintain my Intereſt;   60
That at some time unlook't for you might see
The good intent of seeming Treachery.
What greater Blessing can your Arms attend,
Than t' have your Foes, commanded by your Friend?
I early of *Lucilius* projeƈt knew,   65
And from the neighb'ring parts my Arms withdrew,
That he a Body might of *Romans* form,
The great exploit securely to perform.
    Anto.   'Tis possible thou mayſt be honeſt! yet
    'twere ſtrange,
Men ſtill were doubted, who but seem to change. 70
But say! how came this Tumult to begin?
    Phot.   The people long have discontented been,
Curſt me aloud, and murmur'd at the Queen;
That to your side so firmly we adher'd,
And to their Common Peace your Cause preferr'd; 75
They said they wou'd not be the Viƈtor's prey;⎫
But whom they muſt at laſt, betimes obey: ⎬
And ruine all who ſtop't 'em in their way. ⎭
    Anto.   Where were the Souldiers?
    Phot.   When she sally'd forth—
None ſtay'd, who lov'd the Queen or Martial Worth ;80
But all the Discontents remain'd behind,
And had effeƈted what they long design'd,
Had not those Pow'rs that Treachery prevent,
To your relief the brave *Lucilius* sent:
He in the Town a Band of *Romans* got,   85
And overthrew the Rebels and their Plot.

Anto.   You then are none of 'em——

Phot.   I was by force :
But *Lucrece* ne're cou'd hate vile *Tarquin* worse,
Than I these Forcers of my Loyalty—
                                    [*Points to the Lords.*
And like her too (since not believ'd) I'l dye.   90

Memn.   You durſt not dye by an Egyptian Sword :
What is't this sudden Courage does afford ?

Phot.   I was no Villain thought, but now I hate
My Life, and cou'd rush gladly on my fate ;
And you repent——

Chil.   That e're we truſted thee—   95
Slave ! more uncertain than a Winters Sea.

Anto.   I will believe Death shook thy Loyalty,
And all thou didſt was Fear, not Treachery :
Photinus rise ! thy frailty I forgive.   [*Rises.*
And if thou can'ſt or dar'ſt thus branded, live ;   100
But never more a weighty Charge receive.

Phot.   I wou'd live gladly to redeem my Crime ;
'Tis all the benefit I ask of Time.

Anto.   But you Fierce Lords that dare your Sove-
         raign blame,
And would depose, or govern in Her name,   105
Shall find what 'tis to play with Royalty ;
And fall like *Phaeton* from the borrow'd Skie.

Chil.   We scorn thy Mercy, and our Country love,
And gladly from her dying Cries remove.   109

ACT. V

Scene the Firſt.   The Palace.

Enter Antonius, Cleopatra, Charmion, Iras, *and*
Attendants.

Cleop.   Fortune's afresh fond of *Antonius* grown,
And has this Minute her old Love put on ;

She calls her wonted Charms into her Face,⎫
And hugs him—   ⎬
With the fierce ardor of a first embrace. ⎭   5
   Anto. Of this success, when they at *Rome* shall hear,
They'l change perhaps their Superstitious fear,⎫
And the ill *Omens* on my Foe transfer.   ⎭
His will the Owl bethought, unchas'd away,
Which upon *Concord*'s Temple braves the day.   10
The Ape in *Ceres* Temple will be His,
And his defeat the Eight-foot-Dragon hiss.
The blood my Statue shed, will his be thought;
So are weak minds by Superstition wrought.
   Cleop. What we can't shun, 'twere better not to
     know,   15
Nor do the Gods maliciously foreshow,
To make us feel our Fate before it come;
But men too nicely pry into their doom.
   Anto. Let it fall quick whatever they prepare,⎫
It is the Thunders voice, we cannot bear;   ⎬ 20
Blind to our Fate, let us both hope and fear: ⎭
But thou *Lucilius,* who do'st still outrun
All that we can expect or wish were done;
Like some kind God thou leap'st into the Scale
And turn'st it when all Mortals seem to fail,   25
Take from my hand this Armor of clear Gold.
Let the best Metal the best man enfold.
   Lucil. Me dead or living you anon shall praise.

Enter Messenger.

   Mess. With his whole Force *Octavius,* Sir, moves
     on;
'Tis thought on every part he'l storm the Town.   30
   Anto. His late defeat then stings the restless Boy;
And all at once we shall our Swords imploy.
Let us embrace, then each man to his Post:
We'l meet no more but Conquerors or Ghosts.
The World's at stake, my Queen, and this short
     hour   35

Contains the Fate of all succeeding Pow'r.
If this one day we can our Fate defer,
To morrow's Sun will see *Ventidius* here :
Victorious Legions to my Aid he brings ;
Flesh't all in *Parthian* Blood and spoils of Kings.   40
[*Ex.* Anto. Canid., Lucil.

Enter Photinus *at another Door.*

Cleop. My boading Heart sayes we shall meet no
    more,
And sends up thoughts I never knew before.
My Ears with dismal dying cryes are fill'd,
And my Eyes grow with ghastly Visions wild ;
Methinks I see *Antonius* bleeding there,   45
And all his Souldiers pale with Death or Fear.
    Charm. Your wounded Fancy does these forms
        create,
Expect as you deserve, a better Fate.
    Cleop. O that betimes he had my Cause forsook !
Cæsar with pity on a Queen must look.   50
Defenceless too.   Winds unoppos'd give o're,
And but 'mongst Trees and solid Buildings roar.
The *Romans* against me declared the War,
But caught *Antonius* Vertue in that snare.
    Phot. When two fierce Bulls contend, the doubtful
        Herd   55
Stand gazing by a while, of both afear'd :
But soon as one the fatal strife declines,
The Captive number with the Victor joyns.
And so should we——
    Cleop.   Yes ! it meer Brutes we were—
And knew no Nobler Passion than vile Fear ;   60
Minutes move slowly when such weight they bear,
Each now is more important than a year :
I grow impatient, can bear no delay,
But quickning Fate would through the shell survey.
    Char. The strongest place, and nearest is your
        Tomb ;   65

Hear good news soon, the bad too soon will come.
Be patient Madam——
    Cleop.   Who compos'd can be ?
A Tempeſt heard and their whole Wealth at Sea ?
Each Pile that flies may pierce *Antonius* Heart ;
And they in showrs from meeting *Romans* part.   70
Let us move on, no matter where you lead
A breaking Heart, and a diſtemper'd Head.
                      [*Noise of Arms.*
                      [*Ex.* Cleop. Charm.
    Phot.   Clashing of Arms I heard, and noise of
    Drums,
Nearer and nearer the fierce Clangor comes.
                    [Photinus *ſteals off unseen.*

Enter Antonius, Canidius, Lucilius, *as beaten back into
the Town.*

    Anto.   Gape Hell, and to thy dismal Bottom take 75
The loſt *Antonius* ; this was our laſt Stake ;
Warn'd by my ruine, let no *Roman* more
Set Foot on this inhospitable shoar.
Cowards and Traytors fill this impious Land ;
Faithless and fearful, without Heart or Hand.   80
Some ran to *Cæsar* like an headlong Tyde,
The reſt their fear made useless on our side.
    Canid.   Their Fear ! their Treachery ! we are be-
    trai'd :
By Hands we truſt the sureſt Snares are laid.
The Queen, no doubt, does correspondence hold   85
With *Rome* and *Cæsar*, and we all are sold.
    Anto.   I had but one glad thought within my breſt,
And thou to that one thought, wilt give no reſt.
Fortune hath seiz'd my Empire and Renown ;
Honeſt Old Souldier, let my Love alone :   90
But you my generous Friends to *Cæsar* go,
Too much already to your Love I owe :
Let me now sink alone ; enough y'have done :
A falling Tow'r 'twere madness not to shun.

Your guilt is small, let early penitence,   95
Your Ties and Love to me plead your defence.
   Lucil.   No Sun shall see me living after you;
My Death shall tell you that my Life was true.
   Canid.   For what should I my bending years pre-
      serve ?
Canidius will no second Master serve.   100
                    [*A shout without.*

            Enter a Messenger.

   Mess.   Your Navy, Sir, is joyn'd with *Cæsar*'s Fleet,
And with one voice their Emperor they greet.
Both sides their bloody hatred have laid down,
And in one Body row toward the Town.
   Canid.   Sir, with *Egyptians* it was chiefly mann'd,
And is there yet no dealing underhand ?   106
Still does the Queen so innocent appear ;
Her people guilty, she alone is clear.
   Anto.   Her peoples Love, her Love to me has lost ;
And now her Faith, is by their Treason cros't.   110
Pity, not blame the Queen, who sinks this hour,
Crush't with the ruines of an Emperor.
By Land and Sea betray'd! what shall we do ?   ⎫
   Canid.   Let's fight and die in Arms upon the Foe. ⎬
   Anto.   We of resistance scarce can make a shoe. ⎭
Death shuns the naked Throat and proffer'd Brest ; 116
He flies when call'd, to be a welcome Guest.
I may be tane alive, and made a scorn,
Where I have oft the highest Honours worn.
Rome never shall my conquer'd Face behold :   120
Death I have seiz'd, and will not lose my hold.
                    [*Shout again.*
            Enter Souldier.

   Sould.   *Cæsar* is entred, and we all are lost ;
Some *Roman* Souldiers still make good their Post.
   Anto.   Their number speak.
   Sould.   Two Legions at the most.
   Anto.   Command 'em to yield easie Victory :   125

Their number is
' Too small to conquer, and too great to dye.
    Canid. What means our Emperor ?
    Anto.   To spare your Blood :
Too long you have my angry Fate withstood.
What is Command, for which we so contend ?   130
Danger and Envy the High Charge attend :
A few we please, and Multitudes offend.
                               [*Canid. to the Sould.*
    Canid. Thou art a Coward, fled'st before thy time,
And with pretence of News would'st hide thy Crime.
'Tis false.   135
    Sould. So it were false indeed, I'd gladly die ;
But this shall show I did not basely flie.
                                   [*Kills himself.*
                Enter Photinus.
    Phot. Horror on horror!   Sir, th' unhappy
      Queen
Betray'd by a Report that you were slain !
    Anto. I understand you, she her self has kill'd ; 140
And better knew to die, than how to yield.
    Phot. Alas ! she has, I pull'd the reaking Steel
From her warm Wound, and with it rush't her
    life——
Her latest breath was busie with your name,
And the sweet pledges of your mutual flame :   145
Your Children she embrac't, and then she dy'd.
    Anto. How well had I been with great *Julius* slain,
Or by some flying *Parthians* darted Cane.
Thy gentle Nature, *Brutus,* how I hate,
Through which I live to taste the dregs of Fate.   150
Such is the gloomy state of Mortals here ;
We knew not what to wish, or what to fear :
My Name in Arms, my Friends and Empire gone,
Yet while she liv'd, I was not quite undone :
Methought I still had something to do here——   155
    Canid. Y'have more than ever, Sir : your Souldiers
    chear,

And bid 'em for a bold defence prepare.

   Anto.   Never : let *Romans* now each other love,
Their tedious quarrel I will soon remove.
'Twice has my Sword with *Roman* Blood been dy'd ;160
It draws no more, but from *Antonius* side.
Had the juſt Gods intended I should live,
To hate my life, such cause they wou'd not give.
They had preserv'd my Empire and my Queen.
Enough and more, I have both Fortunes seen.   165
Strike good *Lucilius* ; 'Tis a friendly part :
Lct no Foes weapon picrce thy Maſters Hcart.

           Lucil. goes behind, makes as if he would
                kill him, but passes the Weapon
                through his own Body.

The Nobleſt way : thou show'ſt me what to do.
Thou giv'ſt th' Example, and I'le give the blow.
               [Antonius ⟨*stabs*⟩ *himself.*
        A great shriek is given at his fall. All
           run out of the room except Phot.

   Phot.   I'le call some help——
⟨*Anto.*⟩   'Twill but increase my pain ; 170
For should'ſt thou ſtir, I'd ſtab my self again.
          Phot. *makes towards the door.* Anto.
            ſtabs *himself again, and falls.*
            Phot. *reenters.*

   Canid.   Let others sigh and weep, but let us go
And vent our grief, in rage upon the Foe.
From the ſtrange horror of that dismal sight,
Cowards would rush into the midſt of fight.   175
   Anto.   Let Cowards crowd to force resign their
    breath.
Brave Minds look through it, and make use of Death.
Thou can'ſt not now my fatal Journey ſtay.
   Phot.   Nor wou'd I, Sir, you'r fairly on your way.
   Anto.   Death soon will place me out of Fortunes
    reach ;   180
Why ſtayes my Soul to sally at this breach ?
   Phot.   It is not big enough.

Anto.   Do'ſt mock me now ?
Can my few Minutes a new Torture know——
    Phot.   They may, and to provoke thy parting Soul,
Know that the Queen yet lives, thou loving Fool, 185
And I the Story of her Death contriv'd,
To make thee kill thy self, which has arriv'd
Juſt as I wish't ; by thy own hand thou dy'ſt,
And art at once the Victim and the Prieſt.
    Anto.   Furies and Hell——
    Phot.   Curse on ; but *Cæsar* shall
With *Egypts* Scepter thank me for thy fall.   191
Though decently he cou'd not take thy Head,
He'l inwardly rejoyce to find thee dead ;
And hug the man that eas'd him from the fear
Of such a Rival, yet his guilt did spare.   195
    Anto.   Thou mak'ſt me hate by turns my Life and
          Death !
O for a moments ſtrength ! my Sword to sheath
In thy false Heart——
But 'twill not be, my hand forsakes my Will ;
Only himself can poor *Antonius* kill.   200
    Phot.   'Coud you have liv'd, I had seem'd honeſt
          ſtill,
But now take all ; the Queen her self muſt Bleed ;
Iras and I muſt to her Throne Succeed.
Thy Councills ſtill to *Cæsar* I betray'd,
This laſt revolt I in thy *Navy* made.   205
    Anto.   Triumphant Villian ! What provok't thee
          to't.
    Phot.   Ambition Sir, I had no Armies I ;
Nor was I born of Royal Progeny.
No Crown descended on my Lazy Head,   ⎫
I cou'd no open path to greatness tread :   ⎬   210
But none despis'd that to a Throne did Lead. ⎭
    Anto.   All *Charmion* said of Thee it seems was true ;
    Phot.   And all *Canidius* 'ere suspected too.
I have discharg'd my Conscience at this Laſt.——
Dy thou.——   215
Whilſt I to *Iras* and a Throne make haſt.   [*Ex. Phot.*

Enter Charmion, Iras, *and Attendants.*

Charm. The Queen Entreats——
Anto. Does my Queen Live, and may *Antonius*
    yet,
Above the Earth his *Cleopatra* Meet.   219
    Charm. She lives, but shut up in her Monument;
Her rowling Thoughts on some dire Mischief bent.
By *Isis* Temple, Sir, you know it Stands;
The Rareſt Fabrick made by Mortal hands.
All she holds dear she has throng'd there, but you,
And now intreats that you will enter too.   225
    Anto. With those we love, a Triumph 'tis to fall;
Moſt gladly I obey her fatal Call.
    Charm. Juſt Heaven's! you faint, what is it you
        have done,
That with such Streams these Living Fountains run?
    Anto. It was a sudden qualm: Limbs do but
        bear   230
Me to My Queen and I'l dismiss you there:
I cannot dy till I have paid that Debt.   ⎫
Nor have our Souls appointed where to Meet.   ⎬
Stand off my Fate, and dare not touch me yet.   ⎭
    Charm. Secure from *Cæsar* you a while may be, 235
And there what's fitteſt to be done Decree. [*A shout.*
The place.
    Anto. The Victory comes on, I hear the Noise,
And of prevailing Foes th'insulting Voyce.
Cæsar to spare me did ſtrickt Order give, ⎫   240
I may be taken and compell'd to live;   ⎬
Move on, all Fates but that I can forgive. ⎭
                                        [*Exeunt.*

Enter Cæsar, Agrippa, Mecœnas, *and Souldiers.*

    Mec. Sir, y'are entirely Maſter of the Town; ⎫
All men their Hatred and their Armes lay down, ⎬
And the whole World now bends to you alone.   ⎭ 245
    Agrip. The names of Parties and of Factions cease,
And War has brought forth her fair Daughter Peace.

Cæs. Command the Souldiers Fury be reſtrain'd,
That Rage deſtroy not what their Virtue gain'd.
Th' *Egyptians* now my Clemency shall share ;   250
I would be lov'd in Peace, though Fear'd in War.
In this Confusion where's the haughty Queen ?

   Mec. Since firſt we entred, She no more was seen.

Enter Photinus *with a Sword.*

   Phot. Great *Cæsar* at my hands that Sword receive,
Which his Deaths Wound did to *Antonius* give.   255

   Cæs. Thou haſt not kill'd him Villain ! quickly
     speak,
Thy Limbs upon a Thousand Racks I'l break,
To find the Truth——

   Phot. He is not Dead, but long he cannot Live ;
And his own Arm the Fatal blow did give.   260
By my advice indeed——

   Cæs.   By thy advice—
Thus *Rome* by *Egypt* is defeated twice.
Thou haſt the pow'r of pardoning from me tane,
And empty Wishes now alone remain.
Each Man will think what he himself had done,   265
And my great mind interpret by his own.
Hence from my sight ! since blaſted is by Thee
The faireſt Fruit of all my Victory.

   Phot. I wish *Antonius* blood were yet unspilt ;
But Yours is the advantage, Mine the guilt.   270
Empire and Glory can no Partners bear,
Since you forgive your Foes excuse my care.

   Cæs. Where is the Queen ?

   Phot.   Fled to the Monument :
Which for her laſt Retreat she ever meant.
Where she has all the Jewels of the Crown,   275
And the Chief Wealth of th' diſtracted Town.
There great *Antonius* Bleeding in her Armes,
Takes his laſt Leave of her deſtructive Charmes.
Give me Two hundred Men within an houre,
They shall alive or dead be in Your pow'r.   280

Cæs. Thou Monster of all Villany forbear ;
Thou woud'ſt thy Gods from off their Altars tear,
Who woud'ſt not thy Afflicted Sov'raign spare.
 Agrip. Men say she is Generous, if so our Force
Will only drive her on some desp'rate Course.   285
If Honourable Terms we should refuse,
We shall her Person and her Treasure lose.
She'l both Convert into one spreading Flame,
And shortning hated Life extend her Fame.
 Mec. A *Roman* Mind can only Death command ;
Fear no such Courage from a Barbarous Hand !   291

Enter a Servant.

 Serv. *Octavia*, Sir——
 Cæs.   Poor Soul ! I pity Her,
She ill the news will of *Antonius* bear.
 ⟨*Serv.*⟩ She's paſt all human Grief and human
  Care.
 Cæs. She is not dead ⟨?⟩
 Serv.   Yes, in her way to *Rome,* 295
Of grief and discontent, as we presume.
 Cæs. Ye joyes of Victory a while forbear,
I muſt on my *Octavia* drop a tear.
She was the beſt of Women, Gentleſt Wife,
In every part how vertuous was her life !   300
 Mec. From out the Chriſtal Palace of her⎞
  Brest,   ⎟
Her clearer Soul is gone to endless reſt.   ⎬
What time, what reason can my loss digeſt ? ⎠

Enter Messenger.

 Mess. *Canidius* ſtill does an old Fort defend.
 Cæs. On every spark of War we muſt attend. 305
True Wisdom will no Enemy despise :
From small beginnings mighty Flames arise.

Enter Canidius with his Souldiers.

 Canid. Thus the laſt Sword for Liberty I draw,
And whom Despair thruſts on no numbers awe.

Who knows——   310
But that those nobler Souls of Ancient *Rome*
May ſtrike with us 'gainſt slavery to come.

⟨[*Exeunt.*

Enter Cæsar *with his Souldiers.*

Cæs.   I charge you all the brave *Canidius* spare,⎫
Let not his Blood now ſtain the ended War :   ⎬
His number speaks not terror, but despair.   ⎭ 315
[Canid. *is beaten off the Stage.*
[*He re-enters.*
Canid.   Fight but one Minute longer, whil'ſt that I
And some few nobler Souls like *Romans* die.
[*They kill themselves.*
Then may you all by *Cæsars* mercy live,
[*The reſt yields.*
Whil'ſt we our Freedom from our Swords receive.
Cæs.   What have I done ! that men had rather
dye   320
By their own hand, than truſt my Clemency ?
Mecæn.   *Canidius* to his Maſter was moſt true,
And did for him what I wou'd do for you.
Agrip.   The World does no more Enemies contain,
And *Cæsar* over peaceful *Rome* may raign.   325
[*Ex. Omnes.*

⟨Scene the Second.⟩

Enter Antonius, Cleopatra, Charmion, *and* Iras
in the Monument.

Anto.   'Twas I that pull'd on you the hate of *Rome*,
And all your Ills paſt, present, and to come.
It is not fit nor possible I live,
And my dear Queen, it growes unkind to grieve.
Cleop.   'Twas I that loſt you in each *Roman* mind ; 5
And to your ruine can you ſtill be kind ?
How can you bear this Tyranny of Fate,
And not the Cause, your *Cleopatra* hate.

Anto. So *Venus* look't, when the *Idalian* B⟨oa⟩r
The tender side of her *Adonis* tore :　　　　　　10
Nor yields my Queen in Beauty or in grief,
When half the World under my rule was plac't⎫
Your Love was all the joy that I cou'd taſt,　⎬
It was my chief delight, and is my laſt.　　　⎭
I dye, and have but one short word to say ;　　15
But you muſt swear, my Queen you will obey.
　　Cleop. By all our Love I will, my death command,
And see the eager duty of my hand.
　　Anto. Your death ! it is the only thing I fear :
And Fate no other way can reach me here.　　20
　　Cleop. Down from a Throne to any private State :
It is a dismal Precipice to the Great.
I giddy with the horrid prospeᚃ grow ;
And shall fall in, unless Death help me now.
　　Anto. Heav'n that success does to my Arms
　　　deny,　　　　　　　　　　　　　　　25
Whispers a *Roman* Soul, and bids him dye.
Our case is different ; to *Cæsar* sue,
Thô me he hate, he needs muſt pity you.
Your Beauty and my Love were all your Crime,
And you muſt live my Queen.
　　Cleop.　　　　　　When you are dead—　30
To be despis'd, reproach't, in triumph lead ;
A Queen and Slave ! who wou'd not life renounce,
Rather than bear those diſtant names at once.
　　Anto. But you may live a Queen ; say you obey'd
Through fear : and were compell'd to give me Aid : 35
That all your Subjeᚃs private Orders had
Not to resiſt him, and my Cause betray'd.
Say, that at laſt you did my Death procure ;
Say any thing that may your Life and Crown secure.
　　Cleop. 'Twere false and base, it rather shall be
　　　said　　　　　　　　　　　　　　40
I kill'd my self when I beheld you dead.
　　Anto. Me the unhappy cause of all your wo !
Your own, and your dear Country's overthrow.

Remember I was jealous, rash, soon mov'd,
Suspe&ct;ed no less fiercely than I lov'd :   45
How I *Thyreus* kill'd, your Love accus'd,
And to your kind defence my faith refus'd.
From shame and rage I soon shall be at re&st;,
And Death of thousand ills hath chose the be&st;.

                                         [*He faints.*

    Cleop.   O &st;ay ! and take me with you——
    Anto.   Deare&st; Queen,
Let my Life end before your Death begin.   51
O *Rome* ! thy freedom does with me expire,
And thou art lo&st;, obtaining thy desire.   [*Dies.*
    Cleop.   He's gone ! he's gone ! and I for ever
        lo&st; !
The great *Antonius* now is but a Gho&st; :   55
A wandring shadow on the Stygian Coa&st;.
I'm &st;ill a Queen, though by the Fate of War,
Death and these Women all my Subje&ct;s are ;
And this unhappy Monument is all
Of the whole World, that I my own can call.   60
    Iras.   O name not Death !
Cæsar men say is good, wise, mild and ju&st; ;
So many Vertues how can you di&st;ru&st; ?
    Cleop.   Thô his la&st; breath advis'd me to submit
To *Cæsar*, and his falling Fortunes quit :   65
When I nam'd Death, speechless my hand he pre&st; ;
And seem'd to say that I had chose the be&st;.
    Iras.   He cou'd not be so cruel, you mi&st;ook ;
Too sharply you apply his dying look.
    Cleo.   He does expe&ct; it, and I'le keep my word, 70
If there be Death in Poyson, Fire, or Sword.
    Charm.   Fortune with lighter &st;roaks &st;rikes lighter
        things ;
With her whole weight she crushes falling Kings.
    Cleop.   We shall in Triumph, *Charmion*, be led,
Till with our shame *Romes* Pride be surfeited :   75
Till every finger *Cleopatra* find
Pointing at her, who was their Queen design'd.

 Char. Their Anger they may glut, but not their
  Pride.
They ne'r had Triumph't if men durſt have dy'd.
 Cleop. Beauty, thou art a fair, but fading flow'r, 80
The tender prey of every coming hour :
In Youth thou Comet-like art gaz'd upon,
But art portentous to thy self alone.
Unpunish't thou to few wer't ever giv'n :
Nor art a Blessing, but a Mark from Heav'n.   85
Greatness moſt envy'd, when leaſt underſtood :
Thou art no real, but a seeming good.
Sick at the Heart ! Thou in the Face look'ſt well,
And none but such as feel thy pangs can tell.
By thy exalted State we only gain,   90
To be more wretched than the Vulgar can.
 Iras. Think how he'l use your Sons when you are
  dead,
And none their Cause can like a Mother plead.
 Cleop. Perhaps, when I am dead, his hate may
  cease,
And Pity take declining Rages place.   95
Sure in the Grave all Enmities take end,
And Love alone can to the Dead extend.
Men say that we to th' other World shall bear
The same Desires and Thoughts, imploy'd as here.
The *Hero* shall in shining Arms delight,   100
In neighing Steeds, shril sounds and empty fight :
Poets shall sing, and in soft Dances move,
And Lovers in Eternal Roses Love.
If ſo, *Antonius,* we but change the Scene,
And there pursue what we did here begin.   105
 Charm. I am prepar'd to follow or to lead :
Name but the fatal Path that you will tread.
 Cleop. In yonder golden Box three Asps
  there lie,
Of whose leaſt venomous bite men sleep and die :
Take one and to my naked Breaſt apply   110
Its poysonous mouth——

Charm.   Alone she shall not die.

Iras.   When *Julius Cæsar* in the Senate fell,
Where were these thoughts ? and yet he lov'd as well.

Cleop.   He lov'd me not ! he was ambitious he ;
And but at looser Times took thought of me.   115
Glory and Empire fill'd his restless mind :
He knew not the soft pleasures of the Kind.
Our Joyes were frighted still with fresh alarms,
And new Designs still forc't him from my Arms.
But my *Antonius* lov'd me with his Soul.   120
No cares of Empire did his Flame controul.
I was his Friend, the Partner of his mind ;
Our days were joyful, and our nights were kind :
He liv'd for Me, and I will die for Him. [*Stings her.*
So, now 'tis past !   I feel my eyes grow dim,   125
I am from triumph and contempt secure,
What all must bear I earlier endure.
                              [*Kneels down to* Anto.
To thy cold Arms take thy unhappy Queen,
Who both thy ruine and her own has been :
Other Embrace than this she'l never know,   130
But a pale Ghost, pursue thy shade below.
Good Asp bite deep and deadly in my Brest,
And give me sudden and Eternal Rest.   [*She dies.*
                              [Iras *runs away.*

Charm.   Fool, from thy hasty Fate thou can'st⎫
    not run   ⎪
Iras.   Let it bite you, I'le stay till you have⎬ 135
    done :   ⎪
Alas ! my life but newly is begun——   ⎭

Charm.   No : thou woud'st live to shame thy
    Family ;
But I'le take care that thou shalt Nobly dye.

Iras.   Good *Charmion* !

Charm.   I'le hear no more : faint Hearts that seek
    delay   140
Will never want some foolish thing to say.
                    Charm. *stings her, then puts it to her
                    own Brest.*

At our Queens feet let's decently be found,
And Loyal Grief be thought our only Wound.   [*Dies.*

  Enter Cæsar, Mecœnas, Agrippa, *and* Photinus.

  Cæs.   Yonder's   the   Monument,   that   famous
     Tow'r;
'Tis weak, and may be ruin'd in an hour.   145
Summon the Queen—— 'Tis obstinacy now
                    [*Calls thrice, none answers.*
Not resolution the lost Queen does show;
Call for a Battering Ram——Now down it goes.
                              [*Enter all.*
  Mecæn.   But oh! what horror does that Breach
     disclose?
The Queen, *Antonius*, and her Maids lie dead: 150
From their pale Cheeks the Life but newly fled.
  Cæs.   Am I so cruel and relentless held,
That Women dare not to my mercy yield?
  Phot.   The   Queen your *Roman* Triumphs   ever
     fear'd,
And therefore Poysons of all sorts prepar'd   155
To end her life, and to prevent that shame,
When ever the unhappy prospect came.
                    [*Phot. runs to* Iras.
Some signs of life in that soft Maid remain;
She seems to move her dying lips again.
  Iras.   Is't   thus   your   word   you with   poor *Iras*
     keep——   160
The Crown of *Egypt* now you may dispose
On whom you please —— Death soon my Eyes will
     close;
And *Cæsar* my——   [*Dies.*
  Cæs.   The   Crown   of *Egypt*, Slave, dispos'd by
     thee?
Her dying words contain some Mystery: 165
  Phot.   Aside.   Which I'le take care she never shall
     explain——
She raves: the Poison has disturb'd her brain.
                              [*Kills her.*

Cæs.   Thou haſt not, Slave, the tender Virgin slain ?
Phot.   I lov'd and cou'd not see her lie in pain.
Cæs.   Villain, thou feard'ſt that her laſt breath
  might say   170
Something that might thy treacherous heart betray.
Mecænas, seize on him, see quick Juſtice done.
  Sould.   Quicker than this, great *Cæsar*, there is
   none.   [*Kills* Phot.
  Cæs.   Who art thou that dar'ſt kill and *Cæsar*
   by ?
  Sould.   I'm Brother to that Maid, resolv'd to die 175
By the same hand, if *Cæsar* say the word.
  Cæs.   Put up : it was a kind of Vertue in thy
   Sword.
What cou'd *Antonius* from a Brother fear,
Who owes him all the Honours he does wear ?
Oh ! what a God-like pleasure had it been   180
With thee t' have shar'd the Empire once agen ?
And to have made a second Sacrifice
To Friendship of each others Enemies.
By thee I am whatever I was made,
But thou art proud, and scorn'ſt to be repaid.   185
  Agrip.   The Queens vaſt Treasure, Sir, I blazing
   found ;
A greater Wealth than ever *Thetis* drown'd.
She her fair Person to a Carcass turn'd :
And has her Treasure to vile Ashes burn'd.
Both ways defeating the proud hopes of *Rome.*   190
  Cæs.   Great minds the Gods alone can overcome—
Let no man with his present Fortune swell   ⎫
The Fate of growing Empire who can tell ?   ⎬
We ſtand but on that Greatness whence these fell. ⎭ 194
                                          [*Ex. omnes.*

FINIS

EPILOGUE

'Twere Popish folly for the Dead to pray :
By this time you have damn'd or sav'd our Play :
But Gentlemen, the Poet bad me say,
He claimes his Merit on a surer score :
It' has brought you here together, and what more 5
Could Waters, Court, or Conventicles do ?
'Tis not his fault, if things no further go.
The Gravest Cit that hopes to be Lord Mayor
Must come to a New Play with his None Dear ;
And the kind Girl engag'd another way, 10
Tells all her Friends sh' has been at the New Play.
They ask the Tale which she does for 'em get
Between the Acts, from her dear Friend she met.
The Peacock-Beauty here may spread her Train,
And by our gazing Fops be made more vain. 15
And all kind Lovers that are here to night,
May thank the Poet for each others sight.
Thô all be bad, men blame with an ill grace
The Entertainment of a Meeting Place. 19

EXPLANATORY NOTES

LIST OF SIGLA USED IN EXPLANATORY AND TEXTUAL NOTES

(Catch Titles from the Bibliography are given, see Vol. II, pp. 235–261.)

K = Kemp's Collection, 1672, 8vo. Bibliography, No. 9a.
A = Miscellaneous Works, 1702, 8vo.   ,,   ,, 30.
B1 = The Poetical Works, 1707, 8vo.   ,,   ,, 36.
B2 = The Poetical Works, 1710, 8vo.   ,,   ,, 37.
B3 = The Works, 1722, 2 vols. in 12mo. ,,   ,, 40.
B4 = The Works, 1776, 2 vols. in 8vo.   ,,   ,, 41.
B5 = The Works, 1778, 2 vols. in 12mo. ,,   ,, 42.
G = Gildon's New Miscellany, 1701, 8vo. ,,   ,, 29.
Gent.'s Journ. = " The Gentleman's Journal," 1691/2–4. 4to. Bibliography, No. 24.
I = D'Urfey's " The Intrigues at Versailles," 1697, 4to. Bibliography, No. 26.
Com. = Commendatory Verses, 1700, fol. Bibliography, No. 28.
W = Wit and Mirth, 1719, 8vo.   ,,   ,, 39.
SP = Poems on Affairs of State, 1698, 8vo.   ,,   ,, 27.
D1 = Dryden's Miscellany, 1684, 8vo.   ,,   ,, 16a.
D2 = Dryden's Miscellany, 1692, 8vo.   ,,   ,, ,,
D3 = Dryden's Miscellany, 1702, 8vo.   ,,   ,, 16b.
V = Buckingham's Miscellaneous Works, 1704, 8vo. Bibliography, No. 32.
P = Poetical Recreations, 1688, 12mo. Bibliography, No. 21.
Q, Q1, Q2, etc. = Quarto editions of plays.
Ff. = Folio editions of " The Happy Pair," 1702 and 1705.
etc. = " and all subsequent editions."

EXPLANATORY NOTES

I. A Pastoral Dialogue.

It is highly probable that this poem is a Court allegory.
" Strephon " was the pastoral name usually given to Rochester.
It is used for him in the Elegies by Flatman and Aphra Behn on
his death, and also in Aphra Behn's lines " *To Mr. Creech* (*under
the Name of* Daphnis) *on his excellent Translation of* Lucretius."
In the latter poem " Thirsis " is used for Thomas Sprat, the famous
Wit, afterwards Bishop of Rochester.

l. 35. Mateless.

I retain the reading of A here, although K and the eighteenth-
century editions read the more modern " matchless." Mateless
was used in the seventeenth century occasionally in the sense of
" matchless." Cf. Quarles's " Sion's Elegies," i. 12 (4to, 1624) :

> " Say, if e're your eyes beheld . . .
> More truer Iliades ; more Vnparallel'd,
> And mateless euills, which my offended God
> Reulcerates."

II. l. 10. We'll Game, and give off Savers too.

This line is a metaphor from card or dice playing. Game =
play. Give off = give over, or relinquish, a common seventeenth-
century use : the N.E.D. quotes examples from Shakespeare,
Anthony à Wood, Wither and Locke. Saver = " One who
escapes loss without gain," Johnson. It is a gaming term. (Cf.
" The Mulberry Garden," I. ii. l. 24.)

The whole line may be paraphrased : " We'll play at the game
of love, and, when we stop, we shall not have lost anything."

There is a very close parallel in the song in Act II of Lord
Orrery's " Altemira " (fol., 1702) :

> *But I so wisely things design,*
> *That still in all Amours of mine*
> *I'm a Winner and no Loser.*

It will be remembered that Sedley saw a performance of this
play in 1664, under its original title, " The Generall." (See
" Sir Charles Sedley," pp. 86, 87.)

III. l. 9. All the seventeenth and eighteenth century texts read
" All that is Woman is ador'd," which is impossible both as
grammar and as sense. I have adopted the reading of the many
modern anthologists, who all change the first " is " to " in."

268

Some support is given to this emendation by a very garbled version which was printed in " Poems on Affairs of State " (3 vols., 8vo, 1704, III. 438, Bibliography, No. 33), which reads " For all in woman is ador'd."

K has the following version :

SONG

Not *Celia* that I juster am,
    Or better than the rest;
For I would change each hour like them,
    Were it my interest.

But I am ty'd to very thee   5
    By every thought I have ;
Should you my heart but once set free,
    I would be no more a Slave.

All that is Woman is ador'd
    In thy dear self I find ;   10
For your whole Sex can but afford,
    The handsome, and the kind.

Why then should I seek farther store,
    And still make Love anew ?
When change itself can give no more,   15
    'Tis easie to be true.

The version in " Poems on Affairs of State " (see above) runs as follows :

SONG

Not, *Celia*, that I am more just,
    Or truer than the rest ;
For I would change each hour like them,
    Were it my Interest.

But I am ty'd to very thee,   5
    By ev'ry Thought I have ;
Should you again my Heart set free,
    I'd be again your slave,

For all in Woman is ador'd,
    In thy dear Self I find ;   10
For the whole Sex can but afford
    The Handsom and the Kind.

Then why should I seek further Store,
    And make my Love anew ?
Since Change it self can give no more,   15
    'Tis easy to be true.

V. ll. 9, 10.   So when the Stars in Heaven appear,
                  And joyn to make the Night look clear.

Perhaps imitated from the famous simile in the " Iliad " (VIII. 555–559), englished thus by Ogilby (fol., 1660, p. 193) :

So glorious Stars about the Moon are seen,
When Winds are silent, and the Aire serene ;
Steep Mountain Clefts, Vallies, and Towers appeare,
And Star-bestudded Skies Expansion cleare :
The Swain rejoyceth viewing then the Stars,
And Elements at Truce from civill Wars.

VII. ORINDA.
This was the *nom-de-plume* of Katherine Phillips, the well-known poetess (1631–1664).

IX. CONSTANCY.
This poem was probably addressed to Ann Ayscough. See Preface, p. xxix, and " Sir Charles Sedley," p. 131.

XI. ll. 17, 18.   Like foolish *Indians* we have been,
                    Whose whole Religion is a Sin :

A reference to the prevalent belief that the American Indians worshipped devils.
    Cf. Horace Walpole's Letters, ed. Toynbee, I. 387 :

    " I assure you now that I could worship him as Indians do the devil."

XII. This poem was reprinted in No. 4 of " The Diverting Post " (*Saturday*, November 11, to Saturday, November 18, 1704). " The Diverting Post " was a periodical that was published weekly from October 1704 to February 1706 for Henry Playford by John Nutt, who was the publisher of the 1702 Sedley. Its contents are chiefly *vers de société*. Another poem attributed to Sedley appeared in the 13th number (see " Doubtful Poems and Translations," No. XCVI., note).

ll. 7, 8.   Friendship so high, that I must say,
              'Tis rather Love, with some Allay.

Apparently copied from Voiture :

    Mais d'amitié si sensible qu'un jour
    Ie pensois bien le changer en amour.
                " Œuvres," ed. A. Roux, Paris, 1866, p. 466, Élégie.

XIII. TO AMARANTA, WHOM HE FELL IN LOVE WITH AT A PLAY-HOUSE.
K has the following version of this poem :

Falling in love with a Stranger at a Play.

Fair *Amarillis*, on the Stage whil'st you
Beheld a feigned love you gave a true ;
I like a Coward in the Amorous War,
Came only to look on, yet got a Scar ;
Fixt by your eyes, I had no power to fly,   5
They held me whil'st you gain'd the Victory :
I thought I safely might my sight content,
To which the power to like (not love) I lent ;
And if I ventur'd on some slight Discourse,
It should be such as could no passion nurse :   10
Led by the treacherous lustre of your eyes,
At last I plai'd too near the Precipice :
Love came disguis'd in wonder and delight,
And I was conquer'd e're I knew him right ;
Your words fell on my passion like those showers,   15
Which swell and multiply the rising flowers ;
Like *Cupid*'s self, a God and yet a child,
Your looks at once were awful, and yet mild :

Methoughts you blush'd, as conscious of my flame,
Whil'st your strict vertue did your beauty blame;   20
But rest secure ; y'are from the guilt as free,
As Saints ador'd from our Idolatry ;
And Love, a Torment doe's for me prepare
Beyond your rigour in my own despair.   24

For the occasion to which this poem possibly refers, see " Sir
Charles Sedley," pp. 99, 100.

XIV. l. 9. *Hippomanes.*

More correctly Hippomenes, the suitor of Atalanta, who won
the race by means of the stratagem of the golden apples.   Sedley
probably knew the story from Ovid (Metamorphoses, VIII.).

XV. To a Devout Young Gentlewoman.

These lines appeared in Peter Motteux's " The Gentleman's
Journal; or the Monthly Miscellany " for October 1692, p. 15
(in the Contents, " *Verses to a devout Young Lady*, by Sir Charles
Sedley "). The following words are prefixed to them :

" Indeed it must be granted, that many times Vertue has
a less share than Envy, in the grave Lectures of decay'd Sinners
to the amorous Young.   Here are some Verses by Sir *Charles
Sedley*, that confirm the Assertion : they are addressed
To a Devout YOUNG LADY."

XVI. l. 20.   Like Fire in unmov'd Flints.

This simile was a favourite with Sedley; cf. " The Mulberry
Garden."   Its origin is probably " Julius Cæsar," IV. iii. :

" O *Cassius*, you are yoaked with a Lambe
That carries Anger, as the Flint beares fire,
Who, much inforced, showe a hastie Sparke,
And straite is cold agen."

XVII.   The following version of this poem appears on p. 114 of
Part II of " Westminster Drollery " (8vo, 1672, Bibliography,
No. 8) :

A Song

1 Get you gone you will undo me,
  If you love me don't pursue me
  Let that inclination perish,
  Which I dare no longer cherish,
  Be content y'have won the field   [5]
  'Twere base to hurt me now I yield.

2 With harmless thoughts I did begin
  But in the crow'd love enterr'd in
  I knew him not he was so gay
  So innocent, so full of play   [10]
  I sported thus with young desire
  Chear'd with his light free'd from his fire.

3 But now his teeth and clawes are grown
  Let me this fatal Lyon shun
  You found me harmless, leave me so   [15]
  For were I not you'd leave me too.

But when you change remember still,
'Twas my misfortune not my will. [18]

XIX. A fragment of this song with a musical setting by Henry
Bowman appears on p. 41 of Br. Mus. Add. 30,382, a music-
book containing the book-plate of Katherine Sedley.

Bowman's manuscript is full of corrections and erasures. I
am indebted to Professor G. Leake, B. Mus., for the following
fair copy :—

- light In wine and love we pay our du - ty   In
- light   In wine and love wine and love
- light In wine and love we pay our du - ty In wine and love

wine   and love we   pay   our   du - ty   to   each
(du - ty)   our   du - ty   in   wine   and love   pay . .   our
we   pay   our   du - ty   we   pay   our   du - ty

friend - ly   friend - ly   come - ing night.
du - ty   to each friend - ly friendly come - ing   night.
to   each   friend - ly friendly come - ing   night.

XXI, XXII, XXIII.

These three poems are printed separately in K, but the printer
of A has run XXII and XXIII together as if they were a single
poem, and has separated them only by a very short space from XXI.
The original arrangement of K, which is obviously the correct
one, has been here restored.

XXIV. To CELIA.

This must have been one of Sedley's most popular poems.
Besides appearing in many miscellanies, it survives in two tran-

scripts in contemporary hands (Br. Mus. Sloane 1009, and Bodl. West. MS. e. 4, p. 169). I reprint the Bodleian MS. in full because of its interesting dedication to Mrs. Mary Napp, who is undoubtedly Pepys's friend and Nell Gwynne's colleague, " Mrs. Knipp." (See " Sir Charles Sedley," p. 126.)

To Mrs Mary Napp

As in those Nations where they yet adore
Marble and Cedar, and their aide implore,
Tis not the Workman, nor the precious Wood,
But tis the Worshipper that makes the God.
So (Cruel Fair) though Heaven has given you all,   [5]
We mortals Virtue or can Beauty call;
Tis we give thunder to your empty frowns,
Darts to your eyes, and to our selves the Wounds.
But for our Love, which proudly you deride,
Vain were your hopes, and vainer were your Pride.   [10]
All envy'd beings which the World can shew,
Unto some meaner thing their greatness owe :
Subjects make kings, and we the numerous train
Of humble Lovers constitute thy Reign.
This only difference Beauties Realm may boast,   [15]
Whom most it favoureth it enslaveth most;
And they to whom tis most indulgent found,
Are alwayes in the surest fetters bound.
But besides thee, a Tyrant ne'er was known,
Cruel to him who serv'd to make her one.   [20]
Valour's a Vice, if not with Honour joyn'd ;
And Beauty's a Disease where tis unkind.   [22]

XXVII. This poem is ascribed to " Ld Mulgrave " in Mr. Thorn Drury's, and to " E.M." (*i.e.* ? Earl Mulgrave) in Sir Charles Firth's, copy of K (see Vol. II, p. 241), but it was included by Ayloffe in the 1702 edition. Which is the more reliable, the unknown annotators of K, or Ayloffe ? As nothing is known of the former, it seems better to trust to the latter, who, after all, was an " affinity " and an intimate friend. I have therefore included the piece among Sedley's authentic works and not, like poems which are ascribed to him *only* by the unknown annotators, among the doubtful works.

XXVIII. K has the following very different version :

To a Lady, who told him he could not Love.

Madam, though meaner Beauties might,
Perhaps, have need of some such slight;
Who to excuse their Rigour, must
Say they our passions do mistrust;
And that they wou'd more pity shew,   5
Were they but sure our loves were true :
You shou'd those pretty Arts despise,
Secure of what is once your prize.
We to our Slaves no frauds address,
But as they are our minds express :   10

Tell me not then I cannot Love,
Say, rather, you it ne're can move;
Who can no more doubt of your charms,
Then I resist such pow'rfull arms :
Whose numerous force that I with stood   15
So long, was not through any hope I cou'd
Escape their pow'r, but through despair,
Which oft makes Courage out of fear.
I trembling saw how you us'd those
Who tamely yielded to your blows :   20
Had you but one of all them spar'd,
I might perhaps have been ensnar'd,
And not have thus, e're I did yield,
Call'd Love's whole Force into the Field.
    Yet now I'm Conquer'd I will prove,   25
Faithful as they that never strove.
All flames in matter where too fast
They do not seize, the longer last.
Then blame not mine for moving slow,
Since all things durable are so.   30
The Oak that's for three hundred years
Design'd in growing, one out-wears.
Whilst flowers for a season made
Quickly spring up, and quickly fade.   34

XXIX. On the Birth-day of the Late Queen. A Song.
    These lines appeared on pp. 1 and 2 of " The Gentleman's
Journal " for May 1692 (in the Contents, " *Verses by Sir* C.
Sidley *on her Majesties Birth-day* ") preceded by the following
words :

    " The 30th of *April*, being Her Majesties Birth-day, was
observ'd with all the usual Solemnity. I design'd to have
sent you an Attempt of mine in Verse, on that noble Subject :
But having happily obtain'd a Copy of those writ by Sir *Charles
Sidley*, it would have been an unpardonable Crime, to have
joyn'd my weak Essay to a Piece by so great a Master."

    The title in " The Gentleman's Journal " is as follows :

    " An Anniversary Ode sung before Her Majesty the 29*th*
of *April :* the Words by Sir *Charles Sidley :* Set by Mr *Henry
Purcell.*"

XXX. To Cloris.
    The omission of the final couplet in A (see Textual Note) is
strong evidence that this poem was addressed to Ann Ayscough,
with whom Sedley went through a form of marriage in April 1672.
(See " Sir Charles Sedley," p. 129.)

XXXI. The Soldier's Catch.
    These lines were probably written in the winter of 1691,
after the surrender of Limerick, the last Jacobite stronghold in
Ireland, which took place on October 3 (O.S.).

The following extracts from Luttrell's " Brief Relation "
illustrate Sedley's verses :

" 28*th Nov.* 1691 : Two regiments of horse are landed at Highlake
from Ireland, Coll. Boncourts and Coll. Byerley's."

" *December,* 1691 : General Ginkle is come to town with several
other officers, being lately return'd from Ireland."

" *Saturday, 6th February* [1692]—A great train of artillery . . . are
almost ready in the Tower to be put on ship-board, and
orders are to be given to take up 164 flyboats for transport
vessells for kings service."

l. 5. Teague.
The contemptuous name commonly applied to Irishmen.
There is a " Teg " in Sir Robert Howard's " The Committee "
(fol., 1665), but the name became widely known from Shad-
well's play " The Lancashire Witches, And Tegue o Divelly
The Irish Priest " (4to, 1681). Teague appears again in " The
Amorous Bigotte : with the Second Part of Tegue O Divelly "
(4to, 1690). It is still commonly applied to Roman Catholics in
Northern Ireland.

l. 36. strike sail.
The claim of England that foreign vessels should " strike sail "
to her ships in certain waters was the origin of many disputes in
the latter part of the seventeenth century. See Pepys's Diary,
ed. Wheatley, II. 145 and note.

XXXIV. THE EIGHTH ODE OF THE SECOND BOOK OF HORACE.
Page in his edition of Horace's Odes (ed. 1909, p. 247) writes :
" This Ode has the peculiar interest of being perhaps the only
Ode of Horace of which there is an adequate rendering in English
—that by Sir Charles Sedley."
I have adopted the text of A in preference to that which
appeared the year before in Gildon's " A New Miscellany."
The version of A is not quite so close to the Latin as the earlier
draft, but is more polished, and, I think, certainly the result of a
final revision. It is regrettable, however, that in l. 20 the " burning " of the first draft which translated the Latin " ardentis "
vividly and accurately should have been replaced by the very
weak " pointed."

XXXV. A BALLAD. *To the Tune of* Bateman.
The subject of this poem is undoubtedly the killing of a barrister
named Hoyle by a young spark called Pitts in the early hours of
Friday, May 27, 1692 (O.S.). Luttrell's " Brief Relation " has
the following account of the affair :

(1692) " *Satturday, 28th May.*—Mr. Hoil, of the Temple,
on Thursday night was at a tavern with other gentlemen, and
quarrelling with Mr Pitts's eldest son, a gentleman, about

drinking a health, as they came out Mr. Hoile was stab'd in the belly and fell down dead, and thereon Pitts fled; and the next morning was taken in a disguise, and is committed to Newgate.

"*Thursday, 30th June.*—This day Mr Pitts was tryed at the Old Baily for the murder of Mr Hoil of the Temple, and the jury found it manslaughter; but the next heir has brought an appeal."

The following is a slightly abridged version of the complete account of the trial, which appeared in " The Proceedings on the King and Queen's Commissions Of the Peace, &c. Held for the City of *London* and County of *Middlesex*, at Justice Hall in the Old Baily, the 29th, and 30th days of *June*, and 1*st* of *July*, 1692. &c." fol., London, 1692, p. 5.

" *George Pitts* of the Parish of *St Dunstans* in the West, Gentleman, was Arraigned [*sic*] upon two Indictments for Killing *John Hoyle*, Gent. of the *Temple* in *London*, the first Indictment was laid for the Murther at Common Law, the second upon the Statute of Stabbing, but the Grand-Jury committing an Error, (which was by endorsing *Billa Vera* on that Bill for Stabbing, when it was really agreed by all of them, that it should have been an *Ignoramus*, and *Billa Vera*, should have been upon the Bill at Common Law) this did occasion a great Controversie in Court; the Jury acknowledged that it was a great mistake . . . upon this the Judges did differ somewhat in their Opinions, fearing that if it should be altred it might make a President for the future : So at last did agree to try the Prisoner upon both the Indictments, which set forth that on the 27th day of *May* last, about two of the clock in the Night . . . in the Parish aforesaid, the Prisoner in his Rage and Malice before-thought, In and upon the said *John Hoyle*, did make an Assault, and with a Sword value 5s, upon the left side of the Body of the said *John Hoyle*, did Strike, Stab and Thrust in the said *John Hoyle*, having no Weapon drawn, giving him one Mortal Wound of the breadth of one Inch, and of the depth of five Inches, of which the said *John Hoyle* then and there instantly died : The matter of Fact was thus ; that the said Mr. *Pitts*, and two or three more Gentlemen, being drinking at the *Young Devil Tavern* in *Fleet Street*, Mr. *Hoyle*, was sent for, who came, and after some time, Mr *Hoyle* without any Provocation began to talk very scurrilously against the present Government, and spake very unbecoming words against the Person of *King William*, whereupon Mr *Pitts* replied, That he was very hard to be pleased if this King would not please him who was now hazarding his life for Us, and Mr *Hoyle* continuing to rail against all government, Mr *Pitts* endeavoured to persuade Mr *Hoyle* to lay by such discourse, but he would not, but gave the Prisoner, *Mr Pitts*, very unworthy Language and provoking Words, calling him Coward, or to that effect, thereupon Mr *Hoyle* and Mr *Pitts* rising up Mr. *Clarke* (one of the Gentlemen in the Company) put himself between them, and desired Mr. *Pitts* to be pacified, then said Mr. *Pitts* (Mr. *Clarke*) pray take my Sword for you know it is not fit for a Gentleman to hear this Language with a Sword by his side, then Mr *Hoyle* went away, but after a little time he came back again, and forced himself into the company, and then gave the Lye to Mr *Pitts* three times, when he said nothing to him, whereupon Mr *Pitts* told him this is meer Madness, and took the Glass and said here's to you, Mr *Hoyle*, and drank to him ; then Mr *Pitts* paid for the Wine and went away, and Mr *Hoyle* and the rest followed him, After this there were some Proposals made of a Place to Fight on the Morrow, and then they two going along the street together (the other two Gentlemen going towards *Temple Barr*) when they came over against the *Temple-Gate*, they fell foul upon each other, Mr *Hoyle* first taking Mr *Pitts* by the Cravate, tore it, and almost strangled him, then struck him over the Head with a Stick, upon which Mr Pitts was forced to stand upon his Guard and drew his Sword, not knowing but the Deceased had drawn his ; so at length Mr *Hoyle* received the Wound aforesaid, which the chirurgeon gave account was Mortal, then Mr *Pitts* went off : It was fully proved that Mr *Hoyle* first began, and was the occasion of all the Quarrel, and several Witnesses were called, who gave account that Mr *Hoyle* in his life-time, was a person much addicted to quarrelling &c. Whereas, on the contrary, Mr *Pitts* called seven Peers, and several Persons of Quality, who satisfied the Court that Mr *Pitts* had always been a Gentleman of a very obliging, peaceable, quiet and moderate Behaviour in all Company, no ways given to Passion or Revenge, and the Prisoner himself did very affectionately declare that he had no manner of Antipathy against *Mr Hoyle*, nor never but once before was in his company, and that what he did was in his own defence, for which great Misfortune he was heartily sorry, for he did not intend any such thing that happened : He produced the Gentlemen who were at the tavern with him, and saw all that passed, who gave a fair account of the matter of Fact, as aforesaid, which was of great Satisfaction to the Court, how that Mr *Pitts* was much abused, Mr *Hoyle* calling Mr *Pitts*, *Poultroon*, Rascally Coward, &c telling him his Sword was Rusty with such an aggravating Language &c. The Tryal was very long, and great Care was taken on both sides ; so the Gentlemen of the Jury having withdrawn for a small time, and being returned gave in their Verdict that Mr *Pitts* was only Guilty of Manslaughter.

"After which he petitioned the benefit of his Clergy, and desired his Prayer might be Recorded which was done accordingly, and an Appeal for Murther was brought against him : he gave sufficient Bail to answer the same at the next sessions, &c."

In "The Proceedings on [*sic*] King's and Queen's Commissions of the Peace, &c . . . Held for the City of *London* and County of *Middlesex*, at Justice Hall in the *Old-Baily*, the 31th [*sic*] of *August*, and 1*st* and 2*d* days of *September*, 1692," . . . London, fol., 1692, the following entry occurs on p. 6 : "*George Pitts* Esq ; being Convicted last Sessions of Manslaughter, for killing Mr *Hoyle*, Pleaded his Pardon, and presented the Court with Gloves as is usual in all such Cases." Another account of the affair is given by Bulstrode Whitelocke in his MS. Commonplace Book (now in the possession of G. Thorn Drury, Esq. K.C.).

"27 May 92,
"Mr Hoyle of ye Temple, coming this morning about two of ye Clock fro ye Young Divel Tavern, was killed wth a sword ; He died Instantly : It proceeded fro a quarrel about Drincking a Health ; killed by Mr Pitt of Graies Inne yt Dranck wth them. Mr Hoyle was an Atheist, a Sodomite professed, a corrupter of youth, & a Blasphemer of Christ."

"Mr. Hoyle" was John Hoyle, a lawyer and a well-known wit. A complete account of him will be found in the Memoir prefixed to Mr. Montague Summers's edition of "The Works of Aphra Behn" (pp. xxxiii–xxxvi). He was an intimate friend of Aphra Behn, who alludes to him frequently in her poems. A letter addressed to him by her is extant, and he is said to have helped her in the writing of her plays.

Title. The Tune of Bateman.
"A Warning for Maidens or young Bateman" is the title of a ballad preserved in the Roxburgh Collection (I. 501). The tune, according to Chappell ("Popular Music of the Olden Time," p. 198), is that of "In Peascod Time" and many other ballads. It is given thus by Chappell :

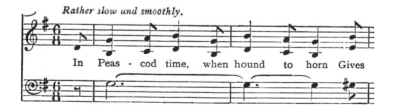

ear, till buck be kill'd : . . And lit - tle lads, with

pipes of corn, Sat keep - ing beasts a - field. . .

l. 13.   All in that very House, where Saint
          Holds Devil by the Nose.

As we learn from the report of the trial, this was the Young
Devil Tavern in Fleet Street, not to be confused with Ben Jonson's
famous Devil Tavern, sometimes called the Old Devil Tavern,
which stood close by. It was here, according to Wheatley
("London, Past and Present," I. 497) that Wanley and Neve
"originated . . . the Society of Antiquaries in 1707."

The subject of the sign, St. Dunstan taking the devil by the
nose with a pair of tongs, would be suggested by the neighbouring
Church of St. Dunstan's.

l. 20. *Namur*
This refers to the capture of Namur by Louis XIV. The
siege was opened on May 14, and the castle capitulated on July 2,
1692 (N.S.).

l. 53. *Hixes's* Hall
Hicks's Hall was the Session House of the County of Middlesex.
It stood in St. John's Street, Clerkenwell, and was named after
Sir Baptist Hicks (afterwards Viscount Campden), at whose cost
it was built in 1612.

XXXVI. THE KNITTING SONG. *The Words by Sir* Charles Sidney.
          [*sic*]
This song was first printed in "The Gentleman's Journal"
(Bibliography, No. 24 *l*) for August and September, 1694,
p. 233 (in the Contents, "*A Song on a Lady Knotting. by* Sir C.
Sedley").

It is there preceded by the following words :

"Happy the Lover who with all his art can warm one of

these cold Beauties into pity, principally now that the Fit of Knotting, (to speak in a Lover's Phrase) possesses the best part of the finer half of human kind, and leaves them as unconcern'd for Sighs and Vows as the fair subject of this song.

Phillis Knotting ; a Song by Sir Ch. Sedley."

It was reprinted in " Wit and Mirth " (8vo, 1719, V. 148) with a musical setting by Henry Purcell, which is also to be found in " English Melodies, Thirteenth to Eighteenth Centuries," by V. Jackson (J. M. Dent, 1910). Purcell's setting is as follows :

The Knotting Song. *The Words by* Sir Charles
Sidney. [*sic*] [1]

The fashion of " knotting " purses was introduced by Queen Mary II and was very fashionable at her Court. Burnet, in his Essay on the Queen, comments upon it as follows :

" When her Eyes were endangered by Reading too much, she found out the amusement of Work : And in all those hours that were not given to better Imployments, She wrought with her own Hands; and that sometimes with so constant a diligence as if she had been to earn her Bread by it." (An Essay on the Memory of the Late Queen by Gilbert, Bishop of *Sarum*, London, 8vo, 1695, pp. 82, 83.)

Cf. the lines entitled " The Royal Knotter " attributed to

---

[1] In the Contents, " Sir Charles Sidley."

Sedley (Vol. II, p. 148), and Dorset's graceful poem entitled
" Knotting," of which I quote the opening stanzas :

> At noon, in a sunshiny day,
> The brighter lady of the May,
> Young Chloris innocent and gay
>   Sat knotting in a shade :
>
> Each slender finger play'd its part,
> With such activity and art,
> As would inflame a youthful heart,
>   And warm the most decay'd.

(" Works of the Minor Poets," 8vo, 1749, I. 132.)

XXXVII. ADVICE TO THE OLD BEAUX.

These lines first appeared on p. 258 of " The Gentleman's
Journal " for August 1693 (in Contents, " *To The Old* Beaux
by a Person of Quality "). No name is appended to them in the
text. The following words are prefixed to them :

" The following Verses, written as I am told by a Person of
Quality, may also serve to shew, that there is a sort of Favours
which young Beauties but seldom grant
                    To the Old *Beaux*."

The same lines are reprinted with a few variants by D'Urfey
in the Epistle Dedicatory to his " The Intrigues of Versailles "
(4to, 1697). He introduces them with the following words
(the play is dedicated to Sir Charles Sedley and his son) :

" . . . there is in this Comedy amongst the Characters One
of an old *Beau*, under the Name of the Count *Brissac*—which
I hear by some offended has been particularly picqu'd at. I
could not recommend its defence, Sir, to a Person who can
better Judge its innocent Nature than your self, having very
lately been diverted by a very good Coppy of Verses which
I am told are yours, and which I beg leave to insert,
          The Young *Lady*'s Advice to the Old *Beaux*,
                    A SONNET."

l 8. dappl'd Greys.
Cf. Macaulay " History of England," ed. Firth, p. 1305 :

" The coaches of the aristocracy were drawn by grey Flemish
mares, which trotted, as it was thought, with a peculiar grace,
and endured better than any cattle reared in our island the
work of dragging a heavy equipage over the rugged pavement
of London."

XXXIX. SONG.
The garden to which " Strephon " took the " charming Fair "
was probably the New Spring Garden at Vauxhall : see note to
" Bellamira," Vol. II, p. 211.

XLII. l. 14. " Belle Dives " must be Annabella Dives (more correctly

Dive or Dyve), daughter of John Dyve, Esquire, Clerk of the Council. She was a Maid of Honour to Queen Mary and married, at the age of about eighteen, Sir Robert Howard, the dramatist and politician, Sedley's old friend of the days of the " Essay of the Dramatic Poesy." At the time of his marriage with this lady (February 1692/3) Sir Robert was seventy. She was his fourth wife and, at his death on September 8, 1698, inherited all his property. These Dyves were probably descended from one of the ancient Northamptonshire families of that name whose pedigrees are given in Baker's " Northamptonshire " (I. 82, 160, 163, 169; II. 254).

(For Annabella Dyve's marriage see Luttrell's " Brief Relation," III. 45, s.d. February 28, 1692/3 ; Chester's " Westminster Abbey Registers," p. 243 n.)

" Stowel " is almost certainly Lady Margaret Stowell (*née* Lady Margaret Cecil), daughter of the third Earl of Salisbury, who married, about May 1691, John, second Lord Stowell (Luttrell's Diary, II. 224).

This poem must have been composed after the marriage of Lady Margaret Cecil and before that of Annabella Dyve, *i.e.* after May 1691 and before February 1692/3.

The chief military operations between William and Louis in 1692 were in Brabant, and included the taking of Namur by the French and the indecisive battle of Steenkirk. The operations on the Rhine referred to in this poem are described by Macaulay in the following sentence : " On the Upper Rhine . . . an indecisive predatory war was carried on, by which the soldiers suffered little and the cultivators of the soil much " (" History of England," ed. Firth, V. 2230).

XLIII. OUT OF LYCOPHRON.

Lycophron, the Alexandrian dramatist, flourished about 260 B.C., and was a contemporary of Callimachus and Theocritus. Of his works there survive a long and obscure monologue called " Alexandra," and a few short fragments of which the following appears to be the basis of Sedley's lines :

> ἀλλ' ἡνίκ' ἂν μὲν ᾖ πρόσω τὸ κατθανεῖν,
> Ἀίδης ποθεῖται τοῖς δεδυστυχηκόσιν·
> ὅταν δ' ἐφέρπῃ κῦμα λοίσθιον βίου,
> τὸ ζῆν ποθοῦμεν· οὐ γάρ ἐστ' αὐτοῦ κόρος.
>
> (Wagner, Tragicorum Graecorum Fragmenta, 1846, p. 153).

XLIV. TO LIBER.

This epigram was also translated by Ben Jonson (Underwoods, fol., 1640, II. 271) :

> *Liber*, of all thy friends, thou sweetest care,
> Thou worthy in eternall Flower to fare,
> If thou be'st wise, with *Syrian* Oyle let shine
> Thy locks, and rosie garlands crown thy head ;

Darke thy clear glasse with old *Falernian* Wine,
And heat, with softest love, they softer bed.
Hee, that but living half his dayes, dies such,
Makes his life longer then 'twas given him, much.

XLVI. This Epigram appeared in "The Gentleman's Journal"
for October, 1692, p. 1 (in the Contents, "*A Translation* of
the 69th Epigram in Martial's *9th Book, by Sir* Charles Sedley"),
where it is preceded by the following words:

"As for those whose over-nice Appetites can never relish
the best of Dainties, I cannot expect they should like my homely
Fare. They are much like those who make it their Business
to rail at all manner of Government, and never live easie under
any. *Martial* hath an Epigram to one of These in his 9th
Book, of which Sir *Charles Sedley* hath made an excellent
Translation, which would be able to reform them, were they
not for the most part Incorrigible."

It is headed "*Dixerat, ô Mores! ô, Tempora!* &c."

The version in "The Gentleman's Journal" is not divided
into quatrains. It may be noticed that this poem is in what for
the period was the rare form of the Shakespearean sonnet. Cf.
No. LXXXI and *n.*

XLVII. Song.

This epithalamion appeared in "The Gentleman's Journal"
for August 1692, p. 14 (in the Contents, "*Verses by Sir* Charles
Sidleys"). It is preceded by the following words:

"The Verses that follow were made for a Nuptial Song:
You will easily know them to be Sir *Charles Sidley*'s, and cannot
but read them with an entire satisfaction."

XLVIII. Another version of this poem appears on pp. 264, 265 of
"Poems Relating to State Affairs," 8vo, 1705 (Bibliography,
No. 35).

On the Infanta of Portugal

I

How Cruel was *Alonzo's* Fate,
To fix his Love so high;
That he must perish for her hate,
Or for her Kindness dye?

II

Tortur'd and Mangl'd, Cut and Maim'd,   5
I' th' minst [*sic*] of all his Pain,
He with his dying Breath proclaim'd
Twas better than Disdain.

III

The Gentle Nymph long since design'd,
For the proud Mounsieurs Bed;   10
Now to a Holy Goal confin'd,
Drops Tears for every Bead.

IV

Tell me, ye Gods, if when a King
Suffers for Impotence;
If Love be such a thing,
What can be Innocence?   15

Title : The Infanta of Portugal.
This is Dona Isabel Luisa, born in 1669, daughter of Pedro II
(then Regent) and his wife, the Queen. Her hand was sought by
various princes, and she was once on the point of being married
to the Duke of Savoy. Among her suitors were Louis XIV and
the Dauphin. The latter is probably the " Proud Monsieur "
of this poem. The affair to which this poem refers is probably
the subject of the following passage in " An Account of the Court
of Portugal Under the Reign of the Present King Dom Pedro II,"
London, printed for Thomas Bennett, 1700 (8vo). After referring
to the slanders cast upon the Princess by " the Partizans of France "
the author continues thus :

" As for the *Conde de Atouguia*, whose Death was perhaps
the cause why these Reports were entertained in the World,
he was advanc'd in Years and, was a married Man so that the
formal story of a Marriage of Conscience must necessarily be
false. It is not deny'd but that he was found dead one Morning
in the Court of the Palace; but the Government did not think
fit to make any strict Enquiry by what hand, or from what
Reason this Nobleman fell, and therefore it becomes not Private
Persons to take that Liberty " (p. 146).

John Sheffield, Earl of Mulgrave, wrote a copy of verses on the
same event :

On Don Alonzo's *being killed in*/ Portugal *upon account of the*
Infanta *in the Year* 1683.

I

In such a Cause no Muse should fail
To bear a mournful Part;
Tis just and noble to bewail
The Fate of fall'n Desert :

II

In Vain, Ambitious Hopes design'd   5
To make his Soul aspire,
If Love and Beauty had not joyn'd
To raise a brighter Fire.

III

Amidst so many dangerous Foes
How weak the Wisest prove !   10
Reason itself would scarce oppose,
And seem agreed with Love.

IV

At worst, he dies for Julia's Charms;
But if no Stars oppose,
He reigns and revels in her arms   15
And laughs at all his Foes.

"The Works of the Most Noble John Sheffield," etc.
Printed for E. Curll, 1721, 4to, p. 125.

l. 12.   Drops Tears with ev'ry Bead.
Imitated by Pope in l. 270 of "Eloisa and Abelard":

"With ev'ry bead I drop too soft a tear."

Elwin and Courthope point out that the force of the line lies
in the phrase "too soft," which Pope added.

ll. 13, 14.   A King
                 Suffers for Impotence.

I.e. Alfonso VI, who was deposed in 1667 on account of his
licentious conduct and his neglect of his brother Dom Pedro,
the Infanta. Pedro became Regent in 1667 and married the
Queen, whose marriage with the King was declared null on account
of the latter's impotence. (See "The Portugal History" by S. P.
(Samuel Pepys), 8vo, 1667.)

XLIX. SONG.

This song appeared in "The Gentleman's Journal" for March
1691/2, p. 8 (in the Contents, "*Verses by Sir* C. S."), where it is
preceded by the following words:

"The following *Verses* are by a Person of Quality. I need
not tell you that it is Sir *C. S.* Whatever flows from him,
discovers its Spring, by its softness and natural turn."

The version that appears in "The Gentleman's Journal"
contains the following additional lines, which are omitted in A
but reprinted in B3, B4 and B5:

Of costly Food it hath no need,
  And nothing will devour :
But like the harmless Bee can feed,
  And not impair the Flow'r.
A spotless Innocence like thine,
  May such a Flame allow ;
Yet thy fair Name for ever shine,
  As doth thy Beauty now.
I heard thee wish my Lambs might stray
  Safe from the Fox's pow'r,
Tho' ev'ry one becomes his Prey,
  I'm richer than before.

L. These lines appeared in "The Gentleman's Journal" for January
1692/3, pp. 21, 22 (in the Contents, "*On a Cock at* Rochester
by Sir Charles Sedley"). They are preceded by the following
words:

"Those who do not understand this *Latin* Epigram, ["De

Parnasso " by Tom Brown, which is printed above] may make themselves amends with one in *English*, by Sir *Charles Sedley*. On a COCK at ROCHESTER."

LI. SONG *A-la-mode.*

Elwin and Courthope suggest that this little parody inspired Pope's " Song by a Person of Quality " :

> Flutt'ring spread thy purple pinions,
> Gentle Cupid, o'er my Heart;
>
> (" The Works of Pope," ed. Elwin and Courthope, IV. 489.)

l. 10. Acrons.

This is a fairly common XVIIth century form of "acorn." According to the N.E.D. it " seems to simulate the Greek ἄκρον." Cf. Lovelace " *The Grasse-hopper* " l. 8.

> " thou dost retire
> To thy Carved Acron-bed to lye."

LII. OUT OF FRENCH.

These lines may have been suggested by the following epigram which appears in a publication with which Sedley may well have been acquainted : " les MUSES Sérieuses, galantes, & enjouées où plusieurs rares esprits font voir les pointes & les graces de la poésie Françoise . . . par J. M. a Jene chez Jean Jacques Bauhofer Avec Privilege L'an 1673." 8vo (Bibl. Ars., B.L. 7261), p. 8.

> Sur Un Chartreux
> travaillé des Gouttes.
>
> Mon cher amy ne me dis plus
> que les plaisirs du Dieu Bacchus
> & ceux qu'on goute avec Sylvie,
> Nous font souffrir des maux sur la fin de la vie;
> que la goutte souvent de ces biens est le fruit,
> Et puis que les Chartreux n'ont de leur continence
> Que la goutte icy bas pour toute récompense,
> Je serois un grand sot d'étouffer mon désir
> Va, va ta rémonstrance est vaine ;
> Quand i'aime & que ie bois, i'en ay tout le plaisir
> Et les Chartreux en ont la peine.

LIII. l. 28. *Pontack's.*

A celebrated French eating-house in Abchurch Lane, City. The proprietor, Monsieur Pontaq, was, according to Pepys, the son of " the famous and wise President of Bordeaux," and Evelyn says he was well read in Philosophy, " but chiefly the Rabbins." Misson, the French traveller, writing in 1697, says that " those that would dine at one or two guineas per head are handsomely accommodated at our famous Pontack's." (Wheatley's " London, Past and Present," III. 102, where this passage is quoted.) See also " Bellamira," IV. vi, l. 52 and note, Vol. II, p. 218.

LIV. The " Physician " is Sir Richard Blackmore (*d.* 1729), author of various epic poems, and a " Satyr against Wit," which was answered by a collection of lampoons entitled " Commendatory Verses On the Author of the Two Arthurs, And the Satyr against Wit " (fol., 1700). On p. 3 of the latter volume this poem first appeared without the final couplet of the version printed in A. For an account of the war between Blackmore and the Wits see " Sir Charles Sedley," pp. 231, 232.

The " Commendatory Verses " were answered by " Discommendatory Verses, Or those which are truly Commendatory On the Author of the Two Arthurs, And the Satyr against Wit " (fol., 1700), which contains the following answer to Sedley's poem by an unidentified author :

> To the Poetical Knight, who would have no Body Spoil Paper but Himself.

>> A P-x on Rhimes and Physick, *S-ly* cry'd
>> (And he had Sense and Reason on his side ;)
>> For both of Rhimes and Physick H'had his fill,
>> And swallow'd more than ev'ry Verse a Pill.
>> A Doctor coming by, and loath to lose
>> A Knight so Famous for his P- and Muse,
>> Offer'd him means to give his Knighthood ease,
>> And make the radicated torments cease.
>> Vile Quack, said he, go patch up Mother *Q-les*,
>> Sir *Richard* turn prescriber to Sir *Ch——ls ?*
>> It shall not be, jog Homeward if you please,
>> I'll have no Paper spoil'd on my Disease.
>> The Doctor cry'd, 'Tis true, th' Infection's such,
>> 'Twill certainly discolour't with a Touch ;
>> But I'll affirm, and so withdrawing smil'd,
>> My Papers may, but thou canst ne'er be *Spoil'd.*

LV. PROLOGUE.

This prologue is not, as far as I can discover, printed with any play. I conjecture that it was written for a comedy called " The Reform'd Wife " by Charles Burnaby. The exact date of the production of this play is unknown, but it was published on April 2, 1700 (Allardyce Nicoll's " Eighteenth-Century Drama," p. 301). " Glorious Dryden " had " withdrawn his light " after the production of the famous Secular Masque on March 25, 1700.

It is clear from ll. 8–10 that the Prologue refers to a first venture, and " The Reform'd Wife " was Burnaby's first play. Although its moral tone is not especially high, its language is clean enough to justify the claim that it is " void of Pagan Wit." The printed epilogue made a very similar claim :

> *Let none hereafter Plays Ungodly call,*
> *For this was writ to mortifie you all.*
> *No Parson's here expos'd, no Brothel storm'd,*
> *But a kind handsome keeping Wife Reform'd.*
>
> (Cf. Sedley's Prologue, ll. 21–23.)

Finally, the last line of Sedley's Prologue fits " The Reform'd
Wife " very well. Women are very prominent in the comedy,
and the vapourings of the absurd Lady Dainty would justify
Sedley's comment.

l. 5. *Ballon* and Tumblers.

The Ballon or Balloon was the seventeenth-century football,
which appears from this passage to have been used by clowns on
the stage.

Elwin and Courthope compare this passage with Pope's " Imitations of Horace," Book II. Ep. I. ll. 47, 48 :

> And learned Athens to our art must stoop
> Could she behold us tumbling through a hoop.

(" Works," ed. Elwin and Courthope, III. 352.)

LVI. Prologue to Epsom Wells.

This Prologue is printed in all editions of Shadwell's comedy.
The present text is that prefixed to the first quarto (1673).

It is there printed entirely in italics except for the proper
name " Ben." The title in the quarto is " Prologue written by
Sir *C. S.*"

LVII. Prologue to the Stroulers. See pp. xxvi, xxvii.

Sedley probably wrote this Prologue for a strolling company
of players that he came across in the country. Another " Strowlers
Prologue at Cambridge " appears in Gildon's " New Miscellany "
(8vo, 1701, p. 248).

An amusing description of such a company is given in " Covent
Garden Drollery " (2mo, 1672) in the poem entitled " *A Lampoon
on the* Greenwich *Strowlers* " (pp. 20–25). The company who are
satirized in these lines act in a stable :

> " This fortunate stable had Faggots in it
> Which serv'd to seat all the House but the Pit,
> For that was more decently spread I confess
> With straw."

They had no scenery :

> " I confess they had never a Scene at all,
> They wanted no copy, they had th' original,
> For the windowes being down, and most part of the roof,
> How could they want Scenes, when they had prospect enough."

They admitted a Londoner for a groat, while

> " The Towns men they let in for drink and good chear,
> The School boys for peace, the Seamen for fear."

The author of the poem interrupts a tragedy that is being acted
by sending the " King " for " a Flagon of Beer " and carrying on
a flirtation with the " Queen " while his Majesty is away.

LVIII. Prologue to " The Wary Widdow or Sir Noisy Parrat."

This Prologue was written for Henry Higden's comedy of this
name, produced at Drury Lane in 1693. Whincop (quoted by

Genest, I. 49) writes : " The author had contrived so much
drinking of Punch in the play that the actors almost all got drunk,
and were unable to get through with it, so that the audience were
dismissed at the end of the 3d act." The text is that printed in
the quarto edition of Higden's play (1693), where the title is
" The Prologue Written by Sir *Charles Sydley*." This Prologue
also appeared in " The Gentleman's Journal " for February
1692/3, p. 61, and in the third edition of " Dryden's Miscellany,"
8vo, 1702, p. 254. The version in " The Gentleman's Journal "
(in the Contents, " *A Prologue by Sir* Charles Sedley ") is preceded
by the following words :

" We have since had a Comedy, call'd the *Wary Widow, or
Sir Noisy Parrat*, by *Henry Higden* Esq ; I send you here the
Prologue to it by Sir *Charles Sedley* ; and you are too great
an admirer of *Shakespear*, not to assent to the Praises given to
the Fruits of his rare *Genius*, of which I may say as *Ovid* to
Graecinus,

Quos prior est mirata, sequens mirabitur Aetas,
In quorum plausus tota Theatra sonant.

A PROLOGUE by Sir *Charles Sedley*."

LIX. This translation appeared in " The Gentleman's Journal "
for September 1693 (in the Contents, " Martial lib. 2, Epigr. 41.
imitated by Sir Charles Sedley "), preceded by the following
words :

" The Toothless Dame on whom *Martial* wrote the Epigram,
of which Sir *Charles Sedley* made the following imitation, ought
certainly to have given the Preheminence to Tears.
TO MAXIMINA, lib. 2. Epigr. 41."

LXI. To Nysus. Perhaps suggested by Martial, Bk. VI. Ep. 65.
These lines appear in " The Gentleman's Journal " for November
1692, p. 2 (in the Contents, " *An Epigram by Sir* Charles Sedley "),
preceded by the following words :

" Thanks to Fortune, I do not know that I have any great
interest in these Reflections against the Censorious : They are
obvious Truths, and even those who never fail'd to please the
most difficult are convinc'd of them. To find it true, you
need but read this
Epigram by Sir CHARLES SEDLEY."

LXIII. l. 13. *Audley.*
This must be Hugh Audley, a famous seventeenth-century
usurer, who died on November 15, 1662. His career is summed
up in the title of a contemporary tract, " The Way to be Rich,
according to the Practice of the great Audley, who began with
£200 in 1605, and dyed worth £400,000, Nov., 1662." (London,

Printed for E. Davies, 1662.) (Pepys's Diary, ed. Wheatley, II.
399 and note.)

LXIV. To POSTHUMUS.
This translation was printed in " The Gentleman's Journal "
for January and February 1694, p. 12 (in the Contents, " *To
Posthumus, by Sir* Charles Sedly "). It is introduced as follows :
   " Here is another of *Martial's* Epigrams. It is englished by
Sir *Charles Sedley*.
                    To *Posthumus. lib.* 2. Ep. 12."

l. 1. *Cashoo*, also spelt " cashou " and " cachou " :
   " A sweetmeat, generally in the form of a pill, made of cashew
nut, extract of liquorice, etc., used by tobacco-smokers to sweeten
their breath."—N.E.D., which quotes an advertisement from
" The London Gazette," No. 1800/4, 1683 : " The best Spanish
Lozenges and Cashu, to be eaten."

LXVII. These lines appear in " The Gentleman's Journal " for
November 1693, p. 365 (in the Contents, " *To* Cloe *by Sir*
Charles Sedley "). They are introduced as follows :
   " I have here several other short pieces that may be properly
enough plac'd by these. The first is an Epigram by Sir *Charles
Sedley*.
                          To *CLOE*."
I follow A in reading " Honesty " in l. 2 ; although " honestly,"
the reading of the " Gentleman's Journal," makes equally good
sense.

LXVIII. l. 4. Child.
   This is Sir Josiah Child (1630–1699), a famous and wealthy
merchant of whom Macaulay gives a vivid account in the eighteenth
chapter of his " History." He began as a merchant's apprentice.
In 1678 he was made a baronet, and in 1683 Evelyn computes his
fortune at £200,000. He was Director and afterwards Chairman
of the Old East India Company, and ruled over it like an Eastern
despot. He wrote several books on trade.

LXX. l. 5. To play " booty " is to " join with confederates in order
to ' spoil ' or victimize another player ; to play into the hands of
confederates in order to share the plunder with them ; hence to
play or act falsely so as to gain a desired object ; *esp.* to play badly
intentionally in order to lose the game."—N.E.D. Cf. Etherege,
" The Man of Mode," III. i. (4to, 1676) :
   Y. Bell. What think you of playing it on Booty ?
   Har. What do you mean ?
   Y. Bell. Pretend to be in Love with one another ;

LXXI. l. 9. " Camblet " or Camlet was originally a rich Oriental
material, but the name was applied later to cheap imitations

which were common in the seventeenth century. Silk, wool and hair all seem to have been used in its manufacture. " It is uncertain whether it was ever made of camel's hair ; but in the sixteenth and seventeenth centuries it was made of the hair of the Angora goat."—N.E.D.

LXXXI. Perhaps suggested by Martial, Bk. I. Ep. 41. This poem is a Shakespearean sonnet ; cf. No. XLVI.

l. 2. self-moving Attoms.

Atheism was commonly associated with Epicurus, Lucretius and the atomic theory of the universe. Epicureanism and atomism had been revived in the seventeenth century by the fashionable French philosopher, Pierre Gassend or Gassendi.

LXXXII. ON ARRIA AND PŒTUS.

This epigram commemorates the heroism of Arria, wife of Cæcina Pætus, who, in A.D. 42, when her husband was ordered by Claudius to commit suicide and hesitated, stabbed herself and offered him the dagger. (Pliny, Epistles, III. 16.)

LXXXIII. l. 5. *Bradbury*

This is George Bradbury, a well-known barrister. He was called to the Bar in 1667, and first won commendation from Judge Jeffreys in 1684 as junior counsel against Lady Ivy. He was one of the leaders of the Bar summoned to consult with the Peers in December 1688 on the political crisis. On July 9, 1689, he was created a Baron of the Exchequer, and continued in that office till his death in 1696. (See D.N.B., *s.a.*, Bradbury, George.)

l. 6. *Conquest*

All that I can discover concerning this physician is the information contained in the following extracts from Luttrell's " Brief Relation " : " Dr Conquest, a Popish Physician haveing lately spoke words of the prince and princesse of Orange occasioned much talk " (Luttrell, I. 303, *s.d.*, February 6, 1686/7). " Dr Conquest the Physitian is dead at Bath " (*Ibid.* III. 190, *s.d.*, September 21, 1693).

l. 7. *W——* is made *B——*.

This must be Thomas Watson (1637–1717), a favourite of James II, who was consecrated Bishop of St. Davids on June 26, 1687. He was deprived of his see and excepted from the Act of Indemnity at the Revolution. His personal character is said to have been painted in the blackest colours by his enemies. The following story throws some light on Sedley's reference. " It is said that when his nephew, Medley, blundered while conducting the service in the cathedral, Watson scandalized the congregation with two loud ' God dammes.' " (See D.N.B., *s.a.*, Watson, Thomas.)

LXXXIV. l. 10. *Burnet's*

I.e. Gilbert Burnet, the famous Whig and latitudinarian divine (1643–1715), who became Bishop of Salisbury after the Revolution. Sedley's friend John Wilmot, second Earl of Rochester, went to him for a " blessed end," of which Burnet left an eloquent account in his " Some Passages in the Life and Death of John Earl of Rochester " (8vo, 1680).

XC. ll. 6, 7. The Subject's humble, but not so the Praise,
    If any Muse assist the Poets Lays.

Elwin and Courthope compare Pope's " Rape of the Lock," I. 5, 6 :

> Slight is the subject, but not so the praise,
> If she inspire, if he approve my lays.

l. 206. Teils

" Teil " is an old word for the lime or linden tree, cognate with Latin *tilia* and French *tilleul*. Sedley uses it here to translate " tiliam."

l. 214. A Sacred Silence reigns throughout the Hive.

Dryden has the same phrase in his translation of this passage :

> 'Tis sacred silence all. Nor dare they stray
> When rain is promised or a stormy day.

There is no parallel in the Latin :

> Post ubi iam thalamis se composuere siletur
> In noctem fessosque sopor suus occupat artus.

As the date of Sedley's version is unknown, it is impossible to say whether he or Dryden is the borrower.

l. 268.

This unmetrical line is made to run smoothly in the eighteenth-century editions by the omission of " same." Probably Sedley left it unfinished ; cf. ll. 503 and 534.

l. 282. Bring our Distempers.

I retain the reading of A, which is shown to be correct by reference to the Latin :

> Si vero quoniam casus apibus quoque *nostros*
> Vita tulit.

l. 503. **For equal, Nymphs the *Dryades* with shrill**
      Complaints.

This line makes no sense as it stands and is probably unfinished. The Latin runs

> At chorus aequalis Dryadum clamore supremos
> Implerunt montes.

It is rendered thus by Dryden :

> But all her fellow nymphs the mountains tear
> With loud laments, and break the yielding air :

l. 534. This awkward alexandrine provides another proof that the translation is unfinished.

XCII.   The following version appears on f. 56 of Br. Mus. Add. MS. 34,744.   Ovid, Bk. II. Eleg. 5.

Taken out of S^r Ch : Sidley's & Mr Oldhams Translations.

Nay then ye Devil take all love ! if I
So oft for its damn'd sake do wish to die !
W^t can I wish for but to dye, when you
Dear faithless thing, I find, cou'd prove untrue ?
Why am I curs'd wth life ?   Why am I fain   5
For thee false Jilt to bear eternal pain ?
False Maid ! thou various torment of my life
Thou flying pleasure, and thou lasting greif ?
Tis not the letters wch thy crimes reveal,
Not secret presents wch thy falshood tell :   10
Wou'd God ! my just suspicions wanted cause,
That they might prove less fatal to my ease :
Wou'd God ! less colour for thy guilt there were
But y^t (alas too much of proof does bear !
Happy's ye man that's handsomly receiv'd   15
Whose Mistress swears, & lies, & is beleiv'd.
Cruel ye man, & uncompassionate,
And too indulgent to his own regret,
Who seeks to have her guilt too manifest,
And with ye murdering secret stabs his breast.   20
I saw, when little you suspected me,
When sleep, you thought gave opportunity,
Your crimes I saw, & these unhappy eyes,
Of all your hidden stealths are witnesses :
I saw in signs your mutual wishes read,   25
And nods ye message of your heart conveigh'd :
I saw ye constant board, wch writ all o're
With scrawls of wine, loves mystick Ciphers bore :
Your glances were not mute, but each bewray'd,
And with your fingers Dialogues were made :   30
I understood ye language out of hand,
(For what's too hard for love to understand ?)
Full well I understood for w^t intent,
All this dumb talke, & silent hints were meant :
When others rose, I saw thee dart a kiss,   35
The wanton prelude to a farther bliss :
Not such as wives to their cold husbands give,
But such as hot Adulterers receive :
Such as might kindle frozen appetite,
And fire ev'n wasted Nature wth delight ;   40
Such as ye God of war, & Paphian Queen
Did in ye height of their embraces joyn.
" What art thou mad I cry'd, before my face,
" To steal my wealth & my new rival grace ?
" I'll rise, & seize my own upon ye place.   45
" There soft Endearments shou'd not farther goe,
" But be ye secret pleasure of us two,
" How comes this third in for a share I'd know ? "
This and much more I said by rage inspir'd,
Whilst conscious shame her cheeks with blushes fired :   50

Such lovely stains yᵉ face of heaven adorn,
When light's first blushes paint yᵉ bashful morn :
So on yᵉ bush yᵉ flaming rose does glow,
When mingled with yᵉ lillies neighbouring snow;
This, or some other colour much like this,   55
The semblance then of her complexion was :
And while her looks yᵗ sweet disorder wore
Chance added beauties undisclosed before :
Upon the ground she cast her jetty eyes,
Her eyes that shot fiercer darts in yᵗ disguise :   60
Her face a sad & mournful air expressd.
Her face more lovely seem'd in sadness dress'd :
Urg'd by revenge I hardly cou'd forbear
Her braided locks, and tender cheeks to tear :
When I beheld her face my anger cool'd ;   65
I felt myself to a meer lover fool'd,
Evn yᵗ fierce outragious thing erewhile,
Grew calm as infant, when in sleep they smile :
And now a kiss am humbly fain to crave,
And beg no worse than she my rival gave :   70
She smil'd & strait a throng of kisses prest,
The worst of wᶜʰ shoud Jove himself but tast,
The brandish'd thunder from his hand wou'd wrest.
Well pleas'd I was and yet tormented too,
For fear my envy'd rival felt them so :   75
Better they seem'd by far than them I taught ;
And she in them shew'd something new methought :
Fond jealous I myself yᵉ pleasure gruch,
And they displeas'd because they pleas'd too much.
When in my mouth I felt her darting tongue,   80
My wounded thoughts it with suspition stung :
Nor is this all, tho I of this complain,
Nor shoud I for a Kiss be so in pain ;
But such ne'er cou'd be taught her but in bed,
And Heaven knows wᵗ reward her teacher had.   85

THE MULBERRY GARDEN

TITLE-PAGE. Sir Charles Sidley : this is the only published work
in which the name is spelt thus. The same spelling occurs in
all editions.

DEDICATION. " Her Grace the Dutchesse of Richmond and Lennox "
is Frances Stuart or Stewart, " La Belle Stuart," born in 1648.
Her father was a doctor attached to the Court of the Queen-
mother, Henrietta Maria, in France, and early in 1663 Frances
was appointed Maid of Honour to Catherine of Braganza. The
king's infatuation for her soon became common talk. According
to Pepys he was " besotted " with her. De Comminges, the
French Ambassador, wrote on June 25/July 15, 1663, that there
had been a great quarrel between " La Dame " (Lady Castlemaine) and " La Demoiselle " (Frances Stuart), and that the king

had threatened never to enter Lady Castlemaine's house again if her rival were not present (Wheatley's " Pepysiana," p. 293). She was also the subject of hopeless passions cherished by Buckingham, Anthony Hamilton, John Roettiers the medallist, and Nat. Lee the poet. She is said, however, to have refused to yield even to the king. Charles even contemplated divorcing the queen and marrying her.

In 1667 she eloped with Charles Stuart, third Earl of Richmond and Lennox, who was a friend of Sir Charles Sedley (see " Sir Charles Sedley," p. 75). For a while the king was mad with jealousy and the duchess did not appear at Court for some time. She attended Mary of Modena at the birth of the Old Pretender and was present at Queen Anne's coronation. She died a Roman Catholic on October 15, 1702, and was buried in Westminster Abbey.

Her portrait by Lely is at Hampton Court and has been reproduced as the frontispiece of this volume.

She appears as Britannia on several medals and is probably the original of Britannia on Roettiers's halfpenny in 1672.

The duchess, as Sedley says, had " 'scapt very well " hitherto from the attentions of dedicators, but her admirer, Nat. Lee, was to dedicate his " Theodosius " to her in 1680.

I. i. l. 1. Well, for all this heat, . . .
   Cf. Molière, " L'Escole des Maris," I. ii. ll. 1, 2, 6–9 :

> " *S_g in. relle.* Mon frère, s'il vous plaist, ne discourons point tant
> Et que chacun de nous viue comme il l'entend ;
>
> .   .   .   .
>
> Ie vous diray pourtant que mes intentions,
> Sont ne prendre point de vos corrections :
> Que i'ay pour tout conseil ma fantaisie à suivre,
> Et me trouve fort bien de ma façon de viure."

l. 5. See Plays, Balls, . . .
   Cf. " L'Escole des Maris," I. ii. ll. 115–116 :

> " I'ay souffert qu'elle ait veu les belles compagnies,
> Les diuertissements, les Bals, les Comedies."

12. My elder Brother, and a Reverend Justice.
   Cf. " L'Escole des Maris," I. i. 20 :

> " Monsieur mon frere aisné, car Dieu mercy vous l'estes."

ll. 25, 26. I'm asham'd to see you every day set out thus powdered . . .
   Cf. " L'Escole des Maris," I. i. 23–28 :

> " Ne voudriez vous point, dy-ie, pur ces matières
> Des jeunes muguets m'inspirer les manières,
> M'obliger a porter de ces petits chapeaux,
> Qui lassent éventer leur debiles cerveaux,
> Et de ces blonds cheveux de qui la vaste enfleure
> Des visages humains offusque la figure ? "

l. 27. Periwig
 Periwigs did not come into fashion till about 1663. Pepys
bought his first on May 30, 1663, but was very nervous about
wearing it for some time. Charles II did not wear his till the
spring of 1663/4. They had, however, been used by elderly
men for many years before the Restoration. Anthony à Wood
bought one from his barber on September 4, 1656 ("Life and
Times," ed. Clark, I. 209).

l. 34. Lord, what pains you take to Quarrel . . .
 Cf. "L'Escole des Maris," I. i. 57–64.

> " C'est un étrange fait du soin que vous prenez,
> A me venir toûjours ietter mon âge au nez ;
> Et qu'il faille qu'en moy sans cesse ie vous voye
> Blasmer l'ajustement aussi bien que la ioye :
> Comme si condamnée à ne plus rien chérir,
> La vieillesse devoit ne songer qu'a mourir,
> Et d'assez de laideur n'est pas accompagnée,
> Sans se tenir encor mal propre & rechignée."

l. 41. Sillabub
 " A drink or dish made of milk (frequently as drawn from the
cow) or cream curdled by the admixture of wine, cider or other
acid and often sweetened or flavoured."—N.E.D. It was a
favourite country dish in the seventeenth century and is often
mentioned in plays, *e.g.* Wycherley's " The Gentleman Dancing
Master," I. i. (4to, 1673), where *Hippolita* complains that she is
never allowed " to eat a Sillybub in new Spring-Gar'n with a
Cousin."

l. 45. Hide-Park Filly
 I.e. a courtesan. Hyde Park had a bad reputation : cf.
Shirley's " Hide Park," IV. i. (4to, 1637), where the scene is laid
in the Park :

> "*Julietta.* I were too much wicked to suspect your honour,
> And in this place.
> *Lord Bonvile.* This place, the place were good enough
> If you were bad enough, and as prepar'd
> As I, there have beene stories that some have
> Struck many deere within the Parke : "

ll. 52, 53. to be all day abroad.
 Cf. "L'Escole des Maris," I. 2. 42, 43 :

> " qu'elle courre, ayme l'oisiuité,
> Et soit de damoiseaux fleurée en liberté."

l. 55. Sedans
 The name and the covered portable chair which it denotes
seem to have been introduced into England in the reign of
Charles I. In the Index to the Patents of 1634 (quoted by
N.E.D.) the word is applied to chairs of this kind, for supplying
which Sir Sanders Duncombe received a grant. According to
Evelyn, Duncombe brought them from Italy (Diary, ed. Dobson,

I. 239). Mr. Austin Dobson, however, in a note to this passage in his edition of Evelyn's Diary, states that Duncombe only popularized them, but that they were actually introduced by the first Duke of Buckingham, to whom Prince Charles (Charles I) gave two out of three presented to him by the Spanish Prime Minister, the Duke of Olivarez. The earliest reference to them in the drama is probably in Brome's " The 'Sparagus Garden " (4to, 1640), where they are mentioned as a novelty :

> " The new Hand-litters: what do yee call it, a Sedan ? "
> (" The 'Sparagus Garden," I. x.)

l. 57. Feathers and Ribands.
  I.e. Fops and Beaux. Cf. Dryden's " An Evening's Love," I. i. (4to, 1671), where *Jacinta* speaks of two gallants as follows : " I guess 'em to be feathers of the English Embassador's Train." These special senses of " Feather " and " Riband " are not noticed by the N.E.D.
  With the whole passage cf. " L'Escole des Maris," I. ii. 153, where *Sganarelle* asks :

> " Et chez vous iront les Damoiseaux ? "

l. 70. O this fine believing Gentleman.
  Cf. " L'Escole des Maris," I. ii. 162 :

> " Que i'auray de plaisir si l'on le fait cocu."

ll. 79, 80. what visits do you intend this Afternoon ? . . .
  Cf. " L'Escole des Maris," I. ii. 10 :

> " Où donc allez vous, qu'il ne vous en deplaise ? "

I. ii. l. 23. *Colebys*
  This person was landlord of the tavern in the Mulberry Garden. There are many references to him in plays, *e.g.* Wycherley's " Love in a Wood," III, ii. (4to, 1672), where Dapperwit says to his mistress *Lucy :* " you have refus'd *Colby's* Mulberry Garden, and the French-houses, for the Green Garret."

l. 27. Stone-horse
  I.e. stallion : cf. Shadwell's " A True Widow," III. i. (4to, 1679), " gold to silver on the bay Stone-horse against the Flea-bitten."

l. 59. *Point de Venie* or *Rome.*
  Point or thread lace is frequently named after the locality of its manufacture, *e.g.* Point de Bruxelles, Point d'Espagne. Lace was a favourite article of attire of both sexes in the seventeenth century, and there are many references to Point de Venice. Sir Fopling Flutter in Etherege's " The Man of Mode " compares it to Point d'Espagne.

> " *Sir Fop.* In ever saw anything prettier than this high Work on your Point D'espaigne—
> *Emilia.* 'Tis not so rich as Point *De Venice* . . .

Sir Fop. Not altogether, but looks cooler, and is more proper for the Season."

(4to, 1676, III. ii.)

l. 63. Gorget

Originally a piece of armour for the throat, hence later an article of female dress covering throat and bosom.

ll. 74, 75. A Ladies heart is . . . easier surpris'd by being well man'd, . . .

Perhaps suggested by " L'Escole des Maris," I. 4 :

Ergaste . . . une femme qu'on garde est gagnée a demy,

l. 104. Kissing the Cards at *Ombre.*

Ombre was a Spanish card game which came into fashion after the Restoration. The earliest reference in the N.E.D. is in a letter of E. Gower written in 1660/61. It was fashionable right up to the nineteenth century. Thackeray's *Marquis of Steyne* wins " a hundred thousand " at a game of " Hombre " in " Vanity Fair."

For the custom of kissing the cards cf. the Epilogue (spoken by Mrs. Knipp) to Wycherley's " The Country Wife " :

In fine, you Essens't Boyes, both Old and Young,

.   .   .   .

May Kiss the Cards at Picquet, Hombre,—and Lu,
And so be thought to kiss the Lady too.

l. 104. presenting Oranges.

Oranges were a common present from lovers to mistresses and husbands to wives. The buying of oranges in the theatre was a common way of treating. On May 11, 1668, Pepys was " vexed " because " the orange woman did come into the pit and challenge me for twelve oranges, which she delivered by my order at a late play, at night to give to some ladies in a box, which was wholly untrue, but yet she swore it to be true. But, however, I did deny it and did not pay her ; but for quiet did buy 4*s*. worth of oranges of her at 6*d*. a piece." (Diary, ed. Wheatley, VIII. 13.)

I. iii. ll. 7, 8, 9. a Wilderness of Sycamores, Orange, and Lemmon Trees.

Evelyn mentions the excellence of China oranges grown in his own garden on September 25, 1679 (Diary, ed. Dobson, III. 37). They are said by Bray in his note to have been grown in England since the reign of James I or before. There were some in the " Physique Garden " in St. James's Park, where they were seen by Pepys on April 19, 1664 (Diary, ed. Wheatley, IV. 113). With the whole passage cf. " L'Escole des Maris," I. iii. 35.

"Avouons que Paris nous fait part
De cent plaisirs charmans qu'on n'a point autre part ;
Les Prouinces auprés sont des lieux solitaires."

l. 24. a saver

See note to Poem No. II.

I. iv. l. 123. *Ring.*

This Stage Direction must have crept in from the marked prompt copy. A marginal " *Ring* " occurs in Rochester's " Valentinian " (4to, 1685), IV. ii., but in that play it may refer to the ring which the Emperor sends to *Lucina* to persuade her to come to Court. A printed prompt copy of Shirley's " The Sisters " (8vo, 1652), made apparently for a revival after the Restoration, is preserved at Sion College, London. It has the MS. Stage Directions " Act Ready " eighteen lines before the end of Act I, with " Ring " at the end of the Act. Act II has " Act Ready " twenty-six lines from the end and " Ring " at the end of the Act. Act III has " Ring " at the end but no " Act Ready." Act IV has the same directions as Act I, and Act V the same as Act III.

" Act Ready " and " Ring " seem to have an intimate connection. " Act Ready " cannot mean " prepare for the next Act," as it comes at the end of an Act in each case. " Act," however, in the seventeenth-century theatre often means not an Act in the modern sense, but the interval between two Acts, and also the music played during the interval, *e.g.* in Marston's " What you will " there is a dumb show at the end of Act II, and we are told in a Stage Direction that " much of this is done while the Acte is playing." This is probably also the meaning of the word in " Henry VIII," Epilogue :

> " *'Tis ten to one, this Play can never please*
> *All that are heere : Some come to take their ease*
> *And sleep an Acte or two ; but those we feare*
> *We have frighted with our Trumpets.*"

This meaning of " Act " certainly survived the Restoration. In " *A Lampoon on the Greenwich Strowlers* " (probably by Joe Haines) in " Covent Garden Drollery " (8vo, 1672), p. 24, we find the following line :

> " I ordered the Drummer to beat a long Act."

" The Drummer " was the entire orchestra of a small strolling company, and the context shows that the speaker has good reasons for desiring a long interval, and therefore tells the drummer to give a lengthy display of his skill.

" Act Ready," then, would mean " music ready," and " *Ring* " would be the direction for the prompter to ring for the music.

II. i. l. 9. the State

I.e., the Commonwealth. Sir Samuel was a Roundhead, and the usual name given to the Republican Government was the " State."

l. 14. the Cause
I.e. the Good Old Cause, as the Puritans called the cause
of republicanism and puritanism. The name seems to have
survived the Restoration, for Algernon Sidney at his execution spoke of " *The Old Cause* in which I was from my youth
engaged."

l. 29. sequester'd.
The usual term for the confiscation of Royalist estates by the
Commonwealth authorities.

ll. 32, 33. Solliciting her Husbands Composition at a Committee.
This is a reference to such bodies as the Committee for Advance
of Money and, more especially, the Committee for Compounding
with Delinquents, before which Royalists could " compound " for
their loyalty by surrendering part or the whole of their estates.
Sedley must have had painful memories of the treatment which
his mother received at the hands of the Committees (see " Sir
Charles Sedley," pp. 30–35).

l. 74. Pater-Noster Row
Famous for mercers. Pepys often visited them, *e.g.* on
November 21, 1660, when he bought " some green watered
moyre for a morning waistcoat " (Diary, ed. Wheatley, I. 289).

ll. 98, 99. a Coach with the Glasses drawn up.
Coaches with glazed windows were a novelty in the reign of
Charles II. Anthony Hamilton, in Chap. VII of the " Memoirs
of Count Grammont " (ed. G. Goodwin), mentions that the
king had one, but that De Grammont brought over an improved
model from France. In a note on this passage Mr. Goodwin
quotes a book called the " Ultimum Vale " of John Carleton,
which describes them as " a new fashion " in 1663.

l. 109. As Papists go to Church for fear of the penalty.
A reference to the fines imposed on Roman Catholic " recu-
sants " who refused to attend the Anglican service.

l. 178. Grayes-Inn-walks.
Gray's Inn Walks or Gardens was a large open piece of ground,
laid out in lawns and planted with trees extending northward
from South Square, Gray's Inn, to King's (now Theobald's)
Road. It was laid out as a garden when Bacon was Treasurer of
the Inn, and he has been credited with its origin. It was a
fashionable promenade under Charles II : cf. Pepys on June 30,
1661 :

  " *Lords Day.* Hence I to Gray's Inn Walk, all alone, and
  with great pleasure, seeing the fine ladies walk there."
  (Diary, ed. Wheatley, II. 61.)

And again on May 4, 1662 :

> " When Church was done, my wife and I walked to Grayes Inne, to observe the fashions of the ladies, because of my wife's making some clothes." (*Ibid.* 230.)

l. 205. *the French House.*
Probably Chatelain's, a famous French tavern in Covent Garden. Pepys calls it " Chatelin's, the French house " (Diary, ed. Wheatley, VII. 361). See note to Act IV. sc. i. l. 150.

II. ii. ll. 25, 26.   But, fair *Althea*, you were much to blame
        With your own breath to blow a hopeless flame.

Sedley practically repeated this couplet in the lines entitled " The Platonick " (No. X of the present edition, ll. 1, 2).

II. iv. l. 37. *They enter the Widows house.*
The previous scene was probably a " carpenter's scene," or perhaps only a painted back cloth set immediately within the proscenium. Sir Samuel and Wildish would have left the stage by a proscenium door ; the scene would then draw and reveal the interior of the Widow's house, and they would immediately re-enter from the wings. The opposite effect is produced at the end of Act IV, where Sir John Everyoung is talking to the 'prentices inside his house, and during the conversation the scene changes from the interior to the street outside, probably by dropping the same street scene in front of the rear portion of the stage. In both cases I have inserted a scene division for the convenience of the modern reader. That scenery of this kind was used is definitely proved by a Stage Direction in Dryden's " The Rival Ladies " (4to, 1663), V. i., where the scene is first laid on the deck of a " Carrack," but afterwards changes to the captain's cabin, the Stage Direction being " The Scene draws and discovers the Captain's Cabin."

ll. 20, 21. a Dish of Coffee.
The word and the drink came into Western Europe at the beginning of the seventeenth century. Coffee became popular in England under the Commonwealth. The first coffee-house was opened in Oxford in 1650, and another was opened in London in 1652. They became very numerous after the Restoration. Coffee was associated with Roundheads and republicanism. The Coffee Club which Pepys visited before the Restoration was a republican debating society.

l. 61. forbearance money,
" Money paid to a creditor (in addition to the interest) for allowing the repayment of a loan to be deferred beyond the stipulated time."—N.E.D., where this passage is quoted.

l. 164. A muss

A muss is a scramble : cf. Shakespeare, " Antony and Cleopatra," III. xiii.

> "Authority melts from me of late. When I cried hoa,
> Like Boyes unto a musse, Kings would start forth,
> And cry, your will."

III. ii. ll. 3, 4. few Plays gain Audience by being in Print.

Restoration plays were nearly always printed after production on the stage. There were, however, a few exceptions, such as Flecknoe's " Damoiselles à la Mode," which was printed in 1667 but probably not produced till September 1668.

ll. 81, 82. a Beggar that begs in a Tone.

Seventeenth-century beggars seem to have asked for alms in a peculiar whining tone. Cf. Letter of the Co. of Dorchester printed in " Sir Charles Sedley," pp. 346, 347 (she is describing the Irish) : " I find them not only senceless but a mallincoly sort of people and speak all in the tone off the cripples off London." It is possible, however, that "Tone" may be a misprint for "Tune."

l. 86. Song.

This song was very popular. It appears in a number of miscellanies such as " The New Academy of Complements " (1671), " Wit and Drollery " (1682), " The Academy of Compliments " (1684), etc. See Bibliography.

l. 176. Scrivener

Originally a professional amanuensis, but commonly used throughout the sixteenth and seventeenth centuries for a notary or lawyer.

III. iii. ll. 14, 15. A true Servant to the State, and a man in Authority ! he shall have three kicks more for that.

This passage is probably an echo of Shakespeare, " Julius Cæsar," III. iii., where the Roman mob use much the same line of argument to the poet *Cinna* when the latter says that he is a bachelor :

> " That's as much as to say, they are fooles that marrie ; you'l beare me a bang for that I feare : "

l. 41. Sympathy-powder

Said to have been invented by Sir Kenelm Digby. It is described in " A Late Discourse made in a solemne Assembly of Nobles and Learned Men at *Montpellier* in *France* by Sir *Kenelme Digby*, Knight, &c. Touching the Cure of Wounds by the *Powder* of *Sympathy* ; With Instructions how to make the said Powder ; whereby many other secrets of Nature are unfolded." The British Museum has the second edition augmented, 12mo, London, 1658. There are also Latin and French versions.

Corneille refers to the powder in " Le Menteur " (1642), IV. iii. :

> "*Dorante.* Alcippe te surprend ! sa gúerison t'étonne
> L'état où je le mis était fort périlleux :
> Mais il est à présent des secrets merveilleux.
> Ne t'a-t-on parlé d'une source de vie
> Que nomment nos guerriers poudre de sympathie ?
> On en voit tous les jours des effets étonnants."

IV. i. ll. 28, 32. Cheese-Cakes . . . a Bottle of Rhenish.

According to Evelyn " Certain trifling *Tartes, Neates-tongues, Salacious meates,* and bad *Rhenish* " were the chief dainties sold in the Mulberry Garden. (" A Character of England," 12mo, 1659, p. 57.)

ll. 57, 59. A friend at Court . . . a Bishop.

Sedley seems to have forgotten for a moment that the scene is laid under the Commonwealth. It is a curious anachronism to speak of a Court before the Restoration and of a Bishop's power of granting livings when the Bishops were in hiding or exile.

ll. 134, 135. all my acquaintance have two or three Names apiece.

It was uncommon for anyone under the rank of royalty to have more than two names in the seventeenth century.

ll. 137–139. Incomparable Ladies, that like Roman Conquerors have two or three names.

Every free-born Roman had at least three names. The nomen, or middle name, distinguishing one gens from another ; the cognomen, or third name, distinguishing one familia from another ; and the prænomen, or first name, one individual from another. Sedley is probably thinking of the fourth name, or title, adopted by victorious generals, such as " Africanus," " Germanicus," etc.

l. 143. *Giffords*

A notorious London brothel. Mrs. Gifford, Mrs. Temple and Mrs. Creswell were all well-known procuresses and are often mentioned in plays. Cf. Etherege, " She Wou'd if she Cou'd," V. i. (4to, 1667) : " pox on your honourable intrigue, Wou'd I were safe at *Giffords.*"

Also Shadwell's " The Miser," V. i. (4to, 1672) : " Gentlemen, I hate the Name of a Muse, as I do that of a Baud : Were I a poet I would invoke *Creswell* or *Gifford* before any Muse in *Christendom.*"

l. 149. *Hoquemore*

I.e. hock. It is an anglicised form of Hochheimer, from Hochheim on the Main. Cf. Shadwell's " Epsom Wells " (4to, 1672), III. i. (Bevil's Letter) : " *I am very well, and drink much Hockamore,*" cf. Bellamira II. i. 192.

ll. 150, 151. *Chaste Ling, . . . La-Fronds.*

Chaste Ling is Chatelain's, a famous French tavern in Covent

Garden, much frequented by Wits and men of fashion. Cf.
Pepys's Diary March 13, 1667/8 (Wheatley's ed., VII. 361):
" At noon all of us go to Chatelin's, the French house in Covent
Garden to dinner," and Shadwell's " The Humorists," V. i.
(4to, 1671): " Raymund, a fellow that never wore a noble or
polite Garniture, or a white Perriwig, one that has not a Bit of
Interest at *Chatolins,* or ever eat a good Fricacy, Sup, or Rogust
in his life."

La Fronds was another French house, apparently near Chatelain's in Covent Garden: cf. Dryden's " Sir Martin Mar-all "
(4to, 1667) IV. i.: " Wine from *Shatling,* and *La Fronds,*" and
the Prologue of Bankes's " Destruction of Troy " (4to, 1678/9):

> *" the rich Banquet is to come, a Treat*
> *Cook'd by your* Chat'lin *and* La Froon *of* Wit."

l. 170. Guittar.
   Cf. " The Memoirs of Court Grammont " Chap. VIII (ed.
Gordon Goodwin, I. 174, 175), where the vogue of the guitar
at the Court of Charles II is vividly described.

l. 195. Angel-beast
   A card game fashionable at the Restoration. It seems to have
been superseded by the more fashionable ombre.
   Cf. " Prologue to the Double Marriage " (as printed in
" Covent Garden Drollery," 1672, p. 15):

> " he found too soon,
> Damn'd Beasts and Umbre, spent the afternoon; "

and " The Feigned Astrologer " (4to, 1668, III. i.):

> " A kind of Lady-ordinary,
> Where they are beasting it, for that game's in
> Fashion still, though *Hombre* be more Courtly."

l. 266. Bubbles
   A bubble is a dupe. Cf. Shadwell's Explanation of the Cant
prefixed to his " Squire of Alsatia " (4to, 1668): *Bubble, Caravan.*
the Cheated.

l. 279. a Padding for Hearts
   To pad was originally merely to tramp along a road, and later
to rob on the highway, which is the meaning here. The earliest
example of this meaning given by the N.E.D. is from Ford's
" The Lady's Trial " (1638):

> " One can Cant . . . and pick a pocket,
> Pad for a cloak or hat, and, in the dark
> Pistol a straggler for a quarter-ducat."

Cf. " Bellamira," III. iv. 67.

l. 279. Vizards ?
   I.e. Masks. Cf. Wheatley's note to Pepys's Diary, s.d., June 12,
1663, III. 166 n.: " Masks were commonly used by ladies in
the reign of Elizabeth, and when their use was revived after the

Restoration for respectable women attending the theatre, they
became general. They soon, however, became the mark of
loose women and their use was discontinued by women of repute."

l. 315. light
The eighteenth-century editions substitute the more modern
word " chance " : cf. V. iv. l. 67.

IV. ii. l. 1. some Souldiers below.
Sedley may well have been thinking of his own mother's arrest
by Parliamentary troops, which must have been one of his earliest
memories. See " Sir Charles Sedley," p. 31.

l. 197. the General will declare like an honest man.
The General is George Monk, who reached London from Scot-
land early in February 1659/60. The king was proclaimed on
May 8.

V. i. ll. 160–163.
These lines were afterwards adapted by Sedley in the lyric
entitled " Constancy " (No. IX of this edition, ll. 3–10).

V. ii. l. 14. return your kind Visit in the *Fleet.*
The Fleet Prison, which dated from Norman times, was used
in the seventeenth century both for debtors and criminals. James
Howell and William Wycherley were among its most distin-
guished temporary inhabitants.

V. iii. l. 18–21. May my Perriwig . . . come off always with my Hat,
if it cost me above twelve pounds.
A periwig which came off with the hat would be a badly fitting
one. Twelve pounds was a very high price. Pepys paid £4 10s.
for two very good ones on March 29, 1667, but he was acquainted
with the maker (Diary, ed. Wheatley, IV. 245).

l. 48. *Machevile*
I.e. Niccolo' Machiavelli (1469–1527), the famous Italian author
and statesman, traditionally regarded as a type of diabolic cunning.

V. iv. l. 27. Hackneys.
" Hackney " originally meant an ambling horse, then such a
horse kept for hire, then a carriage kept for hire, which is the
sense here. Hackney coaches were numerous in the reign of
Charles II, and Pepys mentions a Proclamation to restrain their
abuses on November 7, 1660.

l. 28. black Farrendine
Farrendine (spelt in several ways) was a kind of cloth made of
mixed silk and wool or hair, similar to poplin. It is said to have
been so called from its inventor Ferrand, *circa* 1630. On
January 28, 1662/3, Pepys tells how his wife was robbed of her
new " Ferrandin waistecoate." " Mohair " and " Ferrandine "
were considered cheap materials (Pepys, Diary, ed. Wheatley,

III. 27 and note). *Lucy,* in Wycherley's " Love in a Wood,"
III. i., says that Dapperwit gave her her first " Farrenden Gown."
l. 67. by.
A dicing term, " throw " being understood. The later
editions read " bet," which is certainly more appropriate.
V. v. l. 104. a Flame ⟨that⟩ smil'd
All texts read " a Flame you smil'd."   Sedley probably wrote
" a Flame y^t smil'd," " y^t " being the common abbreviation
for " that."   The compositor apparently mistook it for " y^u "
which was an equally common abbreviation for " you."

ANTONY AND CLEOPATRA

Prologue, l. 2. *fleurets*
" nom d'un ancien pas qui se composait d'un demicoupé et
de deux pas marchés sur la pointe de pied."   Littré, quoted by
N.E.D., which cites this passage.

l. 10. *Saver*
See note to Poem No. II.

I. i. l. 1. an easie Victory
I.e. Actium, 31 B.c., the famous naval battle in which Octavian
defeated the combined fleets of Antony and Cleopatra.

ll. 12. 13. *Armenian* Kings . . . *Parthian* blood
" Kings " in the plural is an exaggeration.   According to
Plutarch, Antony captured Artabazus, king of Armenia, by
treachery and triumphed over him in Alexandria.   He had
previously waged a long war with the Parthians.

l. 21. fair Sister
I.e. Octavia, Octavian's half-sister, married to Antony in
41 B.C.

l. 49. former Wife
I.e. Fulvia, Antony's first wife.

l. 83. *Thyreus*
The name is Thyrsos in Plutarch.   Thyreus is the form found
in North and Shakespeare.

I. ii. l. 41. *Canidius*
Lucius Canidius Crassus, Consul in 40 B.c., commander of
Antony's land forces at Actium.

l. 70. a promiscuous crowd . . .
" for lack of water men his Captaines did presse by force all
sorts of men out of Graece that they could take up in the field,
as travellers, muletters, reapers, harvestmen and younge boyes."—
Plutarch's " Life of Antony," tr. North.

l. 142. *Amintas, Deotorus*—
Amintas (or rather Amyntas), according to Plutarch, was king of Lycaonia.

Deotaurus (Deiotarus) was tetrarch and afterwards king of Galatia. Both are mentioned in the " Life of Antony " as having deserted Antony and gone over to Octavian.

l. 144. *Pelusium* by *Seleucus*
Pelusium was a city of Lower Egypt lying between the seaboard and the deltaic marshes. Seleucus was an officer of Antony and Cleopatra who surrendered it to Octavian. According to Plutarch, " a rumor ran in the citie " that he had done so by Cleopatra's orders. " Cleopatra brought Seleucus wife and children to Antony to be revenged of them at his pleasure."

l. 173. *Cæsarion*
Cleopatra's son by Julius Cæsar.

l. 174. *Antillus*
Or Antyllus, Antony's elder son by Fulvia. The name is probably an abbreviation of the diminutive Antonillus.

l. 210. ⟨find⟩
I read ⟨find⟩ here for the impossible " sate " of all the old texts; " find " in the old script might conceivably been mistaken for " sate " with a long *s* and badly formed *a*.

l. 213. When *Brutus* this *Octavius* over-threw.
I.e. at Philippi where Antony was victorious over Cassius while Brutus at first overcame Octavian.

II. i. l. 115. Passions lye yet within your tender breast.
Cf. note to Poem No. XVI.

II. ii. l. 41. Of *Tuscan* Kings sprung from the glorious race.
An echo of Horace's famous address to Mæcenas : " Mæcenas atavis edite regibus."—Odes, I. i.

l. 52. *Arabia . . . Nabatheans*
Plutarch mentions among the provinces given by Antony to Cleopatra " that parte of Arabia where the Nabatheians doe well, which stretcheth out towards the Ocean."

ll. 54, 55. Moon . . . Sun
" Cleopatra having brought him two twinnes, a sonne and a daughter, he named his sonne Alexander, and his daughter Cleopatra, and gave them to their surnames, the Sunne to the one, and the moone to the other."—Plutarch, " Life of Antony," tr. North.

l. 61. *Bacchus . . . Isis*
" Now for Cleopatra she did not only weare the apparell of the Goddesse Isis but so gave audience unto all her subjects as a new Isis."—*Ibid.*

In an earlier passage Plutarch mentions that Antony and Cleopatra were compared to Bacchus and Venus.

ll. 145, 146. Single pair of inverted commas.
A single pair of inverted commas at the beginning of a line was used to draw attention to proverbs, moral maxims—" sentences " as they were called. See P. Simpson, " Shakespearean Punctuation," § 42, p. 101, where numerous examples from Shakespeare, Jonson and others are quoted. The practice was common enough in the pre-Restoration drama, and occurs as late as Pope's edition of Shakespeare (1725). Cf. III. i. l. 7. etc.

III. i. l. 7. lewd *Cytheris*
Antony's liaison with this woman, according to Plutarch, belonged to the early part of his life before his marriage with Fulvia : " a woman called Cytheride . . . whom he loved derely . . . he caried her up and downe in a litter . . . and had as many men waiting upon her litter, she being a player, as were attending upon his owne mother."

l. 23. *Cinna*
Perhaps a misprint for Sylla or Sulla; but possibly Sedley referred to L. Cornelius Cinna, the friend of Marius, and leader of the popular party against Sulla, whose career certainly justifies the epithet " bloody." In conjunction with Marius he overthrew Sulla's party when that general was in the East. He was Consul in 86 B.C. and died in 83 B.C.

l. 23. *Marius*
Caius Marius (157–86 B.C.), the famous popular leader, conqueror of the Gauls and opponent of Sulla.

l. 24. *Appius*
Appius Claudius Crassus, the decemvir, Consul 451 B.C. The legend of his attempt on Lucretia was the subject of a tragedy by John Webster (*c.* 1609).

l. 25. *Lucullus*
L. Licinius Lucullus (*c.* 106–*c.* 54 B.C.), the famous general and voluptuary, who conquered Mithridates and brought the cherry tree to Italy.

l. 64. in⟨j⟩ur'd
The reading of the quartos, " insur'd," is merely due to the confusion of the *j* with the long *s*.

l. 99. old *Anchises* on *Æneas*
A reminiscence of Verg., *Æn.* II. 707. Incidentally it is an anachronism, as the *Æneid* was as yet unwritten.

III. ii. l. 60. Octavi⟨a'⟩s
All texts read *Octavius's* or *Octavius'*. A badly formed *a* in the copy would easily be mistaken for a *u* by the compositor, and

he made matters worse by transferring the apostrophe to the other side of the *s* and adding another *s*.

ll. 77, 78. *Crassus . . . Babel*
 Crassus is M. Licinius Crassus, whose army was defeated and massacred at Carrhæ in Mesopotamia in 53 B.C.
 Babel is Babylon, supposed vaguely to be the capital of the " Parthians."

l. 103. tender Virgin of low race,
 Perhaps suggested by the Shakespearean Cleopatra's
> " Maid that Milkes
> And doe's the meanest chares."

A good example of the difference between the vivid detailed Elizabethan manner and the general " Augustan " style.

l. 112. *Lepidus*
 M. Æmilius Lepidus, partner with Antony and Octavian in the third triumvirate. See Shakespeare's " Julius Caesar " and " Antony and Cleopatra."

l. 205. I swear upon my Knees . . .
 Sedley follows Shakespeare in dramatizing this incident, which Dryden omits. He borrows from Shakespeare the kissing of *Cleopatra's* hand, which is not in Plutarch. The riot of the soldiers and the rescue of *Thyreus* are inventions of Sedley. Genest's comment is that " Shakespeare has represented the affair as it was, Sedley has made a mountain out of a molehill."

Stage direction after l. 308. Lucilius
 See Shakespeare's " Julius Caesar," V. v. This story of his mutiny is fictitious.

l. 311. Old *Ruffian*
 The phrase is from Shakespeare's " Antony and Cleopatra," IV. i., where Octavian replies to Antony's challenge :
> " *Cæsar* to *Antony :* let the old Ruffian know
> I have many other wayes to dye."

l. 323. *Brutus* to save⟨,⟩
 All texts make nonsense of this line by reading " Brutus, to save myself."

IV. i. l. 56. *Parthian* triumph
 Strictly speaking it was Ventidius, Antony's lieutenant, who was the only Roman who triumphed over the Parthians.

l. 89. *Cateline*
 Lucius Sergius Catilina, the famous revolutionary leader, killed in battle 62 B.C.

l. 90. S⟨u⟩lla
 All texts read the impossible " Scilla." The reference must be to L. Cornelius Sulla, the famous dictator and successful rival of Marius (138–78 B.C.).

ll. 132–134.

These feeble lines are omitted in the eighteenth-century editions. Perhaps Sedley left a revised copy of the play in which they were deleted.

IV. ii, l. 27. Here is the utmost bound of thy success.
        Cf. " Othello " :

> " Heere is my journies end, heere is my butt
> And verie Sea-marke of my utmost Saile."

Cf. note to IV. v. 96–101.

l. 47. ⟨by half⟩

All texts read the impossible " behalf." " By half " does not make very good sense if we are strictly logical, but it was used very loosely in the seventeenth and eighteenth centuries to mean " by a great deal." Cf. Sheridan " School for Scandal," IV. iii.

> " Pshaw ! he is too moral by half."

IV. iii. after l. 8. ⟨Scene the Fourth.⟩

I have inserted this scene division. Probably a back cloth representing Alexandria was dropped in front of the " wood."

IV. iv. l. 121. call ⟨us⟩

All texts read " call in " " ls " in the copy might easily be mistaken for the three digits of " in."

IV. vi. ll. 96–101. Slave ! more uncertain than a Winters Sea.

.   .   .   .   .

But never more a weighty Charge receive.
        Clearly echoes of " Othello " :

> " More fell than Anguish, Hunger, or the Sea."
>   (V. ii. 438.)

and

> " Cassio I loue thee
> But neuer more be Officer of mine."
>   (II. iii. 275.)

V. i. l. 158. Never : let *Romans* now each other love.

The history of this line is a good example of textual degeneration. The compositor of Q2 omitted the colon, and the editor of B4, seeing that the line made nonsense, tried to improve it by reading " Ever let Romans . . ."

l. 170. ⟨*Ant*. 'Twill but⟩

The quarto editions read " But 'twill but." A hastily written " Ant." (perhaps without the stop) might have been mistaken for " But."

l. 292. The real Octavia survived Antony by many years. The reception of the news of her death in Sedley's play is probably suggested by the bringing of the news of *Portia's* death to *Brutus* in " Julius Cæsar."

After l. 325. 〈Scene the Second〉

There must have been a change of scene here. Perhaps a back cloth or curtains were removed and the interior of the " monument " revealed.

V. ii. l. 180. Oh ! what a God-like pleasure . . .

Cf. " Pompey the Great " (4to, 1664, by Buckhurst, Sedley and others) Act III.

> " What publique Joy had our sad Warr ensu'd,
> If I and Pompey o're our former feud,
> Triumphant had in the same Chariot rid."

TEXTUAL NOTES

TEXTUAL NOTES

I. A PASTORAL DIALOGUE BETWEEN THIRSIS AND STREPHON.
        Br. Mus. = Harl. MS. 7332, f. 199.
Title.   (K, *A Pastoral Dialogue.* (Br. Mus. A Pastorall
             Dialogue.
l.   3. Whilome (Br. Mus. while once
l.   4. Envy (Br. Mus. Glory
l.   8. After this line K reads,
             Why do our Woods, so us'd to hear thee Sing,   [9]
             With nothing now but with thy Sorrows ring?
             Thy Flocks, &c. (Br. Mus. as K, except "does"
             for "do" l. [9]   [11]
l.   10. After this line K and Br. Mus. read,
             No loss of these, or care of those are left,   [13]
             Hath wretched *Strephon* of his peace bereft;
l.   12. should (Br. Mus., K did
l.   14. shou'd (Br. Mus. did
l.   15. K reads,
             The hapless *Strephon*: but the Gods I find   [19]
             To no such trifles have this Heart design'd;
             A feller grief, and sadder loss, I plain,
             Then ever Shepherd, or did Prince, sustain;
             Bright Galatea, &c.   [23]
          Br. Mus.,
             The hapless Strephon but the Gods. I finde
             To no such triphles hath this heart design'd
             A fuller greife, a sadder loss I plaine
             Bright Galatea &c.
l.   15. from "Tell me" to l. 34 inclusive K, Br. Mus. omit.
l.   35. Matcless (K, Br. Mus., B3, etc., matchless
l.   37. inimitable (K, Br. Mus. to be adored
l.   38. Virtues (Br. Mus. virtue
ll. 39, 40. K, Br. Mus. read,
             Chaste, without Pride; though gentle, yet not soft;
             Not always cruel, nor yet kind too oft:
             Fair Goddess &c.
l.   42. neglected Courts (K despised Courts, (Br. Mus.
             disspis'd the Court
l.   43. me (K, Br. Mus. one

l.   44.   gone. (K gone : after this line K, Br. Mus. read,
Now I am sure thou wondrest not, I grieve :   [33]
But rather art amazed that I live.

ll. 49, 50.   K,
Yet none so wonderful were ever seen,   [39]
But by as fair they have succeded been. (Br. Mus.
as K except " was " for " were " in l. [39]

ll. 51, 52.   K, Br. Mus. omit.

ll. 53–56.   K reads,
     Strephon
Others as fair, and may as worthy prove,   [41]
But sure I never shall another love ;
Her bright *Idea* wanders in my thought,
At once my Poyson, and my Antidote :   [44]
(Br. Mus. Others are, faire etc.

ll. 57–58.   inclusive (K, Br. Mus. omit, going on to 78–81 :
The Stag shall sooner &c.   [45]

l.   80.   naked on the Shore ; (Br. Mus. on the Naked Shore

ll. 83, 84.   K, Br. Mus. conclude
Then I forget her face ; what once I love,   [49]
May from my eyes, but not my heart remove.   [50]

ll. 85–96.   inclusive : K, Br. Mus. omit

l.   94.   Dastard (B1, etc. Bastard.

II. SONG.

Title.   (B4, B5 *To* Phillis

l. 7.   met, (B4, B5 meet

l. 9.   rash (K grave (B3, etc. rash

l. 14.   After this line K reads
I'le love and hate just where you do,   [15]
And for't no other reason know.
When from this height my Love does fall,
Wee'l bravely scorn &c.   [18]

l. 18.   I will the Blame on Nature lay
(K I'le the whole blame on Nature lay.   [20]

l. 20.   After this line K reads,
I'le grieve as for a friend deceas'd,   [23]
And with the next as well be pleas'd :
Thus we &c.   [25]

III. SONG.

The version found in K is given in full in the note to this poem,
see p. 268.

l. 9.   ⟨in⟩ (K, A, etc. is

IV. " THIRSIS NO MORE . . ."

Title (B3, B4, B5 *The* Answer

l. 9.   feel (K know

l. 18.   native   (K constant
l. 19.   court   (K courts
l. 23.   the tend'rest   (K a gentle
l. 24.   K reads,
    For Beauty else would clogg her innocence :
l. 25.   Subjects   (K servants
l. 27.   what,   (A, B1, B2, B3 what,   (K, B4, B5 what

V.   To Cloris.
   l. 10.   Night   (B4, B5 light
   l. 12.   obliging Gift   (K united work
   l. 13.   K reads,
       He that both lips, or hands adore,

VI.   Indifference Excused.
   l. 2.   nor Oaths   (K nor tears   (B4, B5 or oaths
   l. 7.   Case . . . Pain   (K care . . . pains
   l. 9.   This my *Aurelia*   (K This *Aurelia*
   l. 12.   Heart,   (K Hearts,
   l. 17.   liv'd,   (K live,
   l. 20.   set . . . shew,   (K strive . . . shew

VII.   Orinda to Cloris.
   Title.   (K *To* Cloris
   l.   4.   'em   (K us
   l.   6.   forbears   (K does fear
   l.   11.   they   (K may
   l.   23.   Men   (K We
   l.   32.   rest   (B3, etc. best
  ll. 33–35.   (K reads,
       And even, of them, I'de have thee fly
       All that take flame at every eye.
       All those that light and faithless are,
   l.   39.   pretty'st   (K pretty
   l.   40.   can   (B4, B5 can't

VIII.   The Complaint.
   Title.   (K SONG.
   l.   1.   When fair *Aurelia*   (K When *Aurelia*
  ll. 5–8.   K reads,
       Reserves and care he laid aside,
       And gave his Love the Reins ;
       The headlong course he now must bide,
       No other way remains.
  ll. 9–12.   K reads,
       At first her cruelty he fear'd,
       But that being overcome,
       No second for a while appear'd,
       And he thought all his own :

l.   13. thought   (K call'd
l.   16. K reads,
              What Mortal can have more ?
After l. 24 K has an additional stanza :
              Then he despairing of her heart,   [25]
              Would fain have had his own :
              Love answered, such a Nymph would part
              With nothing she had won.

IX.   CONSTANCY
   l. 3. View but   (K Look on
   l. 6. Now I consider   (K Yet now I look on
   After l. 14 K has the following additional lines :
              The passion I have now shall ne're grow less,   [15]
              No, though thy own fair self should it oppress ;
              I could e'en hazard my Eternity,
              Love but again, and 'twill a Heaven be.

X.   THE PLATONICK.
   l. 1. K reads,
                  Fair *Octavia*, you are much to blame,
   l. 1. *Amaranta*,   (B4, B5 Amarinta,
   l. 14. it   (B4, B5 I
   l. 15. First then, it never   (K First, it never
   l. 20. deathless   (B4, B5 hopeless

XI.   TO CELIA.
   Title. (G To Caelia,
                  Against Honour.
   l. 6. Beast⟨s⟩   (A Beast   (K, B1, etc.   Beasts
   l. 8. As to preserve, and torture Love ?
              (G To Torture thus the Thing you love ?
   l. 12. K omits and substitutes,
              Our greatest torment ? let us break   [12]
              His yoke, and that base power disdain,
              Which only keeps the good in pain :
              In Love &c.   [15]
   l. 16. Devil   (G Daemon
   l. 18. K inserts the following passage between this line and the
              last couplet :
              If we the Laws of Love had kept,   [21]
              And not in dreams of Honour slept,
              He wou'd have surely, long ere this,
              Have crown'd us with the highest bliss ;
              Our Joy had then been as compleat,
              As now our Folly has been great :   [25]
              Let's lose &c.
          G follows K except that in l. [23] it reads for " He would
              have "   (Oh ! he would

XII. HER ANSWER.
    Title. (K *Answer.*
    l. 10. As well my self (B4, B5 Myself as well
    l. 14. in thee. (K on thee.

XIII. The version found in K is given in full in the note to this
        poem, pp. 270, 271.

XIV. THE SUBMISSION.
    l. 4. their (B1, etc. the
    l. 5. long (K due

XV. TO A DEVOUT YOUNG GENTLEWOMAN.
    Title. (K *To a Devout young Woman.*
    l. 1. early (K, Gent.'s Journ. mighty
    l. 15. Kind (K Wise

XVI. TO CELIA.
    l. 2. the Worship (K their worship
    l. 4. heavenly (K mighty
    ll. 15, 16. K reads,
            Say, cruel Fair, then, would you that my flame
            Shou'd for a while move under friendships name?
    l. 20. unmov'd (K quiet
    ll. 20, 21.   small
            Spark, when your self does on that Subject fall?
            (B4, B5
                                   ray
            When your dear heart does on that subject stray:

XVII. SONG.
    For the version of this poem given by "Westminster Drollery"
      see Note, pp. 271, 272.
    After l. 4 K reads,
            It does of late so fast prevail,   [5]
            It must go now, or not at all:
            For should it gather farther strength:
            'Twould give my Honour Laws at length:
              With harmless thoughts I did begin
            But in the Crowd Love &c.
    l. 12. K reads,
            My thoughts for you, and me, did fit.   [15]
    l. 16. K reads,
            Chear'd with his light, free from his fire:
    l. 20. were (B4, B5 was

XVIII. A DIALOGUE BETWEEN AMINTAS AND CELIA.
    l. 2. K reads,
            According as I said;

l. 8. Glow (K Burn
l. 17. might (B1, etc. omit
l. 18. Vigor (K kindness
l. 19. those (K my
l. 20. K reads,
    Or check what you allow.
l. 32. needless (K fruitless
l. 39. Ear (K care
l. 43. obey (K fulfil
l. 46. lose, (K loose
l. 57. farther (B4, B5 further

XIX. Song.
For MS. version in Katherine Sedley's music-book see Note, pp. 272, 273.
l. 4. K reads
    Joyes of Love make too much hast.
l. 8. Beau (K Fool
ll. 9-12. K reads,
    Yet we will have store of good Wenches,
    Whom their own high blouds shall court,
    After two or three good Drenches,
    To out-do them at the Sport.

XX. Song.
l. 4. their (B4, B5 his
l. 12. The (K Their
ll. 21-24. K reads,
    'Tis cruel to prolong a pain;
    And to defer a Bliss,
    Believe me gentle *Hermione*,
    No less inhumane is.
After l. 28 K has the following additional stanza:
    Tis fitter much for you to guess, [29]
    Then me for to explain;
    But grant, O grant that happiness
    Which only does remain. [32]

XXI. Song.
l. 7. K reads,
    Love that can heal the wounds he gives,
l. 9. He laughs (K May laugh
l. 10. his (K it's
l. 11. K reads,
    For in his Chains w'are happier far

XXII, XXIII. Madam, for your Commands . . .
    Awake, my Eyes, . . .
These two pieces, which are separated in K and its successors, are run together in A and subsequent editions.

XXIII.
l. 1. Thought⟨s⟩ (A Thought (K, B3, etc. Thoughts
pursue (A pursues (K, B1, etc. pursue
l. 8. *Amidea*, (K *Flavia*,

XXIV. To CELIA.
For version in Bodl. MS. (West. Eng. Poet. l, 4, p. 169) see
Explanatory Note to this poem, p. 274.
Br. Mus.=Br. Mus. Sloane MS. 1009.
l. 5. you (K thee
l. 10. Br. Mus. reads,
Vaine were your beauty, and now vaine yo͏ʳ pride
l. 15. Beauty's (K Beauties
l. 18. surest (Br. Mus. rudest
l. 19. Br. Mus. reads,
What tyrant yet but there was ever known
l. 22. K reads,
And Beauty a Disease, when 'tis not kind.

XXV. SONG.
l. 2. o're-paid; (K pay'd;
l. 7. near, (B4, B5 dear,
l. 8. Shame. (K Fame.
After l. 12 K has the following additional stanza :
Whil'st no man enjoyes that which I court in vain, [13]
And *Celia* to none is kinder then me ;
To her Honour I'le yield, and never complain,
But dye at her feet, if so it decree.   [16]

XXVI. SONG.
The version of this poem found in K is reprinted with slight
variants in B3 and its successors, which also reprint the version
found in A on a different page. The version found in B3, B4
and B5 which follows K is referred to as " B3, etc."
l. 1. Fair *Aminta*, (K, B3, etc. *Aurelia* (B3, etc. Fair
Aminta
l. 8. Price. (B3, etc. Prize.
l. 11. escape (K escapes (B3, etc. *escape*
After l. 12 K, B3, etc. read,
To be thus for Trifles blam'd,   [13]
Like theirs a folly is,
Who are for vain swearing damn'd,
And know no higher bliss.   [16]
l. 17. Flowers (K flower (B3, etc. flowers

XXVII. SONG.
l. 1. thick (B4, B5 the
l. 2. distant (K dying

l. 23. sure (K e're
After l. 40 K has the following additional stanza :
> Then a wild look the Shepherd cast, [49]
> And falling underneath
> A Beach, where he had seen her last,
> Resign'd his utmost breath.

XXVIII. The Feigned Love.
> The version of this poem given by K will be found in the Note (pp. 274, 275).

XXIX. On the Birth-day of the Late Queen. A Song.
> ll. 13–20. (Gent.'s Journ. reverses the order of these two stanzas, reading,
>> Long may she Reign over this Isle &c. [13]
>> May her blest Example chase &c. [17]

XXX. To Cloris.
> l. 6. Heap (B4, B5 heart
> l. 10. all things (K plots do
>> (Br. Mus. When I forget, &c.
> After l. 22 K has the following additional couplet :
>> What a Priest says moves not the mind, [23]
>> Souls are by love, not word, combin'd. [24]

XXXI. The Soldiers Catch.
> l. 36. th⟨e⟩y (A thy (B1, etc. they

XXXII. The Indifference.
> ll. 9, 10. K reads,
>> I must confess I ne're could find
>> Your equal, or in shape, or mind.
> ll. 15, 16. K reads,
>> But would y'ave kept what you have won,
>> You should have &c.
> l. 24. K reads,
>> But I lose also the desire.
> ll. 26–28. K reads,
>> Wou'd gladly have strange things believ'd ; [26]
>> And if your heart you do defend,
>> Their force against your honour bend. [28]
> l. 29. wou'd (K does
> l. 30. K reads,
>> His own low weakness does confess ;
> l. 31. while (K whilst
> After l. 40 K has the following additional stanza :
>> Yet, cruel Fair, if thou canst prove [41]
>> As happy in some other Love,
>> As I could once have done in thine,
>> The Sun on happier does not shine.

XXXIV. The Eighth Ode of the Second Book of Horace.
l. 3. believe a second time, (G a second time believe
l. 13. G reads,
Sure 'tis not a Crime to swear
l. 16. the (G a
l. 19. G reads,
The decent Nymphs, and cruel God,
That sharpens still his burning Dart
On Hones besmear'd with Blood,
Yet spares thy perjur'd Heart :
l. 23. grows (G grew
l. 25. eldest (G darling
l. 30. Bridegroom (G Bridegrooms

XXXVI. Song.
l. 10. his (W a
l. 11. A, etc. Phillis, *without*, &c. So at the end of each stanza.
l. 19. your (Gent.'s Journ. thy
l. 21. Which he, to sooth (W Which to sooth

XXXVII. Advice to the Old Beaux.
Title. (I The Young Lady's Advice to the Old Beaux
l. 1. I reads,
Scrape, scrape no more your Bearded Chins
l. 2. Beaux, (I Beau's
in hope (I hope (B4, B5 in hopes, in hopes
l. 5. *Young awkard Fops, may* (I Young Fops do daily
l. 6. you (I Old
l. 8. dappl'd (I dapple
l. 9. Gent.'s Journ. reads,
When the old Ogler does look out,
l. 10. our (I the
l. 11. *True Love and* (I Youth and Gay
l. 13. Summer (I The Summer
l. 14. kindly (" Gent.'s Journ." gently
l. 18. *lose both* (I fail in

XLI. To the King on his Birthday.
Bodl. MS. = Bodl. Rawl. MS. D. 361. f. 56.
l. 6. They (Bodl. MS. Thus

XLVI. To Coscus.
l. 4. half the (Gent.'s Journ. the whole
l. 9. now (Gent.'s Journ. omits
l. 14. its (Gent.'s Journ. her

XLIX. Song.
    For extra stanza found in Gent.'s Journ. and B3, etc. see
Explanatory Note, p. 286.

LI. Song A-la-Mode.
    l. 11. Hook⟨s⟩; (A Hook; (B1, etc. Hooks;

LIV. Upon the Author of the Satyr Against Wit.
    l. 10. Actions (Com. Action
    l. 12. Knights⟨.⟩ (A Knights (Com. Knights.
    l. 16. Pills⟨.⟩ (Com., B1, etc. Pills. (A Pills
    ll. 17, 18. Com. omits.

LV. Prologue.
    l. 8. some their (B4, B5 some on their
        ⟨dep⟩end (A pretend (B1, etc. depend

LVI. Prologue to "The Stroulers."
    Br. Mus. = Br. Mus. Eg. MS. 2623 f. 63.
    Title. SP PROLOGUE By Sir Ch— Sydley (Br. Mus. Prologue
        to the Stroulers by Sʳ C. S. Barᵗ.
    l. 3. write⟨.⟩ (Br. Mus. write. (SP write
    l. 6. rise⟨;⟩ (Br. Mus. rise; (SP rise
    l. 8. Li⟨f⟩e's (Br. Mus. life's (SP Live's
    l. 10. our (Br. Mus. the
    l. 16. M⟨e⟩re (Br. Mus. Mere (SP More
    l. 22. *Billet Doux;* (Br. Mus. Billets doux
    l. 24. one (Br. Mus. an

LVIII. Prologue to "The Wary Widdow"
    Q = Quarto ed., 1693.
    l. 1. this (D3, Gent.'s Journ., B3, etc. the
    l. 35. for your selves be wise
        (D3, Gent.'s Journ., B3, etc. read,
            be you not too nice.
    l. 36. Prize⟨.⟩ (Q Prize (D3, etc. Prize,
    l. 36. After this line D3 and Gent.'s Journ. read,
        Then down go half the Artillery of your Eyes. [37]
        For this one Night &c.
        (B3, etc. Then down goes &c.
    l. 37. use⟨,⟩ (Q use (D3, etc. use,

LIX. To Maximina.
    l. 4. has⟨t⟩ (A has (Gent.'s Journ. hast
    l. 10. those (B4, B5 these
    l. 11. the⟨ir⟩ (A these (Gent.'s Journ., B1, etc. their

LXIV. To Posthumus.
    l. 1. That thou dost (Gent.'s Journ. Tho' thou dost
    l. 4. those (Gent.'s Journ. these

LXV. To Scæva.
 ⟨From Martial, *Lib.* 1. *Ep.* 54.⟩ No reference in any text.
 Title. I Scæva (B3, etc. Cæva.

LXVII. To Cloe.
 l. 2. Honesty (Gent.'s Journ. honestly (A, etc. Honesty
 l. 3. Double (Gent.'s Journ. Doubly.

LXXI. To Candidus.
 l. 14. Ye⟨t⟩ (A, B1, B2, B3 Ye (B4, B5 Yet

LXXIII. To Thraso.
 l. 3. know not ⟨thee⟩, (A know not, (B1, etc. know not
   thee,

LXXV. To Bithinicus.
 Title. *Ep.* ⟨26⟩. (A, etc. *Ep.* 12

LXXX. The Maidenhead.
 ⟨From Martial, *Lib.* 1. *Ep.* 58.⟩ No reference in any text.
 l. 2. Guineas (A, B1, B2, B3 Guinea's (B4, B5 Guineas

LXXXI. To Quintus.
 l. 10. the⟨e⟩ (A the (B1, etc. thee

LXXXII. On Arria and Pœtus.
 Title. ⟨From Martial, *Lib.* 1. *Ep.* 13.⟩ No reference in any
   text.
LXXXIII. ⟨From Martial, *Lib.* 2. *Ep.* 54.⟩ No reference in any
   text.

LXXXIV. To Sabinus.
 l. 1. dislik'st Mankind ; (B4, B5 dislik'st all mankind ;

LXXXVI. To Bassa.
 Title. ⟨From Martial, *Lib.* 1. *Ep.* 91.⟩ No reference in any
   text.

LXXXVIII. On Sextus.
 Title. ⟨From Martial, *Lib.* 2. *Ep.* 44.⟩ No reference in any
   text.

LXXXIX.
 l. 44. wrapt (A warpt (B3 wrapt
 l. 74. h⟨u⟩ng (F., A, B, etc. hang (B4, B5 hung
 l. 117. covet, (F. cover
 l. 270. how much that (A, B1, etc. how that (B4, B5 How
   much this house will bring, or cost new hay.
 l. 285. Note⟨,⟩ (F. Note
XC.
 l. 29. on (B4, B5 from
 l. 42. Le⟨s⟩t (A Let (B1, etc. Lest
 l. 67. th⟨ey⟩ A thy (B1, etc. they

l. 135. Y⟨ew,⟩ (A You (B1, etc. Yew,
l. 169. th⟨e⟩y (A thy (B1, etc. they
l. 180. f⟨ro⟩m (A form (B1, etc. from
l. 243. observe, obey, (B4, B5, etc. his will's their law :
l. 251. th⟨e⟩y (A thy (B1, etc. they
l. 268. the same Wound (B3, etc. the Wound
l. 282. our (B3, etc. out
l. 396. *Parth⟨i⟩an* (A, B1, B2, B3 *Parthan* (B4, B5 Parth'an
l. 450. the (B4, B5 thy
l. 496. *Orp⟨h⟩eus* (A *Orpeus* (B, etc. *Orpheus*
l. 503. for equal, Nymphs (B4, B5 for equal Nymphs
l. 534. following behind, unseen, (B4, B5, etc. following, unseen,
l. 624. Me (B3, etc. He
l. 627. Shade, thee, *Tityrus* (B3, etc. shade, the Tityrus,

XCI.
l. 49. frown⟨!⟩ (D1 frown ?
l. 58. gone⟨,⟩ (D1 gone :
l. 64. take⟨;⟩ (D1 take (D2 take ;
l. 106. glass⟨,⟩ (D1 glass,

THE MULBERRY GARDEN

I. i. l. 10. Examples : (Q2, etc. Example :
l. 90. intended (B4, B5 intent
l. 93. not well, (B4, B5 not yet well
l. 102. I'de as lieve (B4, B5 I'd as I live
I. iii. l. 42. sta⟨r⟩ve (Q1 stave (Q2, etc. starve
I. iv. l. 2. Who afford us nothing (B3, etc. Who nothing us afford
II. i. l. 157. Chirurgion, (B4, B5 surgeon
II. iii. l. 37. her House is here hard by. (Q2, etc. Her House is hard by.
II. iv. after l. 1. *Stage Direction* and ⟨she⟩ does (Q1, etc. and does
l. 18. honest, prudent, and a wealthy (B3, etc. honest and a wealthy
l. 31. my pretty Coz. (B4, B5 thy pretty coz,
l. 39. Wi⟨l⟩d (Q1 *Wid* (Q2, etc. *Wild.*
l. 49. time (Q1 times (Q2, etc. time
l. 134. ingenious (Q1 ingenious (Q2, etc. ingenuous
III. ii. l. 39. ⟨of us⟩ : (Q1 off : (Q2 of, (B3, etc. of us :
l. 47. ever open (B4, B5 never open
l. 84. to ⟨stand⟩ allone (Q1, etc. to allone
III. iii. before l. 1. *Stage Direction* ⟨SCENE III A Street.⟩ (Q1, etc. SCENE *changes*

IV. i. l. 37.   Sir *Johns* Daughters, the Ladies. (B3, etc. Sir
                   John's Daughters.

  l. 63.   um (Q1, Q2 u'm (B3, etc. 'em

  l. 89.   Pins matter (B3, etc. pin matter

  l. 110. pound charge, (B3, etc. pounds charge

  l. 126. cou'd see thee. (B3, etc. cou'd see.

  l. 315. light (B3, etc. chance

  l. 351, 352.   *Stage Directions* (All texts "[*alowd*]" after
                   "behalf." As it obviously goes with the first
                   sentence only, I transfer it to the beginning of
                   the speech, substituting "⟨[*aside*]⟩" after
                   "behalf"

V. i. l. 123.   *Stage Direction Perriwig.* (B5 peruke. So throughout
                   Act V

V. iii. l. 43.   S'light⟨! I⟩ (Q1 S'light of (Q2, etc. 'Slight I

V. iv. l. 67.   by, (B3, etc. Bet

V. v. l. 104.   a Flame ⟨that⟩ smil'd (Q1, etc. a Flame you smil'd

  l. 153. Sir Formal (Q1 Sir, Formal (Q2, etc. Sir Formal

  l. 192. you⟨r⟩ guilt (Q1, Q2, B3 you guilt (B5 your guilt

  ad fin. ⟨[Exeunt omnes⟩ (so B3, etc. Qq. omit.

ANTONY AND CLEOPATRA

Persons M⟨r⟩ *Smith* (Q1, M. *Smith* (Q2, etc. Mr *Smith*

I. i. l. 1.   an (Q2, B3 in (B4, B5 an

  l. 19.   redrest⟨,⟩ (Q1 redrest. (Q2 redrest, (B3, B4,
                   B5 redrest

  l. 62.   Empirie (so Q1, Q2 (B3, etc. Empire

I. ii. l. 7.   weake (Q1 week corrected in errata to weake
                   (Q2, etc. weak

  l. 35.   power, (Q1 pow'r, corrected in errata to power,
                   (Q2, B3, B4 power. (B5 pow'r ;

  l. 47.   Boards⟨,⟩ (Q2, etc. Boards.

  l. 109. may (Q2, B3 my (B4, B5 may

  l. 117. sullen (Q2, etc. sudden

  l. 182. reveng⟨e⟩ (Q1 reveng (Q2, etc. revenge

  l. 211. ⟨find⟩ (Q1, etc. sate

  l. 250. grow ; (Q2, B3 grows ; (B4, B5 grow ;

II. i. l. 169.   But Fate⟨,⟩ (Q1, etc. But Fate

II. ii. l. 61.   He does for *Bacchus*, (Q2, etc. He for *Bacchus*

III. i. l. 60.   Seam⟨a⟩n (Q1, etc. seamen

  l. 64.   in⟨j⟩ur'd (Q1, Q2 insur'd (B3, etc. injur'd

  l. 100. you (Q1, Q2, B3 you. (B4, B5 you,

  l. 109. ridiculous⟨ly⟩ (Q1, Q2, B3 ridiculous (B4, B5
                   ridiculously

| | l. 111. | *Stage Direction* transferred from after l. 109 where it occurs in all texts |

l. 111.   *Stage Direction* transferred from after l. 109 where it
          occurs in all texts
l. 112.   Father⟨s⟩   (Q1, Q2 Father   (B3, etc. Fathers
III. ii. l. 6.   acts⟨s⟩   (Q1, Q2 Act   (B3, etc. Acts
l. 24.   won't⟨!⟩   (Q1, Q2, B3 won't   (B4, B5 wont !
l. 35.   his Cause   (Q2, B3, etc. this cause
l. 60.   Octavi⟨a'⟩s   (Q1, Q2, B3 Octavius's   (B4, B5
          Octavius'
l. 135.   an   (Q2, etc. any
l. 142.   ruine   (B3, etc. ruins
l. 221.   she   (B3, etc. he
l. 261.   you⟨r⟩   (Q1 you   (Q2, etc. your
l. 305.   for⟨'⟩t   (Q1 fort   (Q2, etc. for't
l. 323.   *Brutus* to save⟨,⟩   (Q1, etc. Brutus, to save myself,
l. 325.   *Lucilius*⟨.⟩   (Q1 *Lucilius*   (Q2, etc. *Luc.*
l. 325.   same⟨,⟩   (Q1 same   (Q2, etc. same,
IV. i. l.   1.   Caesar⟨.⟩   (Q1 *Caesar,*   Q2, etc. Caesar.
l.   4.   th' *Aegyptian*   (Q1 th *Aegyptian*   (Q2 the *Aegyptian*
          (B3, etc. th' *Aegyptian*
l.   8.   ⟨I⟩ in a   (Q1, Q2 In a   (B3, B4 I in a
l. 15.   un⟨s⟩oil'd   (Q1, etc. unfoil'd
l. 90.   S⟨u⟩lla   (Q1, Q2 *Scilla*   (B3, etc. *Sylla*
ll. 132–4.   inclusive   (B3 omits, giving next three lines to
          Mecaenas   (B4, B5 also omit but give ll. 135–137 to
          Octavia.
IV. ii. l. 24.   the⟨e⟩   (Q1, Q2 the   (B3, etc. thee
l. 47.   ⟨by half⟩   (Q1, etc. behalf
IV. iv. l. 54.   done⟨,⟩   (Q1, Q2 done   (B3, etc. done,
l. 62.   heat,   (Q2, etc. heart,
l. 121.   ⟨us⟩   (Q2, etc. in
IV. v. l.   1.   well⟨,⟩ my Queen⟨,⟩   (Q1, Q2, B3 well my Queen
          doth   (B4, B5 well, my Queen, doth
l. 70.   Traytor⟨s⟩   (Q1, Q2, B3 traytor   (B4, B5 traitors
IV. vi. l.   8.   *Protection*   (Q2, etc.   *Production*
l. 13.   name my Vertue   (Q2, B3 name vertue   (B4, B5
          name that vertue
ll. 45–6.   ⟨*Chil.*⟩   (Q1, Q2, B3 give to *Caes.*   (B4, B5 to *Chil.*
l. 81.   Discontents   (Q2, B3 Discontentments   (B4, B5 Dis-
          contents
l. 89.   Forcers   (Q2 Forces   (B3, etc. Forcers
l. 104.   blame,   (Q1 balme altered in errata to blame
          (Q2, etc. blame
l. 108.   thy Mercy,   (Q2, etc. the mercy
V.   l. 91.   you my generous Friends   (Q2 you generous friends
          (B3 you my generous friends   (B4, B5 you, my
          generous friends,
l. 158.   Never :   (Q2, B3 Never   (B4, B5 Ever

after l. 169. *Stage Direction* ⟨*stabs*⟩   (Q1, etc. *kills*
  l. 170. ⟨Anto.⟩   'Twill but
       (Q1, Q2 read *Phot.*   Ile call some help
               But 'twill but
       (B3, etc. *Ant.*   'Twill but
  l. 190. on;   (Q2 one;   (B3, etc. on
  l. 294. ⟨Serv.⟩   (All texts give this line to Caesar, but also
       print *Caes.* again before 295
  l. 295. *Caes.* dead⟨?⟩   (Q1 *Caes.* dead.   (Q2, B3 dead?
       (B4, B5 dead?
after l. 303. *Stage Direction Enter* a *Messenger*, so Q1, Q2
       (B3, etc. omit *stage direction* and give l. 304 to
       "*Mec.*"
V. ii. l.   9. B⟨oa⟩r   (Q1, Q2, B3 Bear   (B4, B5, Beauty the
       Conquerour, Boar
  l. 165. (Aside)   (All texts read this *Stage Direction* after
       l. 166.

FIRST LINE INDEX TO POEMS